CAMBRIDGE

Official Cambridge Exam Preparation



# PREPARE

STUDENT'S BOOK WITH EBOOK

B1

LEVEL 4

James Styring
Nicholas Tims

Second Edition

**Cambridge University Press**
www.cambridge.org/elt

**Cambridge Assessment English**
www.cambridgeenglish.org

Information on this title: www.cambridge.org/9781009022958



First published 2015
Second Edition 2019
Second Edition update 2021

40 39 38 37 36 35 34 33 32 31 30 29 28 27 26 25

Printed in Italy by L.E.G.O. S.p.A

*A catalogue record for this publication is available from the British Library*

ISBN 978-1-00-902295-8 Student's Book with eBook
ISBN 978-1-00-902296-5 Workbook with Digital Pack
ISBN 978-1-00-902297-2 Teacher's Book with Digital Pack

# CONTENTS

| LISTENING | SPEAKING | WRITING | VIDEO |
|---|---|---|---|
| | | An online profile | |
| A conversation about fashion and music in the past | Talking about yourself | | In fashion |
| | | | Trendsetters |
| | | An informal email (1) | Life events |
| A programme about sport | Describing a past event | | |
| | | | |
| | | | |
| | | A story (1) | |
| An interview about living in the country | Agreeing and disagreeing | | Modern life |
| | | | New York City |
| | | An informal email (2) | |
| A talk about a travel writing competition | Making suggestions | | |
| | | | |
| | | | |
| | | A story (2) | |
| Seven short conversations about food | Ordering food | | Taste this! |
| | | | International food in London |

**Key to symbols:**

✓ *B1 Preliminary for Schools* exam task ▶ Video

# WELCOME TO PREPARE

## LEARN ABOUT THE FEATURES IN YOUR NEW STUDENT'S BOOK!

### ABOUT YOU
Start each unit by talking about you, your life and the unit topic

### PREPARE TO WRITE
Learn useful tips to help you prepare, plan and check your writing

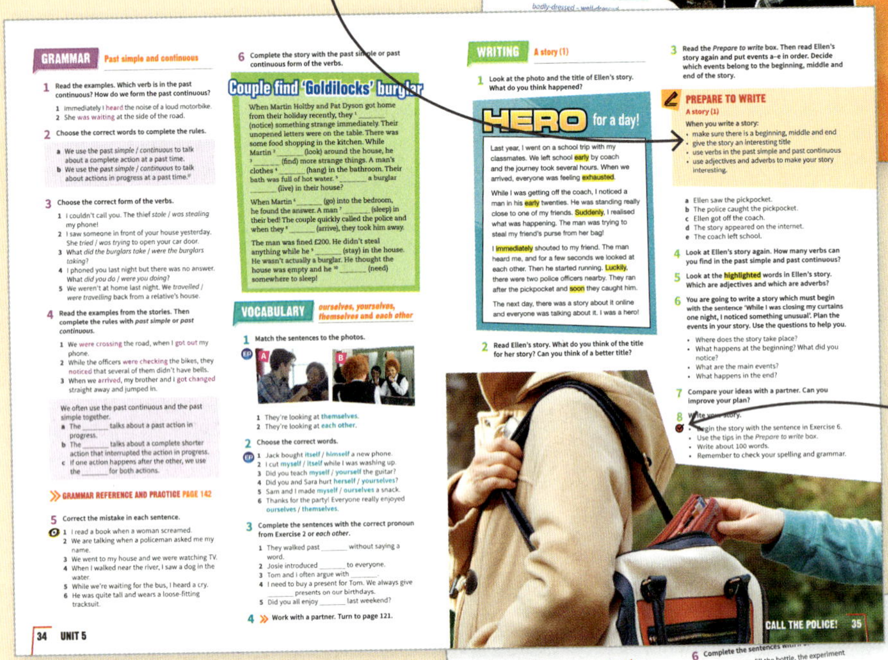


### TALKING POINTS
Say what you think about the topic in the text

### EASY TO FIND EXAM TASKS

### PREPARE TO SPEAK
Learn useful words and phrases for effective communication

### VIDEO
Watch interviews with teenagers like you

## CULTURE

Learn about the culture of English-speaking countries and the wider world

## VIDEO

Watch interesting documentaries about the culture topics

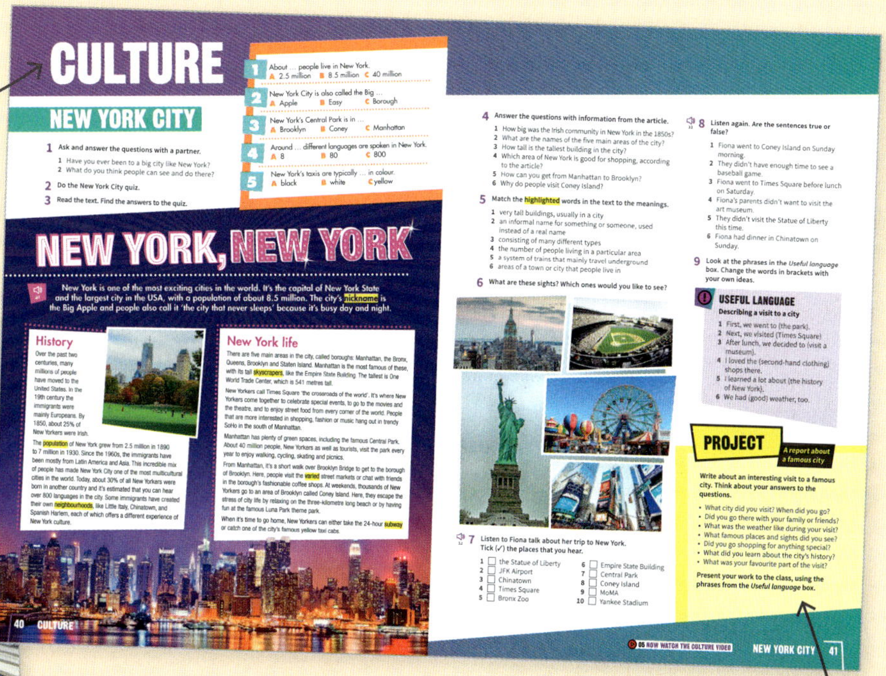

## LIFE SKILLS

Develop important skills that you can use in your daily life

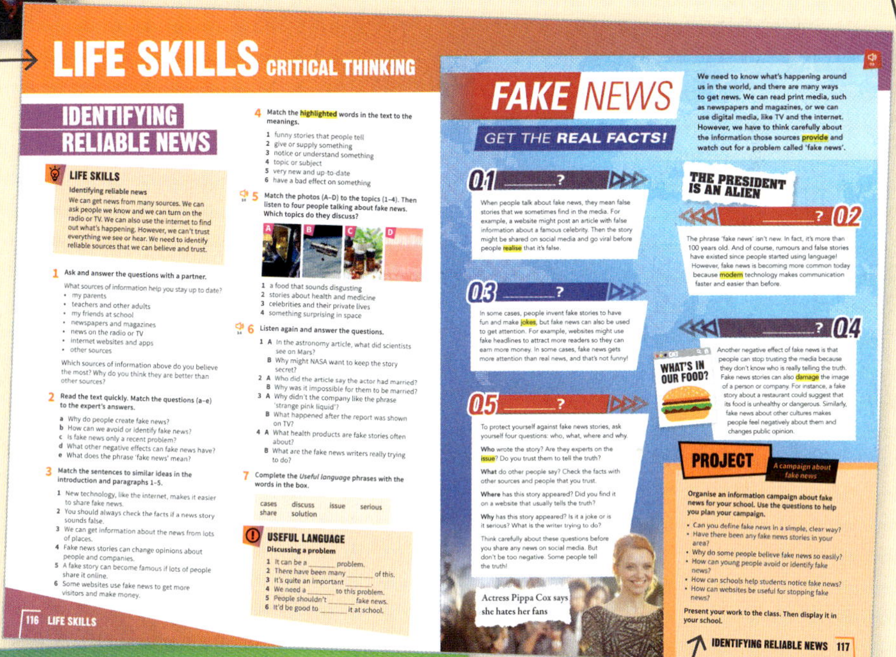


## PROJECT

Work together to create something fun and expand your learning

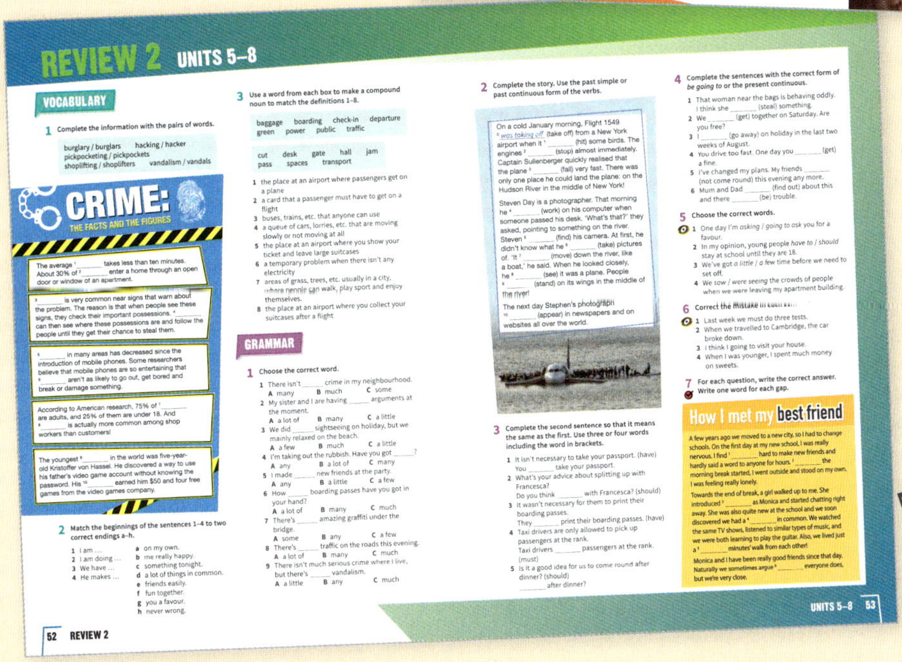


## REVIEW

Check your progress

# 1 ALL ABOUT ME

## ABOUT YOU

What do you look like?
What type of person are you?

Alfie's family

Grace's family

Lucas's family

## VOCABULARY Describing people

01 **1 Look at the photos and listen to three people talking about someone in their family. Who is each speaker describing?**

brother dad sister mum

1 Lucas is describing his …
2 Alfie is describing his …
3 Grace is describing her …

**2 Add the words to the table.**

EP

~~attractive~~ bald blonde curly dark elderly fair good-looking handsome middle-aged pretty straight teenage in his/her (early/late) twenties/thirties

| | |
|---|---|
| Age | |
| Looks | *attractive* |
| Hair | |

**3 Describe someone in the photos. Can your partner guess who it is?**

He's a teenage boy and he's good-looking.

Is it Alfie?

02 **4 Read the descriptions and choose the correct adjectives. Then listen and check.**

EP

1 I think Lucas is really **polite** / **careless**. For instance, when he wants to borrow something, he always says please.
2 My brother's called Alfie. He takes my things without asking. He thinks he's **funny** / **polite**, but he doesn't make me laugh!
3 Grace is very **miserable** / **friendly**. I see her every morning on her way to school. She always says hello.
4 Alfie talks a lot – like his mum! He's sometimes a bit **confident** / **careless** with homework. I try to encourage him to check it, but he doesn't always do it.
5 Grace is a great friend. She's always smiling, and she's never **miserable** / **polite**. She really makes me laugh.
6 Lucas knows what he's good at, so he's quite a **careless** / **confident** boy. He can also be quite a lazy person though. His room is always really untidy!

**5 Match the adjectives to their opposites in Exercise 4.**

EP

careful cheerful rude serious shy unfriendly

**6 Which adjectives in Exercises 4 and 5 describe you?**

**7 Work in pairs. Describe someone you both know. Describe what they look like and what kind of person they are. Can your partner guess who it is?**

She's got straight hair and she's very confident.

Is it Ana?

## READING

**1** **Read the information about part of a school website. Discuss the questions.**

1 Have you got something similar in your school?
2 What do you think of the idea?

**BRYANS HIGH SCHOOL all.about.me**

Would you like to meet other students at Bryans High School who share your hobbies and interests? It's easy with all.about.me.

1 Click here and create an account.
2 Post a photo and your profile – tell everyone about you, your interests and your plans.
3 Read about other students and click on 'Connect' to make new friends.

**2** **Three students have posted information on *all.about.me*. Read the profiles below and ignore any gaps. Match each person to one interest.**

going to the cinema fashion
technology fitness

**3** **Now read Alfie's profile again. Write ONE word for each gap.**

**4** **Read the three profiles again. Write the correct name.**

1 ............ is interested in doing a job related to his/her hobby.
2 ............ is looking forward to learning a new activity.
3 ............ is learning a new skill with help from a relative.
4 ............ agrees with other people about his/her personality.
5 ............ would like to go to another country.
6 ............ might get a prize soon.

**5** **Match the highlighted words and phrases in Lucas's and Grace's profiles with the meanings.**

1 be involved in an activity, with other people
2 become better
3 someone with no brothers or sisters
4 write computer programs
5 be very interested in something
6 able to stay calm and not get angry, especially when something takes a long time

### TALKING POINTS

Who would you most like to spend time with – Alfie, Lucas or Grace? Why?
Is it important to have the same interests as your friends? Why? / Why not?

## BRYANS HIGH SCHOOL all.about.me

Hi everyone. I'm Lucas. I live with my parents, my sister and my two brothers. Some of my classmates think I'm quite serious, but I don't agree. I'm just a bit shy, and I'm quite independent. My main interest outside of school is computers and gaming. But I'm not just a gamer. Right now, I'm taking part in a competition for young game designers. So at weekends, I'm learning to code with my aunt. She's a professional coder. She's also a really patient teacher – I'm finding coding impossible at the moment!

CONNECT

Hello! I'm Grace. I live with my mum and dad. I'm an only child – so no brothers or sisters. My friends and family say I'm a cheerful person. And they're right. I think there's always something to smile about! In my free time, I'm into various typical teenage hobbies, but my favourite is sport. I'm in the school hockey and football teams. And this year I'm having tennis lessons. I'm really making progress, I think. In a few months, I'm going on a kayaking trip with my cousin. We've never done it before but we're really excited.

CONNECT

03

My name's Alfie. I live with my mum, dad and sister, Melissa, right opposite the school. I'm quite friendly and funny, but I [1] ............ be quite serious at times, too. One [2] ............ my biggest interests is film: thrillers, drama, science fiction – I don't mind. I like watching [3] ............ all. One day, I think I'd like to work [4] ............ film.

This year, I want to visit a film studio. There's [5] ............ near London where all eight Harry Potter films were made. My dream is [6] ............ fly to Hollywood and see a studio there.

CONNECT

## GRAMMAR Present simple and continuous

**1** **Match the examples to the rules.**

1 Right now, I'm taking part in a competition for young game designers.
2 In a few months, I'm going on a kayaking trip with my cousin.
3 My friends and family say I'm a cheerful person.
4 This term, I'm having tennis lessons.
5 I live with my parents.

We use the present simple to talk about:
**a** facts.
**b** something that happens regularly.

We use the present continuous for:
**c** something that is happening right now or around now.
**d** temporary situations.
**e** future plans.

» GRAMMAR REFERENCE AND PRACTICE PAGE 138

**2** **Complete the sentences with the present simple or continuous form of the verbs in brackets.**

1 I ________ (get) home at five o'clock every day.
2 Mum ________ (work) late this week.
3 Look at Dan. He ________ (not concentrate).
4 ____ you ________ (do) anything interesting next weekend?
5 She ________ (play) the guitar and the piano.
6 He always ________ (go) swimming on Saturdays.

**3** **Look at Exercises 1 and 2. Are these time words and phrases used with the present simple (PS) or present continuous (PC)?**

at the moment / right now *PC*
never, sometimes, always
every day/week/year
this month/term/week
later, tomorrow, tonight
on Saturdays, at weekends
next week/weekend/month

**4** **Write six sentences about you. Use the time words and phrases in Exercise 3.**

*Right now, I'm having an English lesson.*

**5** **Read the information about the verbs. Check the meaning of the verbs you don't know.**

We don't use some verbs in continuous forms. These verbs are called **stative verbs** and include: *believe, hate, know, like, love, mean, need, own, prefer, understand, want.*
*I don't understand this question.*
NOT ~~*I'm not understanding*~~ *this question.*

**6** **Complete the sentences with the positive or negative form of the verbs in Exercise 5. Sometimes more than one answer is possible.**

0 My uncle *owns* three cars.
1 Ruby's very friendly. We really ________ her.
2 I ________ how old he is. He looks about 14.
3 What ________ this word ________?
4 I'm feeling miserable today. I ________ cold weather.
5 You're speaking too quickly and I ________ you.

**7** **Choose the correct form of the verbs.**

1 We *have* / *'re having* problems with the computers at the moment.
2 I *need* / *'m needing* some new shoes.
3 I *write* / *'m writing* to you about a trip we are planning in November.
4 Tonight she *goes* / *'s going* to the cinema with some friends.
5 This term I *have* / *'m having* some extra maths lessons.
6 I *never forget* / *'m never forgetting* my homework.

**8** » **Work with a partner.** **Turn to page 120.**

## VOCABULARY Prefixes: *un-*, *in-*, *im-*

**1** EP **Read the examples. Then write the opposites of the adjectives, 1–12.**

I'm finding coding **impossible** at the moment!
Lucas's room is always really **untidy**.
I'm quite **independent**.

| | | |
|---|---|---|
| 1 kind | 2 friendly | 3 patient |
| 4 expensive | 5 known | 6 polite |
| 7 visible | 8 healthy | 9 well |
| 10 fair | 11 lucky | 12 correct |

**2** **Agree with these sentences. Use an adjective from Exercise 1 or its opposite.**

0 **A:** I didn't recognise any of the actors in that film.
**B:** They were all *unknown*, I think.
1 **A:** Dad never waits for me!
**B:** You're right. He's very ________.
2 **A:** Mum's still in bed!
**B:** I know. She's feeling really ________.
3 **A:** It's important to wear bright clothing on a bike at night.
**B:** Yes, you need to be ________ to drivers.
4 **A:** We have to be home at 10.30. That's so early!
**B:** Yeah. It's really ________.
5 **A:** I can't believe you found your phone!
**B:** I know. I'm so ________.
6 **A:** The last question in the homework was hard!
**B:** Yes! I got the same answer as you, but Mrs Thomas said it was ________.

**3** » **Work with a partner.** **Turn to page 120.**

## An online profile

**1** Read the two online profiles. Which person is most like you? Why?

USERNAME Snowy
AGE 15
COUNTRY UK/USA
MEMBER SINCE January 2018
NUMBER OF POSTS 79

I'm Tom, but my online name is Snowy – my hair is very blonde! I'm British, but I'm living in the USA right now because my parents are working here. I go to Carson High School in Boston.

I think I'm quite intelligent and very friendly. Some people disagree, of course! I'm really into music and I play the guitar. I practise every day and I'm starting to write my own songs. You can hear a few of them online.

USERNAME Vogue
AGE 16
COUNTRY Australia
MEMBER SINCE March 2018
NUMBER OF POSTS 349

My name's Felicity, but everyone calls me Flic. I'm from Australia. My hobbies are fashion, fashion and fashion – especially from the 1970s and 80s. Oh, and I also love music. I'm learning to play the drums at the moment. They're really loud.

I'm fairly confident, but sometimes I'm a bit careless with my school work. My friends say I'm cheerful and friendly but I know that I can sometimes be impatient. I'm trying to change!

**2** Read the *Prepare to write* box. Which phrases do Tom and Felicity use in their profiles?

### PREPARE TO WRITE
**An online profile**

**In an online profile:**

- introduce yourself: *I'm …, My name's …, I'm from …*
- say what kind of person you are: *(I think) I'm very/quite …, My friends say I'm …, I can sometimes be …*
- talk about your hobbies and interests: *I'm interested in …, I'm (really) into …, My hobbies are …*
- say what you're learning at the moment: *At the moment I'm …, Right now I'm …*

**3** Look at the underlined verbs in the profiles. What verb form do Tom and Flic use for:

**1** their likes and dislikes, and things they do regularly?
**2** things they're doing at the moment?

**4** Look at the highlighted adverbs in the profiles. Add them to the table.

| Make adjectives weaker | Make adjectives stronger |
|---|---|
| *quite* | |

**5** Complete the sentences for you.

**1** I'm very …
**2** I'm fairly …
**3** Sometimes I'm quite …
**4** My friends say I'm …
**5** I think I can be a bit …

**6** Make notes for your online profile. Use the ideas to help you.

- my name
- facts about me
- what I'm like
- hobbies and interests
- things I'm learning at the moment

**7** Write your online profile.

- Use the plan and phrases in the *Prepare to write* box.
- Use adverbs to make adjectives stronger and weaker.
- Write about 80 words.
- Remember to check your spelling and grammar.

# 2 IN FASHION

## ABOUT YOU

01 **Watch the video and then answer the questions.**

What are you wearing today?
What fashions do you like?
Which colours or clothes look good on you?

## VOCABULARY Clothes: adjectives

04 **1** **Look at the photos. Who are the people and what are they wearing? Then listen and check.**

05 **2** **Listen to an interview with three teenagers. Are they talking about:**

**a** what's fashionable at the moment?
**b** what clothes they might buy?
**c** what they like wearing?

05 **3** **Read the questions. Then listen again and write *A* (Ashley), *M* (Molly) or *L* (Luke).** EP

**1** Whose clothes are **comfortable**?
**2** Whose jeans are **skinny**?
**3** Who is wearing something **brand new**?
**4** Who doesn't wear **smart** clothes?
**5** Who isn't interested in **trendy** clothes?
**6** Who is very **well-dressed** today?

**4** **Match the adjectives to their opposites in Exercise 3. How many adjectives can you match to each photo?** EP

| | |
|---|---|
| ~~badly-dressed~~ | casual |
| loose-fitting | second-hand |
| uncomfortable | unfashionable |

*badly-dressed – well-dressed*

**5** **Discuss the questions.**

**1** What do you like wearing? What types of clothing do you never wear? Why?
**2** Do you generally prefer smart or casual clothes? Why?
**3** How important is it for you to wear trendy clothes?

# FASHION and MUSIC

**Before the mid-1950s, there was no such thing as 'youth culture'. Most young people wore the same fashions as their parents, and they listened to the same kind of music. But that all changed with the arrival of rock 'n' roll.**

It started with the 1954 song *Rock Around the Clock* by Bill Haley and the Comets. Although the older generation didn't understand rock 'n' roll, teenagers fell in love with it straight away. It was a new sound – lively and exciting – and with it came new fashions in clothing. Young men wore smart suits with skinny ties, like the popular singers Buddy Holly and Elvis Presley. Young women liked groups such as The Supremes, and they wore loose-fitting skirts which looked great when they danced.

In the 1960s, rock bands like The Rolling Stones became symbols of the growing youth culture. Young women wore very short 'mini skirts' – the older generation was shocked! The mid-1960s to the mid-70s was the hippie era. Young hippies were interested in peace and love, and they listened to The Beatles, Dusty Springfield and Joni Mitchell. Men and women alike had long hair and wore flowery clothing and sandals.

The punk music of the late 70s was loud and angry, and the trends matched the music. Punks wanted to shock people. They dressed in second-hand clothes, which they often tore to look more individual, and their hairstyles were colourful and messy. Teenagers were into bands like The Clash and singers like Debbie Harry and Patti Smith. In the 1980s, long curly hair and bright colours were trendy, and people listened to Michael Jackson, Madonna and U2.

By the 1990s, teens were in love with the look and sound of singers like Britney Spears. It was also the decade of 'boy bands' and 'girl bands' – the Backstreet Boys and the Spice Girls were 'top of the pops'. Black American music called hip hop became popular internationally. Hip hop stars wore tracksuits, gold rings and necklaces, and they sang about having money and driving expensive cars.

Today, people are interested in the styles of their favourite YouTubers and tunes by superstar DJs like Calvin Harris. Hollywood actors or bestselling singers such as Taylor Swift and Ed Sheeran are also popular. There are dozens of genres of rock and dance music and, thanks to the internet, music and clothing fashions are here today and gone tomorrow.

## READING

**1** **How many bands and singers from the last century can you name? Read the article quickly. Does it mention any of them?**

**2** **Read the article again. Choose the correct answers.**

1 Before the 1950s, teenagers
  **A** didn't listen to music very much.
  **B** listened to the same music as adults.

2 In the 1950s, teenage boys
  **A** joined rock 'n' roll bands.
  **B** wore clothes similar to the pop stars.

3 In the 1960s,
  **A** fashions shocked some people.
  **B** hippies wore mini skirts.

4 Punks in the late 70s
  **A** wore colourful clothing.
  **B** didn't wear brand new clothes.

5 Hip hop singers of the 1990s liked
  **A** wearing jewellery.
  **B** wearing smart suits.

6 Nowadays, people
  **A** get their fashion ideas from YouTubers.
  **B** wear similar clothing to Taylor Swift and Ed Sheeran.

**3** **Match the highlighted words in the article to the meanings.**

1 fashions or styles
2 pulled something in order to break it
3 untidy or dirty
4 young people in general
5 someone's appearance
6 what people wear in general

### TALKING POINTS

Why do young people like to dress differently from their parents and grandparents?
Why do you think people choose to dress like music stars?

# GRAMMAR Past simple

**1** **Read the examples and complete the rules with words from the box.**

1 They **listened** to the same kind of music.
2 They **didn't understand** rock 'n' roll.
3 What **did** they **wear**?

| did | didn't | *-d* or *-ed* |
|---|---|---|

We use the past simple to talk about finished past actions and states.
**a** Regular verbs end with ______ in the affirmative, but a lot of common verbs are irregular.
**b** We form negative sentences with ______ + infinitive.
**c** We form questions with ______ + infinitive.

» **GRAMMAR REFERENCE AND PRACTICE PAGE 139**

**2** **Choose the correct words.**

1 I *choosed* / *chose* some new shoes for the party.
2 I *heard* / *heared* the new Harry Styles single.
3 My sister and I *enjoyed* / *enjoied* shopping last Saturday.
4 Did you *get* / *got* any new clothes?
5 He *read* / *red* the lyrics of the songs before he *sung* / *sang* them.
6 I didn't *met* / *meet* your friends at the concert.
7 When did you *go* / *went* shopping?
8 We *planned* / *planed* to go to a concert in Hyde Park but they cancelled it.

**3** **Complete the sentences about you. Use the past simple positive or negative form of the verbs.**

1 I ______ (wear) jeans yesterday.
2 I ______ (get) clothes for my last birthday.
3 My parents ______ (buy) the clothes I'm wearing.
4 My family and I ______ (watch) TV last night.
5 My best friend ______ (text) me this morning.
6 We ______ (go) shopping last weekend.
7 I ______ (have) a music lesson last week.
8 I ______ (see) my friends last weekend.

**4** **Complete the conversation with the past simple form of the verbs.**

**A:** Hey, where [1] ______ (you / get) that T-shirt? It's really cool!
**B:** My brother [2] ______ (give) it to me for my birthday.
**A:** I really like it. Where [3] ______ (he / find) it?
**B:** Well, he [4] ______ (not find) it exactly. He [5] ______ (design) it.
**A:** Really? How [6] ______ (he / do) that?
**B:** He [7] ______ (use) this app called UTme, on his phone. He [8] ______ (take) a photo and then added the colours and the writing. He [9] ______ (show) me the app. It's really cool.
**A:** Wow! I [10] ______ (not know) you could do that. Can you show me the app?

**5** **Make questions about last weekend.**

0 what / you / do / last weekend?
*What did you do last weekend?*
0 you / go / shopping?
*Did you go shopping?*
1 which friends / you / meet?
2 you / play / any sports?
3 what / watch / on TV?
4 you / go / to bed late?

**6** **In pairs, ask and answer the questions in Exercise 5.**

**A:** *What did you do last weekend?*
**B:** *We went to London.*
**A:** *Did you go shopping?*
**B:** *Yes, we did. / No, we didn't.*

# VOCABULARY Adverbs

**1** **We can form adverbs from adjectives. What are the adjective forms of the adverbs in the examples?**

1 Hip hop became popular **internationally**.
2 He shouted at us **angrily**.
3 You need to work **hard**.

**2** **Complete the table with adverbs from the adjectives in the box.**

| ~~amazing~~ | bad | careful | early |
|---|---|---|---|
| fast | good | healthy | heavy |
| honest | lazy | lucky | polite |
| quick | rude | serious | |

| + *-ly* | *y* + *-ily* | Irregular adverbs |
|---|---|---|
| *amazingly* | | |

**3** **Complete the sentences with adverbs formed from the adjectives.**

1 The sisters were chatting ______ (happy).
2 She was late, so she was walking ______ (fast).
3 You mustn't talk ______ (loud) in the cinema.
4 My grandma is old. She walks quite ______ (slow).
5 What did he say? He's talking very ______ (quiet).
6 I'm studying ______ (hard) for the exam.
7 He plays the piano really ______ (good).
8 Alana won the tennis match ______ (easy).

**4** » **Work with a partner. Turn to page 120.**

# LISTENING

**1** **Look at the photo. What do you know about The Beatles? What are they wearing in this photo?**

07 **2** **Listen to a conversation between Sara and her grandma. What does Sara's grandma talk about?**

**a** her favourite band from the 1970s
**b** music and fashion in the 1960s
**c** women's clothes fashions in the 1960s

08 **3** **Listen to the first half of the conversation again. Choose the correct answers.**

1 People *watched / didn't watch* colour TV in the 1950s.
2 Sara's grandma *listened to / didn't listen to* pop music in the 1960s.
3 Sara's grandma watched The Beatles play *on TV / at a concert.*
4 Sara's *dad / grandma* still plays The Beatles' *Abbey Road* album.

09 **4** **Listen to the second half of the conversation again. Complete the sentences. Listen again and check.**

| | | | | |
|---|---|---|---|---|
| beards | blue | dresses | hair | jacket |
| jeans | loose-fitting | | necklaces | tights |

1 Grandma's .......... jacket matches Sara's .......... .
2 Girls wore short .......... and colourful .......... in the 1960s.
3 By the end of the 1960s, the fashion for men was for long .........., .......... and colourful, .......... clothes.
4 Grandma made her own .......... .

# SPEAKING Talking about yourself

**1** **Discuss the questions.**

1 Do you enjoy shopping for clothes? Why? / Why not?
2 Who do you usually go shopping with?
3 What do you usually buy?

**2** **Choose the correct words to make questions.**

1 What clothes *do you like / you like* wearing?
2 How often *you buy / do you buy* new clothes?
3 Where *do you usually / you do usually* buy your clothes?
4 How much *are / do* you spend on clothes?

10 **3** **Listen to Harry answering the questions in Exercise 2 and make notes on his answers.**

10 **4** **Listen again to Harry answering the questions and complete Harry's sentences. Listen again and check.**

1 I .......... jeans always look good.
2 I don't go shopping .......... .
3 I .......... shopping in department stores because the clothes are too expensive.
4 I .......... spend more when I get money for my birthday.

10 **5** **Read the *Prepare to speak* box. Then listen again. Which phrases does Harry use?**

## PREPARE TO SPEAK
### Talking about yourself

When you answer questions:

- use the present simple and adverbs of frequency to talk about habits: *I usually …, I always …, I often …*
- add reasons for your answer: *because …*
- talk about your likes and dislikes: *I like …, I don't like …, I really like …*
- give your opinion: *I think …, I don't think …*

**6** **Ask and answer the questions in Exercise 2. Use phrases from the *Prepare to speak* box.**

# CULTURE

## TRADITIONAL CLOTHES

A

**1** **Discuss the questions.**

1. What four countries are part of the United Kingdom?
2. What are the nationalities of those four countries?
3. How do you think people dress in those countries? Do you know of any traditional clothes from the United Kingdom?

**2** **Read the text. Match photos A–D to countries in the UK.**

## UK CULTURE *Traditional clothes*

In many countries there are traditional clothes that people wear for special occasions, such as national holidays and popular folk festivals. The United Kingdom includes four different countries – England, Wales, Scotland and Northern Ireland – and each country has its own history and special customs.

B

One of the most traditional items of clothing in the UK is the kilt. There are many versions, but the most famous ones are the kilts that men wear in Scotland on special occasions. Traditional Scottish kilts are made with five metres of tartan, which is a fabric with vertical and horizontal lines in different colours. Many Scottish families have a tartan with their own special colours. At the front of their kilts, Scottish men usually wear a small bag called a sporran to carry money and personal items. Scottish women wear a tartan skirt with a blouse and a tartan cloth on their shoulders called a shawl. They may also wear tartan dresses.

C

In Wales, some women wear a traditional costume on important occasions, such as St David's Day, on 1st March. On those special days, many women wear a long dress with a red shawl over their shoulders. However, the most unusual part of the costume is a tall, black hat. It looks like the very formal hats that men wore in the past. Welsh men haven't got a special costume for festivals, but they often wear old-fashioned trousers called breeches.

England hasn't got a national folk costume, but some people wear special clothes for traditional events, such as Morris dancing shows. Morris dancers can wear many different things, but they typically have white or black trousers or breeches. Some people also wear hats and short jackets called waistcoats, with long, colourful ribbons that move when they dance. It's quite spectacular!

In Northern Ireland, traditional Irish step dancing is very popular, and the dancers usually wear special clothes for their performances. Women and girls typically wear a short dress so they can kick up their feet quickly and easily. They sometimes wear tights on their legs, especially when the weather is cold. Men and boys usually wear simple clothes to step dance, such as black trousers, a shirt and a colourful jacket.

D

**3** **Are the sentences true or false? Correct the false sentences.**

1 The kilt is traditionally a clothing item for Scottish men.
2 A sporran is a cloth that woman wear on their shoulders.
3 Welsh men and women wear tall black hats for special events.
4 Breeches are trousers that some men wear to festivals.
5 There's an official costume for all Morris dancers in England.
6 Irish women must wear tights when they do step dancing.

**4** **Match the highlighted words in the text to the meanings.**

1 material for making clothes
2 very exciting to see and watch
3 special days or moments
4 normal habits in a culture
5 things or objects
6 shows for an audience

**5** **Look at the guards in the photos. What are they wearing? Where do you think they work?**

12 **6** **Listen to a presentation about the Beefeaters. Match the names of the uniforms to the photos.**

1 state dress uniform
2 undress uniform

12 **7** **Listen again and answer the questions.**

1 Where can tourists usually see Beefeaters?
2 How long ago were the Beefeaters established?
3 Why are these special guards called Beefeaters?
4 When do the Beefeaters wear the two uniforms?
5 What colours are these parts of the state dress uniform?
 a collar
 b stockings
 c bonnet

**8** **Read the *Useful language* phrases. Complete them with the words in the box.**

| collar | costumes | custom |
|---|---|---|
| dark | decorations | occasions |

## USEFUL LANGUAGE

**Talking about traditional clothes**

1 People wear traditional ________ .
2 This is a very important ________ in my country.
3 They wear ________ blue trousers.
4 The coat's got lots of gold ________ .
5 For important ________ the (Beefeaters) wear (the state dress uniform).
6 There's a big ________ at the top of the coat.

## PROJECT *A poster about traditional clothes*

**Create a poster about traditional clothes where you live. Use the questions below to help you.**

- What festivals do people celebrate where you live?
- Do people wear special clothes on those occasions?
- What do those clothes look like? Are they popular?
- Are there any unusual uniforms where you live?
- Who wears those uniforms? What do they look like?

**Present your poster to the class.**

02 NOW WATCH THE CULTURE VIDEO

# 3 MY WAY OF LIFE

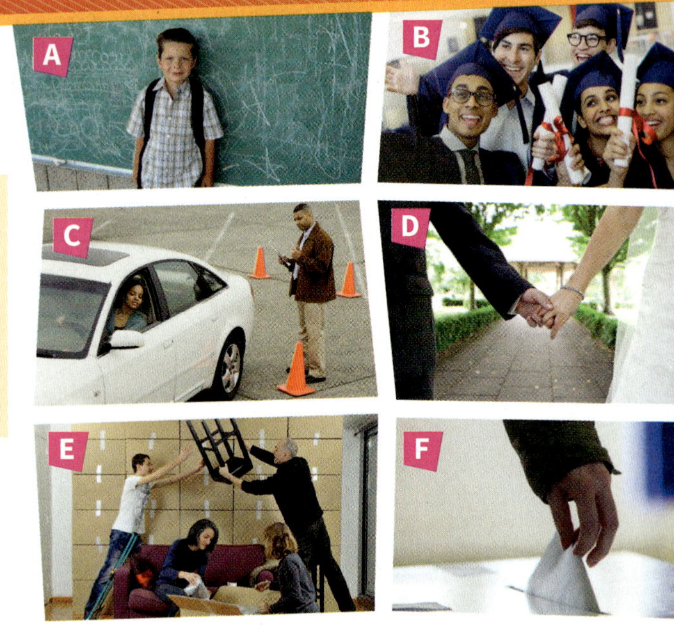


## ABOUT YOU

03 **Watch the video and then answer the questions.**
When did you learn to walk and talk?
How old were you when you learned to swim?
What are the most important events in a person's life?

## VOCABULARY Life events

**1** **Match six of the phrases to the photos.**

EP

be born · get a degree · get a driving licence · get a job · retire · get married · go to university · have children · leave home · leave school · move home · start school · vote

**2** **Put the life events in Exercise 1 in order. There is more than one possible answer. Then compare your answers.**

**3** **Read the quiz. Which four events in Exercise 1 are not mentioned in the questions?**

## Around the world: Age and events

**1** In England, children usually start school when they are ________.
A 4 B 5 C 6

**2** In Belgium and Germany, students cannot leave school before they are ________.
A 14 B 16 C 18

**3** In some states in the USA, the youngest age you can get a driving licence is ________.
A 14 B 16 C 17

**4** In England, around ________% of young people go to university. About 6% of these students leave university before the end of their course and don't get a degree.
A 33 B 43 C 53

**5** In almost all European countries, ________ leave home before ________.
A men, women B women, men

**6** In the UK, children of ________ are allowed to get a part-time job.
A any age B 13 or over C 16 or over

**7** In ________, the average age at which women and men get married is 33.
A Spain B India C Japan

**8** In Brazil you can vote in elections from the age of ________.
A 16 B 18 C 21

13 **4** **Listen and choose Charlie's answers to the quiz.**

**5** » **In pairs, choose *your* answers to the quiz. Then check your answers on page 120. Did you get more points than Charlie?**

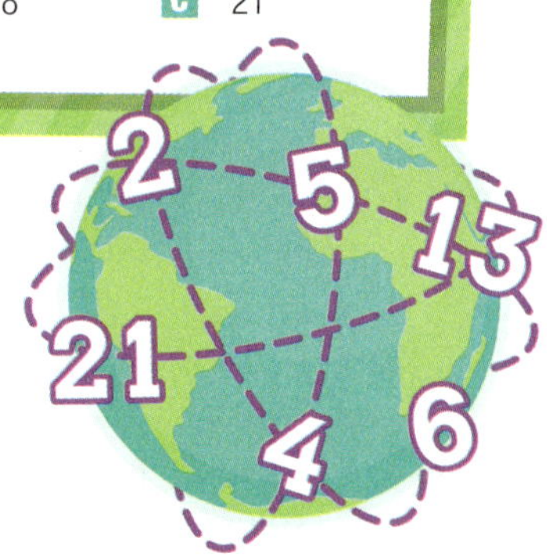


**6** **Look at the events in Exercise 1 again. Make six sentences with *I want to …* .**

*I want to leave home before I'm 25.* *I want to retire before I'm 40!*

**7** **Discuss the questions.**

1 When can you leave school in your country?
2 At what age can you get a job?
3 How old do you have to be to get a driving licence?
4 What do you think is the best age to get married?
5 Is it important to go to university and get a degree? Why? / Why not?
6 Which of your relatives have retired?

Simon, 47, and his daughter Emily, 16, answer today's question ...

# Is teenage life better now than in the past?

home → life → teenagers

14

**Simon** Everything is so different from when I was a teenager. Technology is the greatest change. I had a computer – but only for games, really. And I remember my dad's first mobile phone in the car – it was huge! But the internet and smartphones changed teenage life forever. *We* wrote letters; *they* are texting each other all day. *We* bought a few CDs every month; *they've* got almost every song in the world – in a tiny device in their pocket! When we moved home, we often never saw old friends again. Now it's simple to stay in contact with anyone, anywhere. To me, teenage life looks more exciting than it was.

Not everything is positive, of course. I don't think teenagers now are as healthy as we were in the past. They don't do enough exercise. Without technology, we were more active and spent a lot of our free time outside. Roads were safer, of course, but it's unbelievable to think that often our parents didn't have any idea where we were!

**Emily** Yes, technology makes our lives easier and is now essential for entertainment and school. But it brings problems too – the worst are awful things like bullying on social media ...

My problem is that teenage life is too busy now. On weekdays, as well as normal lessons, there are clubs at lunchtimes. Then after school on Mondays I have Spanish lessons, trumpet on Wednesdays and our band practises on Fridays. And weekends are just not long enough! On Saturday there's yoga club and on Sunday we often see relatives. Then there's homework, of course. Sometimes I'm exhausted on Sunday evenings!

The future will be harder for us, too. And I get worried about that. My friends and I feel the most important thing is to get a good degree – or we won't be able to leave home and get a job. And that means we have to get good marks in everything now. It's stressful.

I think my parents' teenage years were more relaxed than ours are today.

## READING

**1** **Read the article quickly. Who thinks teenage life ...**

1 is better now? 2 was better in the past?

**2** **Read the article again. Choose the correct answers.**

1 When Simon was a teenager,
- A his dad owned a computer and a mobile phone.
- B he owned a computer.
- C he played games on his dad's phone.

2 Simon thinks that before the internet
- A teenagers spent a lot of money on music.
- B it was hard to stay friends with people you didn't see.
- C teenagers enjoyed writing letters.

3 Why does Simon think that teenagers spent a lot of time outside?
- A because their parents weren't worried about them
- B because the roads weren't as dangerous
- C because phones and computers didn't exist

4 Emily thinks that teenagers
- A need technology for their school work.
- B shouldn't use social media.
- C aren't as happy as they were.

5 During the week, Emily
- A has extra music and language lessons.
- B never has time for lunch.
- C doesn't do any sport.

6 Why does Emily think she has to go to university?
- A because her friends want to go
- B because jobs will be harder to find in the future
- C because she always gets good marks at school

**3** **Match the highlighted words in the text to the meanings.**

1 difficult to think is true
2 calm and not busy
3 very tired
4 very bad
5 very small
6 very big

### TALKING POINTS

How was your parents' teenage life different from yours?

What problems can modern life bring for teenagers?

## GRAMMAR Comparatives and superlatives

**1** **Complete the table with the correct comparative and superlative adjectives. Check your answers in the article on page 21.**

| Adjective | Comparative | Superlative |
|---|---|---|
| | one-syllable adjectives | |
| big | bigger | the biggest |
| great | greater | 1 ........ |
| safe | 2 ........ | the safest |
| | two-syllable adjectives with *-y* | |
| easy | 3 ........ | the easiest |
| | other two-syllable and longer adjectives | |
| important | more important | 4 ........ |
| | irregular adjectives | |
| good | 5 ........ | the best |
| bad | worse | 6 ........ |
| far | further | the furthest |

**2** **Read the examples. Then complete the rules with *comparative* and *superlative*.**

1 Teenage life looks more exciting than it was.
2 Technology is the greatest change.

We often use:
**a** *than* after ........ adjectives.
**b** *the* before ........ adjectives.

**3** **Complete the facts with the comparative or superlative form of the adjectives. Remember to use *than* or *the*.**

### IT'S A FACT!

1 ........ (old) woman in the world lived until she was 122.

2 The university with ........ (large) number of students, over four million, is in Delhi, India.

3 The average US teenage boy is 4 kg ........ (heavy) he was 25 years ago.

4 Research says that Norway is ........ (happy) country in the world and also one of ........ (good) countries for children to grow up in.

5 Homes in Hong Kong, China, are now ........ (expensive) in any other city in the world.

6 ........ (young) age at which people can vote in Scotland is 16.

7 The north of England is generally ........ (cheap) the south of England.

### *not as … as*

**4** **Read the example and choose the correct option.**

Teenagers aren't as healthy as they were in the past. (= *they were healthier in the past*)

We use ***not as … as*** to say that people or things are *the same / not the same*.

» GRAMMAR REFERENCE AND PRACTICE PAGE 140

**5** **Compare the people and things with *not as … as*. Use the adjectives in the box or your own ideas.**

| comfortable | hard | old | serious | untidy |
|---|---|---|---|---|

**0** English / maths *English isn't as hard as maths.*
**1** children / adults
**2** you / your best friend
**3** your dad / your mum
**4** you / one of your relatives

**6** **Correct the mistake in each sentence.**

**1** They live in a house bigger than us.
**2** My mum is more relaxed that my dad.
**3** Coffee is the more popular drink in the UK.
**4** This area is more quiet than the city centre.
**5** My most happiest time was when I lived abroad.
**6** I'm not as taller as you.

## VOCABULARY *too, enough, not enough*

**1** EP **Read the examples and choose the correct options. Then match the rules to the sentences.**

**1** Weekends are just not long enough!
**2** They don't do enough exercise.
**3** Teenage life is too busy now.

**a** We use too *before / after* adjectives or adverbs to mean 'more than is necessary, possible, etc.'.
**b** We use enough *before / after* adjectives or adverbs to mean 'as much as is necessary'.
**c** We use enough *before / after* nouns.

**2** **Write replies. Use *too* or *enough* and the words in brackets. Be careful with the position of *enough*.**

**1** **A:** Did you buy the trainers?
**B:** No. They weren't ........ (big). They felt ........ (tight).
**2** **A:** Why didn't you do the homework?
**B:** I didn't have ........ (time) and I was ........ (tired).
**3** **A:** Are you getting a new laptop?
**B:** Yes. Mine is ........ (slow) and it hasn't got ........ (memory).

**3** » Turn to page 120.

## WRITING An informal email (1)

**1** **Read the email Jamal received from his friend Mark and the notes he made. What did Jamal do recently?**

From: Mark
Subject: Back to school …
Reply Forward

Hi Jamal,

How's it going? We miss you on the football team – I'm the new captain! — *Say congratulations.*

*Describe …* — Tell me about your new home. What's your room like?

What do you like doing in your free time where you live now? — *Explain …*

What's your new school like? Have you got any new friends yet? — *Tell Mark about Simon.*

Speak soon,
Mark

**2** **Read Jamal's reply. Does Jamal answer all of Mark's questions?**

From: Jamal
Subject: RE: Back to school …
Forward

Hi Mark,

It's great to hear from you. Congratulations on becoming captain! **Awesome** news!

I love our new house. It's brighter, bigger and there's a garden. Brighton isn't as big as Manchester, but there are **loads** of things to do. There's a **really** good football team here. They're great! I go to watch them play every weekend with my dad and sister.

My school is the largest in Brighton, but it isn't as modern as Victoria Park. In ICT, for example, there aren't enough laptops for everyone. I met a boy called Simon on my first day. He**'s into** computer games like me. **I guess** he's my best **mate** at the moment!

Speak soon,
Jamal

**3** **Read the *Prepare to write* box. Which phrases does Jamal use to begin and end his email?**

### PREPARE TO WRITE
**An informal email (1)**

**In informal emails:**

- use an informal phrase to begin your email: *Hi …, Hello …, It's great to hear from you*
- use short forms: *it's, he's, I'll*
- use informal words and expressions: *Great!, loads of things, He's into …, I guess …*
- use an informal phrase to end your email: *Love, Write soon, Speak soon, See you soon*

**4** **Find six different short forms in Jamal's email.**

**5** **Rewrite the sentences using short forms.**

1 He is really nice and we are good friends.
2 How is school? I hope you are getting on well.
3 I am getting to know everyone and they are all really friendly.
4 We have got tickets and we are going to a game together.

**6** **Match the highlighted informal words and phrases in Jamal's email to the meanings.**

1 I think
2 very
3 likes
4 very good
5 friend
6 a lot

**7** **Imagine you have moved to a new town and started a new school. Read Mark's email again and plan your reply. Use Jamal's notes in Exercise 1 to help you.**

**8** **Write your email to Mark.**

- Use the phrases and tips in the *Prepare to write* box.
- Write about 100 words.
- Remember to check your spelling and grammar.

# 4 CHAMPIONS

## ABOUT YOU

Which sports do you play regularly?
Which sports do you watch?

## VOCABULARY Sports

**1** 15 EP **Match the photos to some of the sports in the box. Then listen and check. Check the meaning of the other sports.**

athletics boxing climbing cycling gymnastics ice hockey ice skating jogging rugby squash surfing swimming table tennis tennis volleyball windsurfing

**2** 16 **Listen to six interviews and match the sentence halves.**

1 We go
2 We do
3 I don't play
4 I go
5 My mates and I go
6 We never play

a athletics in the summer.
b cycling all the time.
c jogging quite often.
d ice hockey.
e tennis together.
f windsurfing on the lake.

**3** **Add the sports from Exercise 1 to the table.**

| do | go | play |
|---|---|---|
| *athletics* | *climbing* | *ice hockey* |

**4** **What other sports and activities can you think of? Add them to the table in Exercise 3.**

*play basketball* *go snowboarding*

**5** **Do the quiz in pairs. The answers are all from Exercises 1 and 2.**

### RACE AGAINST THE CLOCK

**Answer the questions about the sports in Exercise 1.**

**Be quick!** You've got a time limit of five minutes!

1 Which nine sports can you do on your own?
2 Which four sports are for two or four players?
3 Which three sports are for teams of more than four?
4 Which five sports do you do on or in water or ice?
5 In which two sports do you use a racket?
6 In which four sports is there a net?
7 Which sport is not in the Olympic Games?
 a cycling b table tennis
 c ice hockey d squash
8 What sports do people do in these competitions?
 a Wimbledon b Tour de France
 c IAAF World Championships

**6** **Discuss the questions.**

1 What's your favourite sport? Why? When do you do it?
2 What are the most popular sports in your country?

## READING

**1** **Read the text quickly and answer the questions.**

1 Who are the new BMXers?
2 Do they like racing or 'freestyle' BMX?

17 **Did you think that BMX racing was just for men? Think again …**

# Meet the new BMXers

**It was a dark, rainy, winter's day at the National Cycling Centre in Manchester (UK) and I was taking photographs of the girls' BMX team. They were riding around the track with apparently no fear. They all obviously had a real passion for the sport.**

Olivia, aged 15, has long, brown hair. She's smart and confident, and the way she was smiling showed how much she loved it. How did she first become interested in BMX? [1] ________ . Although all the racers were boys, she knew instantly it was the sport for her. 'It's not harder for girls to get into the sport,' she said – anyone can do it. 'BMX gives you knowledge. When you come to the track, you learn something new every day.'

So what is a BMX? A BMX is a bike with small wheels and a low seat. Small wheels actually go faster than big wheels at speeds of up to 20 km/h. [2] ________ These mean that a bike can travel quickly without the rider using their legs too much. But there are no gears on a BMX, so the rider has to pedal a lot to go fast. [3] ________ .

Some BMXers love doing jumps and crazy stunts – this is called 'freestyle'. Other riders prefer racing. BMX races are fast but short. [4] ________ Both riding styles have something in common: riders fall off their bikes a lot. That's why they all wear a helmet, as well as knee and elbow guards under their racing clothes.

Many people think that BMX is scary or dangerous, but fear isn't a thought that goes through this BMX team's minds. [5] ________ They don't see the difference between male and female, not while they are out on the track doing what they enjoy the most.

**2** **Read the article again. Five sentences have been removed from the text. For each space choose the correct sentence. There are three extra sentences which you do not need to use.**

**A** She laughed because some of the riders were moving their legs so quickly.
**B** They usually only last for about 40 seconds.
**C** BMX race bikes can be very expensive.
**D** She was watching her older brother race.
**E** They weren't worried by the rain either.
**F** They see BMX as a fun sport, a way of life, a good social activity.
**G** Normal bikes have at least 20 gears.
**H** This is the biggest problem with BMX races.

**3** **Match the highlighted words in the text to the meanings.**

1 part of a bicycle that controls the speed of the wheels
2 tricks or difficult jumps on a bike
3 a path, often circular, used for races
4 a hard hat that protects your head
5 things you wear to protect parts of your body when playing a sport

### TALKING POINTS

Should schools offer the same sports to girls and boys? Or are some sports for boys and others for girls?

Do you think there is too much sport on TV? Why? / Why not?

## GRAMMAR Past continuous

**1** **Read the examples. Then choose the correct words to complete the rules.**

1 I **was taking** photographs of the girls' BMX team.
2 They **were riding** around the track.

a We use the past continuous to talk about actions in progress at a particular time in *the present / the past*.
b We form the past continuous with the correct *present / past* form of *be* and the *infinitive / -ing* form of the verb.

» **GRAMMAR REFERENCE AND PRACTICE PAGE 141**

**2** **Choose the correct form of the verbs to make past continuous sentences.**

1 They *were wearing / were wear* dark helmets.
2 He *isn't playing / wasn't playing* ice hockey last night.
3 My friends *wasn't talking / weren't talking* about sports.
4 What was he *doing / do* on the court?
5 *Were / Was* she watching the games?
Yes, she *was / were*.
6 Mark *is climbing / was climbing* yesterday.
7 My parents *was going / were going* to a bike race.
8 Were they *listening / listen* to the match?
No, they *weren't / wasn't*.

**3** **Look at the picture of a park last Saturday morning. Write positive and negative past continuous sentences about what the people were and weren't doing.**

0 Kim / play tennis / swim
*Kim was playing tennis. She wasn't swimming.*
1 Adam and Pete / run / skate
2 Myla / throw a ball / hit a ball
3 Karl and Liam / play squash / kick a ball
4 Megan and Ana / cycle / climb
5 Lucy / catch a ball / do athletics

**4** **Write questions in the past continuous.**

0 you / do / sports at 3.30 yesterday?
*Were you doing sports at 3.30 yesterday?*
1 what / you / do / at 8.30 yesterday evening?
2 you / read / at 10.30 / yesterday evening?
3 what / you / wear / last / Sunday?
4 you / sleep / at midnight last night?
5 you / have / breakfast at 8.00 this morning?
6 what / do / five minutes ago?

**5** **Ask and answer the questions in Exercise 4.**

## VOCABULARY Words with different meanings

**1** **Read the sentences. Choose the correct meaning of the words.**

EP

1 I did the extra maths **exercise**. Did you?
a noun: physical activity to get stronger
b noun: written work to practise something
2 Does this tracksuit **fit** you?
a verb: be the right size
b adjective: healthy and strong
3 Who won the Chelsea–Arsenal **match**?
a verb: be the same
b noun: a sports competition
4 The Bulls won the basketball game by 20 **points**.
a noun: the score (e.g. the number of goals/baskets) at the end of a match
b verb: indicate using your finger
5 The basketball team has got a new **trainer**.
a noun: a sports shoe
b noun: a person who prepares players for an event
6 I can't **work out** what to do next.
a verb: to exercise to make the body stronger
b verb: to find the answer to a problem
7 We got a **coach** to the volleyball match.
a noun: a type of bus
b noun: someone who teaches people a sport
8 We **train** at the football club twice a week.
a noun: a long, thin vehicle that travels on rails
b verb: to practise a sport

**2** **Complete the sentences. Use the correct form of the words in Exercise 1.**

0 This green colour *matches* your top.
1 You aren't ________ enough. Do some ________!
2 We go jogging with the rugby ________ every day, but we never ________ in the gym.
3 I can't see the captain. Can you ________ to her?
4 I bought some white ________ but they don't ________ me. They're a size 7 but I take an 8.
5 I need help with the last ________ on page 144.
6 How many ________ has your team got? Did they play any ________ last week?
7 Let's get a ________. The railway station is closed, so there aren't any ________ today.
8 I can't ________ how to play this game.

**3** » **Work with a partner. Student A turn to page 121. Student B turn to page 126.**

A

B

C

## LISTENING

18 **1** **Listen to the show and look at photos A–C. Which is the photo of the week? What happened next?**

18 **2** **Number the events in the order you hear them. Then listen again and check.**

**a** The football went into the goal.
**b** The Sunderland player kicked the football.
**c** A fan threw a beach ball onto the field.
**d** A Sunderland player was running towards the goal.
**e** The referee decided to allow the goal.
**f** The football hit the beach ball.

18 **3** **Listen again. Complete the sentences.**

Liverpool (x3) Manchester Sunderland (x2)

1 The *Sports Review* studio is in ______.
2 A ______ fan threw a beach ball onto the field.
3 ______ won the match 1–0.
4 The ______ players weren't playing well.
5 Chloe thought ______ played better than ______.

## SPEAKING Describing a past event

**1** **When was the last time you watched a sports event (in person or on TV) or took part in one? What was it?**

19 **2** **Listen to Max and Rachel talking about sports. Who took part in an event? Who watched one?**

19 **3** **Read the *Prepare to speak* box. Complete the sentences with the past simple or past continuous form of the verbs. Then listen again and check.**

1 Manchester City ______ (win) for most of the game.
2 Real Madrid ______ (score) two goals in the last five minutes.
3 Lots of people ______ (watch) the competition.
4 I ______ (come) third in one race.

### PREPARE TO SPEAK

**Describing a past event**

When you describe a past event:

- use the past simple to talk about the main things that happened
- use the past continuous to talk about actions in progress
- add your opinion: *It was an amazing …, It was really exciting, It was the best … ever, It was so cool, I really enjoyed …*
- add reasons for your opinion: *because …*

19 **4** **Listen to the whole recording again. Which phrase from the *Prepare to speak* box do they *not* use?**

19 **5** **Complete the reasons that Max and Rachel give. Listen again to check.**

1 I was very happy because …
2 I really enjoyed taking part because …

**6** **Think about a recent sports event. Read the questions and plan your answers.**

1 What was the event and when was it?
2 Did you watch it or take part in it?
3 What happened during the event?
4 What was the final result?
5 Did you enjoy it? Why? / Why not?

**7** **Ask and answer the questions in Exercise 6. Use the past simple and past continuous, and use phrases from the *Prepare to speak* box.**

# LIFE SKILLS PHYSICAL WELL-BEING

## KEEPING FIT

### LIFE SKILLS

**Keeping fit**

Fitness is an important part of a healthy lifestyle. If you want to keep fit, you need to care for your body and do physical activity every day.

**1** **Ask and answer the questions with a partner.**

1 What activities do you enjoy doing in PE class?
2 What physical activities do you do in your free time?

**2** **Read the text quickly. Match the sentences with the types of training.**

1 It's good for warming up before exercising.
2 It's exercise that gives you stronger muscles.
3 It's a typical activity for professional athletes.
4 It includes physical activities like cycling.

**3** **Read the text again and answer the questions.**

1 How can lifting smaller weights help you keep fit?
2 What two ways can people lift weights at the gym?
3 How does aerobic exercise keep your heart healthy?
4 What type of training can help you cycle faster?
5 Why is balance important for some types of exercise?
6 Why is interval training a good idea for tennis players?

**4** **Match the highlighted words in the text to the meanings.**

1 regular programme of activities
2 stop something from happening
3 in a good or correct way
4 move something to a higher place
5 pull something to make it longer
6 ability to exercise for a long time

20 **5** **Listen to Anna and Tom talking about their fitness habits. Who is usually more active?**

20 **6** **Listen again. Complete the sentences with one or two words.**

1 Tom usually plays ________ after school.
2 Tom sometimes goes to ________ with friends.
3 Anna's got ________ practice twice a week.
4 Anna also ________ on Tuesdays and Fridays.
5 Tom and Paul usually play ________ at the weekend.
6 Anna says Tom should ________ with his friend Danny.

**7** **Complete the *Useful language* phrases with the words in the box.**

| about | active | after school |
|---|---|---|
| could | go swimming | stairs |

### USEFUL LANGUAGE

**Making a fitness plan**

1 I usually play (basketball) ________.
2 I don't usually ________ on weekdays.
3 I do ________ an hour of exercise most days.
4 I'm not very ________ at weekends.
5 I ________ ride my bike to school more often.
6 We should always walk up the ________.

# 4 ways to keep fit

Scientists say that people should do one hour of physical activity every day. It can be sports, exercise or everyday activities, such as walking. In the USA, only 25% of teenagers do enough physical activity, and that's a problem. In addition, teens need three types of training to keep fit: weight, aerobic and flexibility training. They also need to train well for specific sports. Good coaches understand athletes' needs and help them to train properly.

1

**Weight training** gives you stronger, healthier muscles. If you lift big weights, your muscles get larger. You can also use smaller weights and lift them more times. This trains your body to exercise for a longer time. At the gym, some people use weight machines, but other people prefer free weights. In both cases, they must lift the weights carefully to prevent accidents.

2

**Aerobic training** is good for you because it makes your heart work harder. You can do light exercise for a longer time, such as cycling slowly for an hour. This gives you stamina so you can exercise longer. You can also cycle hard for five minutes and then rest for a minute. Then you cycle for another five minutes and rest again. This is interval training and it helps you become faster.

3

**Flexibility training** is also important for fitness. For example, athletes need to warm up and stretch their muscles before they exercise. Martial arts, such as Tai Chi, are great for flexibility training. People also need balance for these activities so they don't fall down. In flexibility training, it's best to go slowly and be careful. You don't want to hurt yourself!

4

**Sport-specific training** is a special exercise routine that helps athletes play one sport better. For example, professional football players run a lot and do extra weight training for their legs. In contrast, tennis players do more exercises for their arms. They also stop and start a lot during matches, so interval training is helpful for them. This is when you quickly change between doing high-intensity exercise and low-intensity exercise.

## PROJECT *An exercise plan*

**Make a plan for doing exercise in your free time. Think about the questions and make notes.**

- What sports can you do after school?
- What other exercise can you do on school days?
- What activities do you usually do at the weekend?
- What sports or exercise can you do with friends?
- What other activities can help you to keep fit?

**Present your exercise plan to the class.**

# REVIEW 1 UNITS 1–4

## VOCABULARY

**1 Write the opposite adjectives.**

1 What's wrong? You look **miserable**. You're usually very c.......... on Fridays.
2 Diana's very **polite**. She's never r.......... .
3 'Is Jacob **confident**?' 'No, he's quite s.......... .'
4 It was **careless** of you to lose your phone again. You need to be more c.......... with your things.
5 Marcus is really **friendly** today. He can sometimes be quite u..........!

**2 Find the words (→ ↘ ↗ ↓).**

| u | p | r | e | t | y | i | n | e | u | d | w |
|---|---|---|---|---|---|---|---|---|---|---|---|
| g | o | o | d | l | o | o | k | i | n | g | t |
| f | w | t | r | e | n | d | y | a | f | b | e |
| a | e | u | o | b | n | o | h | d | a | r | e |
| i | c | o | b | a | r | d | l | r | s | a | n |
| s | m | a | r | t | n | a | n | r | h | n | a |
| t | i | i | s | o | b | e | n | i | i | n | s |
| r | p | n | c | u | d | g | r | d | o | p | m |
| a | t | e | e | n | a | g | e | p | n | r | a |
| i | s | e | o | k | a | l | d | e | a | e | r |
| g | e | l | d | e | r | l | y | e | b | t | w |
| h | b | c | a | s | a | l | g | i | l | t | t |
| t | s | k | i | n | y | c | u | r | e | y | e |

Find words to describe someone's:

age
1 t *eenage*
2 e..........

looks
3 p..........
4 g..........-l..........

hair
5 b..........
6 c..........
7 s..........
8 b..........

clothes
9 c..........
10 s..........
11 u..........
12 t..........
13 s..........-h..........
14 b.......... n..........

**3 Choose <u>two</u> correct options for each verb.**

1 **play** volleyball boxing rugby ice skating
2 **do** surfing gymnastics athletics cycling
3 **go** table tennis climbing squash jogging
4 **leave** home school to university married
5 **get** born married university a degree
6 **have** children home confident long hair
7 **get** school a child a job a driving licence

**4 Read the text opposite and choose the correct word for each space. For each question, choose A, B, C or D.**

| | A | B | C | D |
|---|---|---|---|---|
| 1 | be | get | take | have |
| 2 | tiny | few | little | narrow |
| 3 | teams | coaches | members | teachers |
| 4 | finish | miss | stop | retire |
| 5 | method | road | kind | way |
| 6 | degree | university | grade | practice |

## GRAMMAR

**1 Complete the conversations. Use the present simple or continuous, or the past simple or continuous form of the verbs.**

1 **A:** I .......... (spend) a lot of time on homework at the moment.
**B:** Me too. It's unbelievable! Last term, we .......... (not have) as much work.
2 **A:** Why ...... you .......... (stop) having guitar lessons?
**B:** I .......... (not make) any progress and I didn't like the teacher.
3 **A:** Why ...... Tom .......... (be) so unfriendly at the moment?
**B:** I .......... (not know). He usually .......... (say) hello in the mornings.
4 **A:** .......... (you / go) cycling next Saturday?
**B:** No. I .......... (usually / go) cycling on Saturdays, but I .......... (lose) my helmet yesterday.
5 **A:** How old .......... (be) you when you .......... (get) your driving licence?
**B:** Eighteen. But I .......... (not own) a car until I was 25.
6 **A:** I .......... (send) you loads of messages last night but you .......... (not read) any of them.
**B:** No, sorry. I .......... (train) for a swimming competition. It's on Sunday. ...... you .......... (come) to watch?

# GAME OVER

## LIFE AFTER THE OLYMPICS

For athletes, the Olympic Games is often considered the most important event of their career. It is the chance to compete with the best sportsmen and women from around the world. But what happens to athletes when they are too old to [1] ______ part at this level? At this point many athletes are still young: often between 25 and 35 years old.

This can be a difficult time for many athletes. Only a [2] ______ number of them are as famous as Usain Bolt and can earn a lot of money as a celebrity. Others are lucky enough to start a career connected with their sport, for instance as [3] ______ for the next generation of Olympians. But for most athletes, when they [4] ______ from being a professional sportsperson, their whole [5] ______ of life changes. They often start studying again and go to university. In fact, nowadays many athletes study for a [6] ______ while they are training. This means they are better prepared for the time when their sports careers are over.

**2** **Complete the second sentence so that it means the same as the first. Use no more than three words.**

| | | |
|---|---|---|
| **1** | Your room is messier than mine. | My room isn't ______ yours. |
| **2** | I'm not as good at climbing as my dad. | My dad is ______ at climbing than me. |
| **3** | I don't own a warmer jacket. | This is ______ jacket I own. |
| **4** | My old boots aren't as comfortable as these ones. | These boots are ______ my old ones. |
| **5** | My hair isn't as curly as my sister's. | My sister's hair is ______ mine. |
| **6** | You're more patient than me. | I'm ______ as you. |
| **7** | There isn't a player on the team as bad as me. | I'm ______ player on the team. |
| **8** | My brother and I are the same height. | I'm ______ as my brother. |

**3** **Choose the correct words.**

**1** Tonight she *meet* / *'s meeting* some friends at the cinema.
**2** Thank you for the gift you *sent* / *send* me recently.
**3** She got the *better* / *best* mark in the class.
**4** I was looking online because I *needed* / *was needing* some new clothes.

**4** **Correct the mistake in each sentence.**

**1** We are having fun when we are together.
**2** I didn't heared my phone so I missed your call.
**3** Our new home is more near the school.
**4** My dad wasn't going to university.

# 5 CALL THE POLICE!

## ABOUT YOU

How much crime is there in your town or city?
Which crimes are the biggest problem where you live?

## VOCABULARY Crimes and criminals

**1** **Match the crimes to the photos.**

EP

burglary hacking pickpocketing
shoplifting theft vandalism

22 **2** **Listen to six people talking about crime and decide which crime the speakers are talking about.**

23 **3** **Complete the sentences with the missing crimes from Exercise 1 and the correct type of criminals in the box. Use the plural form where necessary. Then listen and check.**

EP

burglar hacker pickpocket shoplifter thief vandal

1 Three weeks ago a ______ stole over 100 million email addresses and passwords from a bank in the United States. Experts believe that ______ costs businesses over two trillion dollars every year.
2 We have a problem with ______ in our area. ______ have smashed the window of my parents' car three times in the last year.
3 We think that only 10% of ______ are professionals. For these people ______ is a job. They typically rob large stores and steal expensive items like designer clothes or bags.
4 I'd like to report the ______ of a car. I saw it happen. And I can describe the ______.
5 Please be careful of ______ in crowded areas. ______ is common at stations.
6 My neighbour doesn't know when the ______ happened. The ______ took TVs, computers, things like that.

**4** **Read the example and complete the definitions with the verbs *steal* and *rob*.**

EP

Professional shoplifters typically **rob** large stores and **steal** expensive items like designer clothes or bags.

1 Thieves ______ something from a place or person.
2 Thieves ______ a place or a person of something.

**5** **Complete the sentences with the correct form of *steal* or *rob*.**

1 The thief ______ my phone from the table in the café.
2 Do any of these photos show the man who ______ you?
3 My parents once came home and a burglar was ______ their flat. He ran away immediately.
4 Is downloading films the same as ______ them?

# That isn't ALLOWED HERE …

*In Singapore, few people chew gum on the streets. You can't bring it into the country and you can only buy it from the chemist's with an ID card! What unusual rules or laws have you come across around the world? And how did you find out about them?*

I was away with my parents in Honolulu, Hawaii last year. One afternoon, we were leaving a restaurant when it started raining hard. My mom suggested visiting the Natural History Museum as we were directly opposite it. We were crossing the road, when I got out my phone. I wasn't really thinking. I wanted to check my messages. Anyway, almost immediately I heard the noise of a loud motorbike. My first thought was: phone thief! But when I looked up, I saw a police officer. We looked at each other for a few seconds and then I noticed she was pointing at my phone! I had no idea, but it's actually illegal to look at your mobile phone on a pedestrian crossing in Honolulu. I'm only 16 but I had to pay a $15 fine! It was really unfair!

**Alexa, San Diego, US**

We went camping in Italy last year and the campsite had a huge pool. When we arrived, my brother and I got changed straight away and jumped in. We were really enjoying ourselves when suddenly we heard a loud noise. Everyone was looking at us and two lifeguards were shouting in Italian. There was probably a rule about jumping in, we thought. It *was* quite crowded. But then the lifeguards started pointing to their heads. For a few seconds we were really confused. Then we realised: *everyone* was wearing swimming caps! We looked it up online later. It's actually the law there. Even my dad had to wear one, and he's completely bald!

**Martin, Dublin, Ireland**

When my dad got a job in Sydney, Australia, we moved there from the UK for two years. We were living close to the centre and Dad started going to work by bike. He didn't even have one back in the UK! We knew that bike helmets are compulsory in Australia. And Dad always wore one. So when the police stopped him and some other cyclists at a traffic light one morning, he was feeling relaxed. But can you believe this? While the officers were checking the bikes, they noticed that several of them didn't have bells – including Dad's. And all bikes must have them in the city. They were each fined $106 – about £60! That feels so unfair.

**Louise, Brighton, UK**

24

## READING

**1** **Read the stories quickly. Complete three sentences about each story.**

1 In Honolulu, Hawaii, you mustn't …
2 In Italy, you must …
3 In Sydney, Australia, all bikes must …

**2** **Read the stories again. Are the sentences true or false?**

1 Alexa had the idea to go to the museum.
2 The police officer stopped Alexa near the museum.
3 Martin and his brother understand Italian.
4 Jumping into the pool was allowed at the campsite.
5 Louise's dad has always been into cycling.
6 Her dad had to pay $106.

**3** **Complete the sentences with the highlighted words in the stories.**

1 We were once ________ for cycling at night without lights.
2 ________ downloading of music, TV and films is a common problem throughout the world.
3 ________ in Brazil says that everyone between 18 and 70 must vote in an election.
4 At my school, it's ________ to wear the uniform.
5 The minimum ________ for driving and texting in the UK is £200.
6 There's a ________ in our house about using phones at the dinner table.

### TALKING POINTS

Do you know any unusual laws?
What rules do you disagree with at your school?

## GRAMMAR Past simple and continuous

**1** Read the examples. Which verb is in the past continuous? How do we form the past continuous?

1 Immediately I heard the noise of a loud motorbike.
2 She was waiting at the side of the road.

**2** Choose the correct words to complete the rules.

a We use the past *simple* / *continuous* to talk about a completed action at a past time.
b We use the past *simple* / *continuous* to talk about actions in progress at a past time.

**3** Choose the correct form of the verbs.

1 I couldn't call you. The thief *stole* / *was stealing* my phone!
2 I saw someone in front of your house yesterday. She *tried* / *was trying* to open your car door.
3 What *did the burglars take* / *were the burglars taking*?
4 I phoned you last night but there was no answer. What *did you do* / *were you doing*?
5 We weren't at home last night. We *travelled* / *were travelling* back from a relative's house.

**4** Read the examples from the stories. Then complete the rules with *past simple* or *past continuous*.

1 We were crossing the road, when I got out my phone.
2 While the officers were checking the bikes, they noticed that several of them didn't have bells.
3 When we arrived, my brother and I got changed straight away and jumped in.

We often use the past continuous and the past simple together.
a The ________ talks about a past action in progress.
b The ________ talks about a completed shorter action that interrupted the action in progress.
c If one action happens after the other, we use the ________ for both actions.

» GRAMMAR REFERENCE AND PRACTICE PAGE 142

**5** Correct the mistake in each sentence.

1 I read a book when a woman screamed.
2 We are talking when a policeman asked me my name.
3 We went to my house and we were watching TV.
4 When I walked near the river, I saw a dog in the water.
5 While we're waiting for the bus, I heard a cry.
6 He was quite tall and wears a loose-fitting tracksuit.

**6** Complete the story with the past simple or past continuous form of the verbs.

### Couple find 'Goldilocks' burglar

When Martin Holtby and Pat Dyson got home from their holiday recently, they [1] ________ (notice) something strange immediately. Their unopened letters were on the table. There was some food shopping in the kitchen. While Martin [2] ________ (look) around the house, he [3] ________ (find) more strange things. A man's clothes [4] ________ (hang) in the bathroom. Their bath was full of hot water. [5] ________ a burglar ________ (live) in their house?

When Martin [6] ________ (go) into the bedroom, he found the answer. A man [7] ________ (sleep) in their bed! The couple quickly called the police and when they [8] ________ (arrive), they took him away.

The man was fined £200. He didn't steal anything while he [9] ________ (stay) in the house. He wasn't actually a burglar. He thought the house was empty and he [10] ________ (need) somewhere to sleep!

## VOCABULARY ourselves, yourselves, themselves and each other

**1** Match the sentences to the photos.

EP

A

B

1 They're looking at themselves.
2 They're looking at each other.

**2** Choose the correct words.

EP
1 Jack bought itself / himself a new phone.
2 I cut myself / itself while I was washing up.
3 Did you teach myself / yourself the guitar?
4 Did you and Sara hurt herself / yourselves?
5 Sam and I made myself / ourselves a snack.
6 Thanks for the party! Everyone really enjoyed ourselves / themselves.

**3** Complete the sentences with the correct pronoun from Exercise 2 or *each other*.

1 They walked past ________ without saying a word.
2 Josie introduced ________ to everyone.
3 Tom and I often argue with ________.
4 I need to buy a present for Tom. We always give ________ presents on our birthdays.
5 Did you all enjoy ________ last weekend?

**4** » Work with a partner. Turn to page 121.

# WRITING A story (1)

**1** **Look at the photo and the title of Ellen's story. What do you think happened?**

## HERO for a day!

Last year, I went on a school trip with my classmates. We left school early by coach and the journey took several hours. When we arrived, everyone was feeling exhausted.

While I was getting off the coach, I noticed a man in his early twenties. He was standing really close to one of my friends. Suddenly, I realised what was happening. The man was trying to steal my friend's purse from her bag!

I immediately shouted to my friend. The man heard me, and for a few seconds we looked at each other. Then he started running. Luckily, there were two police officers nearby. They ran after the pickpocket and soon they caught him.

The next day, there was a story about it online and everyone was talking about it. I was a hero!

**2** **Read Ellen's story. What do you think of the title for her story? Can you think of a better title?**

**3** **Read the *Prepare to write* box. Then read Ellen's story again and put events a–e in order. Decide which events belong to the beginning, middle and end of the story.**

### PREPARE TO WRITE

**A story (1)**

When you write a story:

- make sure there is a beginning, middle and end
- give the story an interesting title
- use verbs in the past simple and past continuous
- use adjectives and adverbs to make your story interesting.

**a** Ellen saw the pickpocket.
**b** The police caught the pickpocket.
**c** Ellen got off the coach.
**d** The story appeared on the internet.
**e** The coach left school.

**4** **Look at Ellen's story again. How many verbs can you find in the past simple and past continuous?**

**5** **Look at the highlighted words in Ellen's story. Which are adjectives and which are adverbs?**

**6** **You are going to write a story which must begin with the sentence 'While I was closing my curtains one night, I noticed something unusual'. Plan the events in your story. Use the questions to help you.**

- Where does the story take place?
- What happens at the beginning? What did you notice?
- What are the main events?
- What happens in the end?

**7** **Compare your ideas with a partner. Can you improve your plan?**

**8** **Write your story.**

- Begin the story with the sentence in Exercise 6.
- Use the tips in the *Prepare to write* box.
- Write about 100 words.
- Remember to check your spelling and grammar.

# 6 CITY LIFE

## ABOUT YOU

04 **Watch the video and discuss the questions.**
Would you prefer to live in a big city or a village? Why?
What are the good and bad things about where you live?

## VOCABULARY City problems

25 EP **1 Match the words to the photos A–F. More than one word can match some photos. Then listen and check.**

| crowds | graffiti | green spaces |
|---|---|---|
| pollution | power cut | |
| public transport | rubbish | |
| rush hour | traffic jam | |

**2 Complete the sentences with some of the problems in Exercise 1.**

0 If we leave for the shopping centre early, we can avoid the *crowds*. It gets really busy there by lunchtime.
1 There was a ________ in our building last night. We had to use torches to see.
2 Can you take out the ________? They'll collect it tomorrow morning.
3 There's a huge problem with ________ in our city from cars and lorries. Many of the buses are electric now.
4 There is always a ________ outside our school in the mornings. More children should walk to school. It's dangerous!
5 I go to school by ________. I often catch the bus but there's also a train.
6 We never go on the underground during the ________ in summer. The trains get too hot.

26 **3 Listen to four people describing where they live. Answer the questions about each person.**

- Do they live in a city or in a village?
- What problem from Exercise 1 is each person talking about? Choose from the words in the box.

| graffiti | green spaces | public transport | rush hour |
|---|---|---|---|

27 **4 Listen and write one or two words in each space.**

1 There's a lot of graffiti on a ________ near the man's house.
2 When the girl lived in a village, she ________ to school.
3 The boy usually gets ________ into the city.
4 The woman says she avoids ________ during the rush hour.

**5 Complete the sentences about where you live. Use the problems in Exercise 1. Discuss your sentences in pairs.**

1 There's a serious problem with …
2 We don't have a problem with …
3 There are lots of …
4 There isn't/aren't enough …
5 One of my favourite places is …
6 One thing I don't like is …

## READING

1 Look at the photos. What do you think these teenagers invented? Read the article quickly and check your answers. Ignore any spaces.

# City problems – TEENAGERS' SOLUTIONS

28

*These two teenagers noticed two everyday problems in cities. And they decided to do something about them.*

While Ben Gulak was visiting Beijing, China, he was shocked at the air pollution in the city. He soon realised one of the main causes: transport. In Ben's home town in Canada, the traffic is quite light, but Beijing has a lot of traffic. Some people drive cars, but a lot of people ride scooters. They're cheaper and they don't need much petrol. They're also lighter and easier to drive through traffic jams. There is one problem: petrol scooters can produce ten times more air pollution than cars.

Back in Canada, Ben started thinking about the problem. He wanted to design a new type of transport – something as small as a scooter, but cleaner. He called his invention the Uno – a motorbike which looks like … half a motorbike! It doesn't use any petrol – just electricity.

Ben won a prize for his invention and now he's completed three different versions of the bike. Will we one day see it on our roads?

When Ann Makosinski was young, she only had a few toys to play with. Instead, she loved inventing new things from rubbish around the house. They didn't work, of course, but Ann soon [1] ________ an interest in science and electronics.

The idea for her first successful invention came from a friend in the Philippines. Ann, who is half Filipino, half Canadian, [2] ________ that her friend was doing badly at school. The [3] ________ was that she couldn't study at night because there wasn't any electricity. Ann was amazed to discover that many people, over a billion in fact, don't have [4] ________ to electricity. And then she remembered a fact from her science class: the heat in a person means each of us is like a walking 100W light bulb. So Ann designed a torch that uses just the heat from a human hand. It wasn't as powerful as a normal torch and only [5] ________ a little light. But Ann's invention won an international science competition with a prize of $25,000 to [6] ________ her education in the future.

2 Now read the part about Ann Makosinski again and choose the correct word for each space. For each question, choose A, B, C or D.

| | A | B | C | D |
|---|---|---|---|---|
| 1 | A developed | B grew | C made | D increased |
| 2 | A informed | B heard | C told | D called |
| 3 | A trouble | B event | C complaint | D rule |
| 4 | A opportunity | B way | C chance | D access |
| 5 | A did | B brought | C produced | D achieved |
| 6 | A own | B carry | C keep | D support |

3 Read the article again and complete the sentences with one or two words in each space.

1 Ben was on holiday in ________ but he is actually from ________.
2 Cars use ________ than scooters.
3 Scooters create more ________ than cars.
4 The Uno is cleaner than a normal scooter because it uses ________.
5 When she was a child, Ann used rubbish ________ new things.
6 Ann's friend wasn't doing well at school because it was impossible ________ at night.
7 Ann's torch works by changing ________ into electricity.
8 Ann won $25,000 for her ________ of the torch.

4 Match the highlighted words in the article to the meanings.

1 largest
2 something you know is true
3 plan something before making it
4 surprised and upset
5 very strong
6 in place of something else

### TALKING POINTS

What problem or situation would you like to solve where you live?
How could you improve the problem or situation?

# GRAMMAR *some/any, much/many, a lot of, a few / a little*

**1** **Read the examples. Then complete the rules with *some* or *any*.**

1 **Some** people drive cars.
2 The Uno doesn't use **any** petrol.
3 Have you got **any** ideas?

We use:
**a** ________ before nouns in positive sentences.
**b** ________ before nouns in negative sentences and in questions.

**2** **Complete the sentences with *some* or *any*.**

1 Do you need ________ help with the rubbish?
2 I like ________ graffiti but not all of it.
3 There's ________ heavy traffic on the motorway.
4 Is there ________ information about bus times?
5 There isn't ________ electricity at the moment. I think there's a power cut.
6 I've got ________ rubbish here. Where can I put it?

**3** **Read the examples. Then complete the rules with the words.**

1 Beijing is like **a lot of** big cities around the world.
2 The city has **a lot of** traffic.
3 **A lot of** people ride scooters.
4 Scooters don't need **much** petrol.
5 When Ann was young, she only had **a few** toys.
6 **Many** people don't have access to electricity.
7 Ann's torch only produced **a little** light.

**a** We use *many*, ________ and ________ to talk about large amounts.
**b** We don't usually use *much* or *many* in positive sentences: *There is ~~much~~* ***a lot of*** *time.*
**c** We use ________ and ________ to talk about small amounts.
**d** We don't use *a few* or *a little* in negative sentences: *He hasn't got ~~a little~~* ***much*** *money.*

» **GRAMMAR REFERENCE AND PRACTICE PAGE 143**

**4** **Look at the underlined nouns in the examples in Exercise 3. Are they countable or uncountable?**

**5** **Complete the table with *a lot of*, *a little* and *much*.**

| Countable nouns | Uncountable nouns |
|---|---|
| There aren't **many** cities. | There isn't [1] ________ water. |
| There are **a lot of** scooters. | There's [2] ________ traffic. |
| There are **a few** people. | There's [3] ________ petrol. |

**6** **Choose the correct words.**

1 **A:** Do you like living in the country?
**B:** Mostly. There are *a few / a little* bad things. There isn't *many / much* entertainment.
2 **A:** I got *much / a lot of* tips from my aunt about visiting the UK.
**B:** My brother gave me *a little / a few* information about *a / some* good things to see in the UK.
3 **A:** Have you got *a few / some* minutes? I'm doing a questionnaire on pollution.
**B:** I'm sorry. I haven't got *much / many* time. Are there *many / much* questions?
4 **A:** Do you have *some / any* problems with crime?
**B:** There's *a little / a few* graffiti, but not really.

**7** **Think about your perfect place to live and complete the sentences. Compare your ideas.**

1 My perfect place to live has got *a lot of / a few* …
2 There are *some / a lot of* …
3 There aren't *any / a lot of* …
4 It hasn't got *much / many* …
5 There's only *a little* …

# VOCABULARY Compounds: noun + noun

**1** **Make a word from A and B for each photo 1–8 below.**

EP

**A** ~~apartment~~ bus pedestrian post recycling speed taxi road

**B** bin box ~~building~~ crossing limit rank sign stop

1 *apartment building*

**2** **Compete the sentences with the correct compound from Exercise 1.**

1 There's a lot of people at the ________. Maybe we should catch a bus instead.
2 What's the ________ on motorways?
3 Can you take this letter to the ________ for me?
4 I live on the fourth floor of that ________.
5 It's compulsory for cars to stop at a ________.
6 Is this your ________? Is it OK to put plastic in it?
7 Let's meet at the ________. There are lots that go into the centre from there.
8 The ________ says turn right.

**3** » **Work with a partner. Turn to page 121.**

# LISTENING

**1** **What are the advantages and disadvantages of living in the country?**

29 **2** **Listen to an interview with Bess and Mr Evans. In general, do they agree or disagree?**

29 **3** **Read the sentences carefully and check any new words. Then listen again and choose the correct words.**

1. Mr Evans lives in the *country* / *city*.
2. Bess *lives* / *lived* in the same place as Mr Evans.
3. Mr Evans thinks Bess is *sometimes* / *never* late for school.
4. Mr Evans thinks villages need better *roads* / *public transport*.
5. Bess thinks the problem with rubbish is *worse* / *better* where she lives now.
6. Bess thinks we should do more *cleaning* / *recycling* in this country.

# SPEAKING Agreeing and disagreeing

**1** **Look at the two photos below. What can you see?**

30 **2** **Listen to Alice and Oliver talking about the places. What do they agree on?**

30 **3** **Read the *Prepare to speak* box. Then listen again.**

**Which phrases do Alice and Oliver use? Write *A* or *O* next to each phrase.**

## PREPARE TO SPEAK
### Agreeing and disagreeing

**Giving your opinion**
Personally, I think …
I (don't) think …
It seems to me …
If you ask me, …

**Asking for an opinion**
What do you think?
Do you agree?
Do you think …?

**Agreeing**
That's true.
Yes, maybe you're right.
I completely agree with …

**Disagreeing**
I'm not sure I agree.
I don't think so.
I don't agree.

**4** **Discuss which place in the photos below you would prefer to live in. Use phrases from the *Prepare to speak* box to agree and disagree.**

**5** **Prepare your ideas on two of the topics below.**

1. going to the cinema / watching films at home
2. going to a concert / listening to music on headphones
3. cycling / using public transport
4. living in an apartment building / living in a house
5. holidays at the beach / holidays in cities

**6** **Discuss the topics in Exercise 5. Use phrases from the *Prepare to speak* box to agree and disagree.**

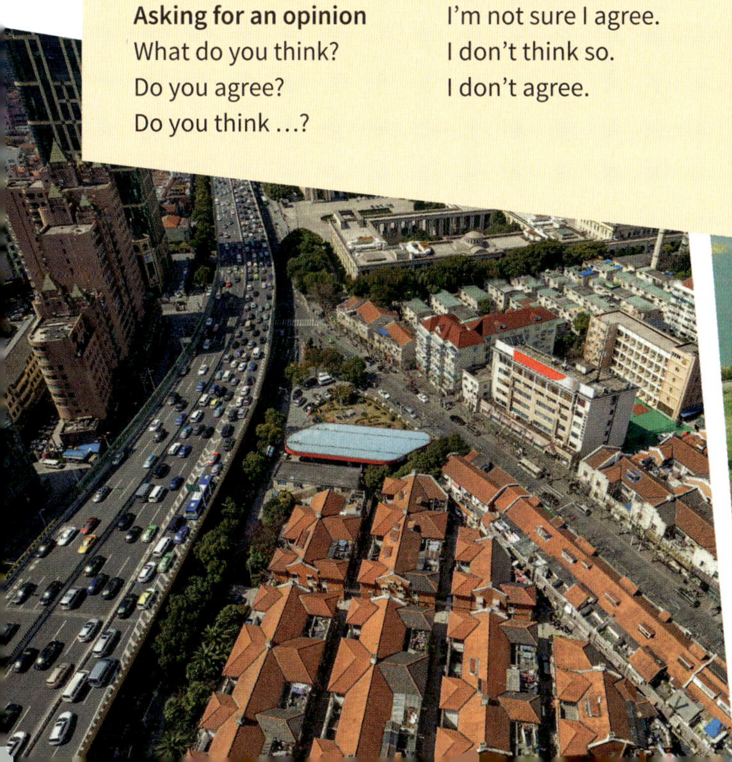

# CULTURE

## NEW YORK CITY

**1** **Ask and answer the questions with a partner.**

1 Have you ever been to a big city like New York?
2 What do you think people can see and do there?

**2** **Do the New York City quiz.**

**3** **Read the text. Find the answers to the quiz.**

**1** About … people live in New York.
**A** 2.5 million **B** 8.5 million **C** 40 million

**2** New York City is also called the Big …
**A** Apple **B** Easy **C** Borough

**3** New York's Central Park is in …
**A** Brooklyn **B** Coney **C** Manhattan

**4** Around … different languages are spoken in New York.
**A** 8 **B** 80 **C** 800

**5** New York's taxis are typically … in colour.
**A** black **B** white **C** yellow

# NEW YORK, NEW YORK

31

**New York is one of the most exciting cities in the world. It's the capital of New York State and the largest city in the USA, with a population of about 8.5 million. The city's nickname is the Big Apple and people also call it 'the city that never sleeps' because it's busy day and night.**

## History

Over the past two centuries, many millions of people have moved to the United States. In the 19th century the immigrants were mainly Europeans. By 1850, about 25% of New Yorkers were Irish.

The population of New York grew from 2.5 million in 1890 to 7 million in 1930. Since the 1960s, the immigrants have been mostly from Latin America and Asia. This incredible mix of people has made New York City one of the most multicultural cities in the world. Today, about 30% of all New Yorkers were born in another country and it's estimated that you can hear over 800 languages in the city. Some immigrants have created their own neighbourhoods, like Little Italy, Chinatown, and Spanish Harlem, each of which offers a different experience of New York culture.

## New York life

There are five main areas in the city, called boroughs: Manhattan, the Bronx, Queens, Brooklyn and Staten Island. Manhattan is the most famous of these, with its tall skyscrapers, like the Empire State Building. The tallest is One World Trade Center, which is 541 metres tall.

New Yorkers call Times Square 'the crossroads of the world'. It's where New Yorkers come together to celebrate special events, to go to the movies and the theatre, and to enjoy street food from every corner of the world. People that are more interested in shopping, fashion or music hang out in trendy SoHo in the south of Manhattan.

Manhattan has plenty of green spaces, including the famous Central Park. About 40 million people, New Yorkers as well as tourists, visit the park every year to enjoy walking, cycling, skating and picnics.

From Manhattan, it's a short walk over Brooklyn Bridge to get to the borough of Brooklyn. Here, people visit the varied street markets or chat with friends in the borough's fashionable coffee shops. At weekends, thousands of New Yorkers go to an area of Brooklyn called Coney Island. Here, they escape the stress of city life by relaxing on the three-kilometre long beach or by having fun at the famous Luna Park theme park.

When it's time to go home, New Yorkers can either take the 24-hour subway or catch one of the city's famous yellow taxi cabs.

## 4 Answer the questions with information from the article.

1 How big was the Irish community in New York in the 1850s?
2 What are the names of the five main areas of the city?
3 How tall is the tallest building in the city?
4 Which area of New York is good for shopping, according to the article?
5 How can you get from Manhattan to Brooklyn?
6 Why do people visit Coney Island?

## 5 Match the highlighted words in the text to the meanings.

1 very tall buildings, usually in a city
2 an informal name for something or someone, used instead of a real name
3 consisting of many different types
4 the number of people living in a particular area
5 a system of trains that mainly travel underground
6 areas of a town or city that people live in

## 6 What are these sights? Which ones would you like to see?

## 7 Listen to Fiona talk about her trip to New York. Tick (✓) the places that you hear.

32

1 ☐ the Statue of Liberty
2 ☐ JFK Airport
3 ☐ Chinatown
4 ☐ Times Square
5 ☐ Bronx Zoo
6 ☐ Empire State Building
7 ☐ Central Park
8 ☐ Coney Island
9 ☐ MoMA
10 ☐ Yankee Stadium

## 8 Listen again. Are the sentences true or false?

32

1 Fiona went to Coney Island on Sunday morning.
2 They didn't have enough time to see a baseball game.
3 Fiona went to Times Square before lunch on Saturday.
4 Fiona's parents didn't want to visit the art museum.
5 They didn't visit the Statue of Liberty this time.
6 Fiona had dinner in Chinatown on Sunday.

## 9 Look at the phrases in the *Useful language* box. Change the words in brackets with your own ideas.

### USEFUL LANGUAGE

**Describing a visit to a city**

1 First, we went to (the park).
2 Next, we visited (Times Square)
3 After lunch, we decided to (visit a museum).
4 I loved the (second-hand clothing) shops there.
5 I learned a lot about (the history of New York).
6 We had (good) weather, too.

## PROJECT

*A report about a famous city*

**Write about an interesting visit to a famous city. Think about your answers to the questions.**

- What city did you visit? When did you go?
- Did you go there with your family or friends?
- What was the weather like during your visit?
- What famous places and sights did you see?
- Did you go shopping for anything special?
- What did you learn about the city's history?
- What was your favourite part of the visit?

**Present your work to the class, using the phrases from the *Useful language* box.**

05 NOW WATCH THE CULTURE VIDEO

# 7 GETTING ON

## ABOUT YOU

When you have a problem, who do you ask for help? Friends or family? Why?

Do you consider any members of your family to be a friend as well?

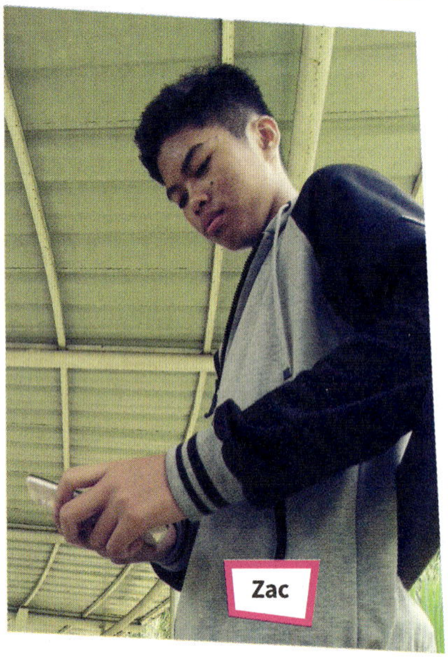

## VOCABULARY *be, do, have* and *make*

33 **1 Look at the photos and listen to two conversations. Complete the sentences with the correct name.**

1 ______ has a problem with family.
2 ______ has a problem with non-family members.

33 **2 Choose the correct option to complete the sentences. Then listen again and check.**

EP

1 He *does / makes* me angry.
2 You're always *making / having* problems with him.
3 We *had / made* an argument this morning.
4 *I'm / I've* annoyed with him!
5 *Are you / Have you* on your own?
6 Why don't we *make / do* something later?
7 You need to *make / have* fun.
8 Can you *make / do* me a favour?
9 What *is / has* wrong?
10 It's hard to *do / make* friends.
11 It *doesn't / isn't* my fault.
12 You *have / are* lots in common.

**3 Complete the table with the phrases in Exercise 2. Can you add any more?**

| | |
|---|---|
| be | *be annoyed* |
| do | |
| have | |
| make | |

**4 Complete the sentences with the correct positive or negative form of *be*, *do*, *make* or *have*.**

1 Oh, no! Something ______ wrong with the TV. It isn't working!
2 Can you ______ me a favour, please?
3 Some people find it easy to ______ new friends.
4 I'm really sorry that the glass broke, but it ______ my fault!
5 You should talk to someone if you ______ problems.
6 Let's ______ something together on Saturday.
7 Our coach ______ really annoyed with the referee at our last match.
8 What were they saying? Were they ______ an argument?
9 Thanks for your party last night. We ______ a lot of fun.
10 I get on OK with Noel, but we ______ much in common.
11 My cousin is always rude. She ______ me really angry.
12 Is Piper feeling OK? She ______ on her own again.

**5 Discuss the questions.**

1 Who or what makes you angry?
2 When and why do you have arguments?
3 When do you like being on your own?
4 How do you have fun? Who with?
5 What do you have in common with your best friends?

READING

1 Read problems 1–3 quickly. Who isn't annoyed with a family member?

# TROUBLESPOT

*don't get angry – get advice*

34

LOGIN HOME ASK US VIDEOS LINKS

## 1 KAITLIN, 15, DERBY

I'm quite a shy person and I haven't got a lot of friends. I was walking home from school yesterday, when I saw some boys from my class. They were laughing at me. One of them said, 'She's always on her own!' and he pointed at me. It was unbelievable! Why do I have to be with someone all the time? What's wrong with being on your own?

## 2 DYLAN, 14, PENZANCE

My little brother is really annoying. Yesterday, I found him in my room. He knows he mustn't go in there. And he was reading my diary! It made me really angry. Then we had an argument because he took my phone. He sent about 50 texts and now I haven't got any credit. Help!

## 3 ALEX, 15, LONDON

My best mates, Sasha and Mandy, are just like me. They're often late and they forget things, but they **behave themselves** (most of the time!). I was hanging out with them last Saturday and I had to get home by 10 pm, but we were having fun and I didn't realise the time. I was a bit late because they didn't have to get home until 11 pm.

Now my parents say I can't spend time with my mates because they can't **trust** me, and I have to get home by 9.30 pm. It isn't **fair**! I don't want to fall out with my parents, but they think I'm still a child. What should I do?

## What you think ...

**A** I agree. Sometimes you don't have anything in common with other people, and that's fine.

**B** He should **apologise**. Maybe you should **lock** your door.

**C** You shouldn't get angry. It's important to talk to your parents. Then you'll understand why they're worried.

**D** You must show them you can change, so try to be really sensible for a month – or forever!

**E** Maybe you should put a **password** on your phone.

**F** Friendship is important, but you don't have to be with someone all the time. It's good to be independent.

**2** **Read the problems again and complete the sentences with the correct names, *Kaitlin*, *Dylan* or *Alex*.**

1 .................. has a problem as a result of a mistake.
2 .................. had a problem after class one day.
3 .................. had an unwelcome visitor.
4 .................. likes being alone sometimes.
5 .................. doesn't agree with someone else's decision.
6 .................. can't use something essential.

**3** **Read the problems again and then read advice A–F in the 'What you think ...' section. Match two pieces of advice to each person.**

**4** **What advice would *you* give to each person?**

**5** **Match the highlighted words to the meanings.**

1 a secret word that protects you online
2 shut something with a key
3 say sorry to someone
4 treating people in a way that is right
5 be polite and not do things that are unhelpful
6 believe someone is good, reliable and honest

### TALKING POINTS

Are internet forums good places to get advice? Why? / Why not?

In what ways can you help or support your friends when they have problems?

## GRAMMAR *have to* and *must*

**1** **Read the examples. Then complete the rules.**

1 You **must** show them you can change.
2 He knows he **mustn't** go in there.
3 I **have to** get home by 9.30 pm.
4 You **don't have to** be with someone all the time.
5 Last Saturday, I **had to** get home by 10 pm.
6 My mates **didn't have to** get home until 11 pm.

**a** We use *have to* and ________ to talk about rules and things that are necessary.
**b** We use ________ when something isn't allowed by a rule.
**c** We use *don't have to* when something isn't necessary. We use ________ when something wasn't necessary in the past.
**d** We use ________ for rules in the past.
**e** Remember: *You **mustn't** go.* = You aren't allowed to go. *You **don't have to** go.* = It isn't necessary for you to go.

**2** **Make two sentences for each idea. Compare your answers.**

0 things you have to do at school
*I have to wear a uniform. I have to study for my exams.*
1 things you don't have to do at school
2 things you mustn't do at school
3 things you must do at home
4 things you mustn't do at home
5 things you had to do when you were younger
6 things you didn't have to do when you were younger

### *should*

**3** **Read the examples. Then complete the rules.**

1 What **should** I do?
2 He **should** apologise.
3 You **shouldn't** get angry.

We use:
**a** ________ to say something is a good idea.
**b** ________ to say something isn't a good idea.
**c** ________ in questions to ask for advice.

» GRAMMAR REFERENCE AND PRACTICE PAGE 144

**4** **Take turns to read out the problems and give advice. Use *You should* or *You shouldn't.***

1 I can never find my phone.
2 I find it hard to make friends.
3 I have a lot of arguments with my cousins.
4 My parents think everything is my fault.
5 My sister/brother uses my things without asking.

**5** **Correct the mistake in each sentence.**

1 We wanted to chat, but we must go to school.
2 I'm sorry we had ask you.
3 In my opinion, all schools has to have a uniform.
4 Studying is great, but you don't have to sit down all day.
5 I don't must go to bed early at weekends.

## VOCABULARY Phrasal verbs: relationships

**1** **Read the examples. Then match the phrasal verbs in 1–8 to the meanings a–h.**

EP

1 We **hang out** in the park after school.
2 Do you **get on** well with your sister?
3 I **get together** with my mates on Saturdays.
4 I don't want to **fall out** with my parents.
5 Let's play on my computer. **Come round** at 4.30.
6 Friends should always **look after** each other.
7 Did your cousins **make up** after they had that argument?
8 The band were together for a year, but then they **split up**.

**a** have a good relationship and not argue
**b** spend a lot of time somewhere
**c** end a relationship
**d** visit someone in their home
**e** make sure someone is well or happy
**f** become friends again after a disagreement
**g** spend time with, or go to meet, a friend
**h** have an argument with someone

**2** **Complete the sentences with the phrasal verbs from Exercise 1.**

1 I don't ________ very well with my brother. We had a big argument last week. I don't know if we'll ever ________.
2 Some of my friends ________ at the youth centre, but I don't go there.
3 Tom and Harriet weren't together for long. They ________ after six weeks.
4 I know you're nervous, but you mustn't worry. I'll ________ you.
5 I always ________ with my friends after school, but they never ________ to my place.
6 It isn't a serious problem, and I'm sure we won't ________ about it.

**3** **Discuss the questions.**

1 When do you and your mates get together? Where do you usually hang out?
2 What kind of people do you get on with?
3 How should friends look after each other?

**4** » **Work with a partner. Student A, turn to page 121. Student B, turn to page 126.**

## WRITING An informal email (2)

**1** **Read the email. Where do Ana and Nicole live?**

From: Ana Salinas
To: Nicole Mason
Reply Forward

Hi Nicole,

How's it going? I'm really looking forward to visiting you in England on the school exchange trip next month! I have a few questions:

*Me too!* —

What's the weather going to be like?

*Explain* —

I'll buy some adaptors. What else should I bring?

*Suggest …* —

What will I have to do while I'm at the school?

*Tell Ana* —

Hugs from Spain!
Ana

**2** **Read Nicole's reply to Ana. Underline the parts of Nicole's email that match the four notes in Exercise 1.**

From: Nicole Mason
To: Ana Salinas
Reply Forward

Hi Ana,

I'm great, thanks. I'm really looking forward to your visit too!

February is the coldest month here in the UK! Remember to pack a hat, gloves and your warmest coat. You should also bring some money for shopping and going out.

You don't have to do homework, but during the trip it's a good idea to make a note of things to tell your classmates in Spain. I did that on my trip to your school.

Bye for now!
Nicole

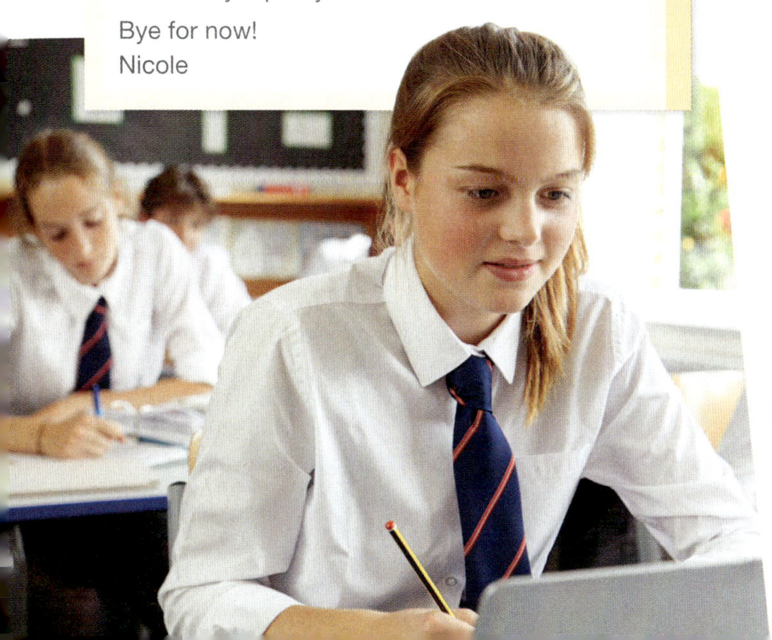

**3** **Read the *Prepare to write* box and find the phrases that are in Nicole's email.**

### PREPARE TO WRITE

**An informal email (2)**

**In replies to emails:**

- start with a greeting: *How's it going?, How are you?, It's great to hear from you.*
- answer all of the questions you were asked
- to give advice, use: *You should / shouldn't … , Remember to …, It's a good idea to …*
- end with a closing phrase: *I'm really looking forward to your visit / to meeting you / to seeing you, I can't wait to meet you / see you again.*

**4** **Complete the sentences using phrases from the *Prepare to write* box.**

1 It's very cold here in winter so it's ________ to visit in summer.
2 I know you love cycling, so ________ bring a helmet and gloves.
3 Thank you for your email. It's great ________ again.
4 We got together two years ago but I didn't see you last year, so I can't ________.
5 The weather changes all the time, so you ________ pack an umbrella and sunglasses!

**5** **Read the email from Sam. How many questions does he ask?**

From: Sam Morris
To:
Reply Forward

Hi,

How are you? It's nearly the school holidays. I can't wait to travel to your country! I'll be at your house in three weeks!

*Great* —

What's the weather like at this time of year in your country?

*Explain* —

What should I bring with me?

*Suggest …* —

I'd love to give your family a gift for letting me stay. I'd like to bring something special from my country. What would your family like?

*Tell Sam* —

See you soon,
Sam

**6** **Write your email to Sam.**

- Use the notes beside Sam's email.
- Use the tips in the *Prepare to write* box.
- Write about 100 words.
- Check your spelling and grammar.

# 8 GOING AWAY

## ABOUT YOU

Has your family ever travelled abroad? Where did you go?
Where in the world would you most like to visit? Why?

## VOCABULARY International travel

**1** **Match the words in the box with A–K in the photos.**

EP

| | | |
|---|---|---|
| baggage | baggage hall | |
| boarding pass | check-in desk | |
| customs | departure gate | |
| passport | passport control | |
| queue | security check | sign |

**2** **Work in pairs. Number the photos in order and then use them to describe what you do at an international airport.**

*1 You arrive at the airport and you go to the check-in desk. You show …*

35 **3** **Listen and check your answers to Exercise 2.**

**4** **Complete the sentences with words from Exercise 1.**

1 You have to show your ________ and your ticket at the check-in desk.
2 There's often a ________ for the security check.
3 You need to follow the ________ to your departure gate, where your ________ and your ________ are checked.
4 As you walk through customs, officers might ask to check inside your ________.

**5** **Discuss the questions.**

1 What's the difference between a boarding pass and a ticket?
2 What's the difference between a security check and a customs check?
3 What are the best and worst things about air travel?

## READING

36

1 Read Olivia's blog entry. What does she plan or intend to do in Tokyo?

2 Read the online guide to Tokyo. Which paragraphs mention things that are in the blog?

## WE'RE OFF TO TOKYO

Posted 3.16 pm

I can't wait! We're leaving on Saturday – a taxi is picking us up at 8 am and we're going straight to the airport. We're going to have a great time! On the first day, we're going sightseeing in and around the Roppongi district. We're going to visit a cat café and have a go at gaming. Apart from that, I'm not sure. Mum says we're going to look around the shops but I'm not so sure about that. I've found this great guide to the city, but has anyone got other suggestions?

**Olivia Burton**

## TOKYO

CITY MAP

● PLACES TO VISIT ● THINGS TO DO ● WHERE TO STAY

1 *FAST FOOD HEAVEN* › **THE STREETS ARE FULL OF RESTAURANTS** selling noodles and sushi. Noodles look like spaghetti and they're served with fried meat, seafood or vegetables. Sushi is rice served with uncooked fish or vegetables. The flavours are incredible. You can even take a class to learn how to prepare your own sushi.

2 *TECH CULTURE* › **IF YOU WANT TO DISCOVER** the Japanese love of technology, spend some time in a gaming café. Try the Internet Comic Café Manboo, where you can admire thousands of *manga* comics for sale as well as play all the latest computer games. They rent rooms with sofas where gamers can lie down after long sessions. They even have showers – you'd probably need one after an 8-hour overnight gaming session!

3 *FASHIONISTAS* › **BE SURE TO VISIT** the Harajuku district. It's where all the trendy Japanese teens hang out, so be prepared! You're going to see a lot of people wearing 'cosplay' clothing. Cosplay is short for 'costume play' and it's a Japanese pop tradition. Girls and boys dress in incredible costumes inspired by their favourite anime (manga cartoon) or computer game character.

4 *WEIRD AND WONDERFUL* › **TOKYO IS FULL OF UNUSUAL THINGS** to see and do. It's hard to walk a block in Tokyo without seeing loads of vending machines! Most sell cold drinks but others sell things like dog food, umbrellas and hamburgers! How about going to one of the famous cat cafés, where you can play with a cat or a kitten while you drink your coffee? There are around 60 cat cafés in Tokyo! There's even a hedgehog café in Roppongi.

3 **Read the online guide again and choose the correct answers.**

1 What is sushi?
- **A** a meat and rice dish
- **B** fresh fish and vegetables
- **C** rice with fish or vegetables
- **D** a type of noodle

2 At Manboo, you can't
- **A** buy modern sofas.
- **B** play computer games all night.
- **C** get manga comics.
- **D** have a shower.

3 What happens in the Harajuku district?
- **A** Teens play computer games.
- **B** People go to cosplay cafés.
- **C** Japanese pop stars hang out.
- **D** People wear unusual clothes.

4 A vending machine is something that
- **A** makes drinks.
- **B** sells drinks.
- **C** cooks food.
- **D** sells sushi.

5 Tokyo's cat cafés
- **A** serve Japanese tea.
- **B** have hedgehogs as well.
- **C** are well-known.
- **D** are in the Roppongi district.

### TALKING POINTS

Would you like to visit Tokyo? What would you like to see and do there?

What sightseeing would you recommend to visitors to your town or country?

## GRAMMAR Future: *be going to* and present continuous

**1** **Read the examples. Then complete the rules with *be going to* or *present continuous*.**

1 We're going to look around the shops.
2 We're leaving on Saturday.
3 Be prepared! You're going to see a lot of people wearing 'cosplay' clothing.

We use:
**a** ________ to talk about future plans and arrangements, usually with a specific time reference (for example, *next week, in August*).
**b** ________ for things we intend to do some time in the future, sometimes with a non-specific time reference (for example, *one day, some time*).
**c** ________ when we predict things that we know are likely.

» GRAMMAR REFERENCE AND PRACTICE PAGE 145

**2** **Complete the conversation with the correct form of *be going to* and the verbs in brackets.**

**Olivia:** We [1] ________ (fly) to Tokyo on holiday! I'm really looking forward it.
**Zayne:** I was in Japan a few years ago. Tokyo's amazing. You [2] ________ (have) a great time! What [3] ________ (you / do)?
**Olivia:** We [4] ________ (visit) a cat café.
**Mum:** And we [5] ________ (go) shopping!
**Olivia:** What? I [6] ________ (not walk) around the shops! I [7] ________ (find) a good gaming café.
**Zayne:** [8] ________ (you / try) sushi with fish?
**Mum:** No way! I [9] ________ (not eat) uncooked fish!

**3** **Choose the correct form of the verbs.**

1 Next month, I *going to* / *'m going to* return your bicycle.
2 We *'re going to* / *going to* visit Argentina
3 They aren't going to *meet* / *met* at the bus stop.
4 I *'m going to working* / *'m going to work* in a sports shop. That's my plan.
5 You're going to *come* / *coming* to the UK one day.
6 They *aren't going* / *not going* to join us.

**4** **Make sentences with the present continuous or *be going to*.**

0 we / visit / Turkey one day
*We're going to visit Turkey one day.*
1 I / get / the bus at 6.45 pm
2 I / cycle / to your house next time
3 they / not buy / a new TV
4 we / walk / home after school today
5 The sky is dark and cloudy. I think / it / rain
6 we / not catch / the 5.30 train / tomorrow

**5** **Make notes about your plans and arrangements for next weekend. Use the ideas in the box or your own ideas. Discuss your plans and arrangements in pairs.**

| go shopping | go to a gig or to the cinema |
|---|---|
| hang out in town | meet some friends |
| study | visit my grandparents |
| watch a football match | |

**A:** *What are you doing next weekend?*
**B:** *I'm going shopping on Saturday. I'm going to buy some new jeans.*

## VOCABULARY Phrasal verbs: travel

**1** **Read the sentences. Choose the correct meanings of the phrasal verbs.**

1 We're going away at the weekend.
**a** staying at home **b** visiting another place
2 They set off at 9.30 this morning.
**a** left a hotel **b** started a journey
3 When are you getting back?
**a** arriving in another place
**b** returning
4 What time did the plane take off?
**a** leave the ground **b** arrive after a flight
5 We're going to check in early.
**a** arrive at a hotel or for a flight
**b** reserve a hotel or a flight
6 See you at 4.00. My flight is getting in at 3.45.
**a** arriving **b** leaving
7 I can't wait to look around Moscow.
**a** visit a place and look at the things in it
**b** feel happy that something is going to happen
8 My dad is going to pick up my mum at the station.
**a** call **b** collect

**2** **Complete the questions. Use the correct form of the phrasal verbs in Exercise 1.**

1 What time do you ________ for school every morning?
2 Who normally ________ you and your friends from school?
3 Do you usually ________ or stay at home in the holidays?
4 Do you like ________ old places?
5 What time do you ________ from school in the afternoon?
6 When did you ________ from your most recent holiday? Where did you go to?
7 How do you feel when your flight ________ and lands?
8 Can you explain what you have to do when you ________ to a hotel?

**3** **Ask and answer the questions in Exercise 2.**

**4** » **Work with a partner. Turn to page 121.**

## LISTENING

**1** **Look at the photo and make predictions.**

1 Where do you think this is?
2 What is the person doing?
3 Where is the person going?

**2** **Read the notes and look at the spaces. What kind of information is needed for each space?**

### TRAVEL WRITING *Competition*

First prize: Trip to (1) ________.

Length of trip: two (2) ________.

**Competition details**

What you must mention: the people, (3) ________ and the local environment.

Maximum number of words to write: (4) ________.

Closing date of competition: 19th (5) ________.

What information to include when you apply: (6) ________.

37 **3** **Listen and complete the notes.**
**Compare answers with your partner.**

37 **4** **Listen again to check, and correct any mistakes.**

## SPEAKING Making suggestions

**1** **Discuss the questions in pairs.**

1 What do you usually do at the weekend?
2 What are you planning to do next weekend?

38 **2** **Listen to two friends planning their weekend. What do they decide to do?**

38 **3** **Read the *Prepare to speak* box. Then listen again. Which phrase don't you hear?**

### PREPARE TO SPEAK

**Making suggestions**

**Suggesting ideas**
Why don't we …?
What about …?
How about …?
We could …

**Agreeing with ideas**
That's a good idea.
That sounds great!

**Disagreeing with ideas**
I'm not sure.
The problem with that is …
… might be a better idea.

**Making a decision**
Yes, let's do that.

**4** **Work in pairs. Choose three possible activities for the weekend. Use the ideas in the box or your own ideas.**

| | |
|---|---|
| go walking in the mountains | go to the beach |
| hang out in a country park | go sightseeing |
| visit a cool museum | |

**5** **Discuss the three activities and agree what to do. Use phrases from the *Prepare to speak* box.**

# LIFE SKILLS INTERPERSONAL SKILLS

## DEALING WITH CONFLICT

**LIFE SKILLS**

**Dealing with conflict**

We never have exactly the same ideas or opinions as our friends or family members. We often disagree with people and sometimes we get angry or have arguments. When that happens, we need to deal with conflict in a positive way and work together to solve the problem.

**1** **Ask and answer the questions with a partner.**

1 Do you get along well with most people?
2 What things make you feel upset or angry?
3 What do and your friends argue about?

**2** **Read the text quickly. Match the titles (A–D) to four of the tips.**

A Live and learn
B Be clear and kind
C Stay calm
D Think together

## Friends *and* arguments

### Tips for dealing with conflict

39

**What happens when you and your friends argue? How should you react when they get angry or upset with you? Follow these helpful tips to deal with conflict in your friendships and find a solution that works for everyone.**

**1** ______. When we're angry, we might say or even scream things that aren't kind. It's always better to keep cool and think carefully before we speak. Count to ten in your head, and if you can't relax, then walk away. Sometimes you have to do that!

**2** **Listen first.** Give the other person a chance to speak without interrupting them. You have to listen carefully and pay attention to your friend's face and body language. Try to imagine how your friend is probably feeling at that moment.

**3** ______. You have to be honest about your thoughts and feelings. Explain the problem clearly and say what you need from your friend. You should choose your words carefully and try to be nice to the other person. You don't want to start a new argument!

**4** **Admit your mistakes.** Remember that even the best people make mistakes and nobody is perfect. It's OK to make mistakes, but we have to admit them and then say we're sorry. We should also forgive other people when they apologise for their own mistakes.

**5** ______. Two heads are always better than one. You should have a conversation with your friend about how you could solve the problem. And you don't have to keep it a secret. You can get help from another friend or an adult if that's helpful.

**6** **Cool down.** After you've had a serious argument, it's good to relax and cool down. When you feel better, you should go for a walk with your friend or maybe you can do something fun. Why not play a sport or watch your favourite TV show together?

**7** ______. Arguments are a normal part of life, and we don't have to worry about every disagreement. But we should try to learn from them. After all, we don't want to repeat the same mistakes again! Think about what happened, and remember that lesson for the future.

**3** **Match the sentences to similar ideas in the text.**

1 Nice people sometimes do things that aren't right.
2 You should do something to make you feel calm after an argument.
3 We sometimes say bad things to people when we're angry.
4 We don't want to have the same problem twice.
5 Try to put yourself in the other person's place.
6 A third person could help you find an answer.

**4** **Match the highlighted words in the text to the meanings.**

1 say that something is true or real
2 stopping someone who is speaking
3 find the answer to something or stop a problem
4 when people have a different opinion about something
5 shout something very loudly, in a high voice
6 movements and positions of your body and face that show other people how you are feeling, without using words

**5** **Discuss the questions.**

1 When was the last argument you had with a friend? What did you argue about?
2 How did you deal with the conflict? Did you use any tips from the article?

40 **6** **Listen to a conversation. Why is Michael upset with Amy? Do they use any of the suggestions in the article to find a solution?**

40 **7** **Listen again and answer the questions.**

1 What time did Amy arrive?
2 Who has got Amy's bicycle right now?
3 When did Michael and Amy plan to meet?
4 Why does Amy usually arrive late?
5 What solutions do Michael and Amy discuss?
6 What does Michael want to do right now?

**8** **Complete the *Useful language* phrases with the words in the box.**

about always fault idea tired why

## USEFUL LANGUAGE

**Dealing with conflict with a friend**

You've ________ got an excuse.
I'm getting ________ of this.
________ are you so angry?
I'm sorry ________ that.
It wasn't my ________.
I've got an ________.

## PROJECT

*Resolving a conflict*

**Work with a partner. Write a dialogue about two friends who are having an argument. Use the situations and questions below to help you.**

- forgetting someone's birthday
- not inviting someone to a party
- borrowing and losing something
- always arriving ten minutes late

1 Who are the people in your dialogue?
2 What are the people arguing about?
3 Which person started the argument?
4 How could they solve the problem?
5 What can they do after the argument?

**Act out your dialogue for the class.**

# REVIEW 2 UNITS 5–8

## VOCABULARY

**1** **Complete the information with the pairs of words.**

burglary / burglars hacking / hacker
pickpocketing / pickpockets
shoplifting / shoplifters vandalism / vandals

### CRIME: THE FACTS AND THE FIGURES

The average 1 ________ takes less than ten minutes. About 30% of 2 ________ enter a home through an open door or window of an apartment.

3 ________ is very common near signs that warn about the problem. The reason is that when people see these signs, they check their important possessions. 4 ________ can then see where these possessions are and follow the people until they get their chance to steal them.

5 ________ in many areas has decreased since the introduction of mobile phones. Some researchers believe that mobile phones are so entertaining that 6 ________ aren't as likely to go out, get bored and break or damage something.

According to American research, 75% of 7 ________ are adults, and 25% of them are under 18. And 8 ________ is actually more common among shop workers than customers!

The youngest 9 ________ in the world was five-year-old Kristoffer von Hassel. He discovered a way to use his father's video game account without knowing the password. His 10 ________ earned him $50 and four free games from the video games company.

**2** **Match the beginnings of the sentences 1–4 to two correct endings a–h.**

**1** I am …
**2** I am doing …
**3** We have …
**4** He makes …

**a** on my own.
**b** me really happy.
**c** something tonight.
**d** a lot of things in common.
**e** friends easily.
**f** fun together.
**g** you a favour.
**h** never wrong.

**3** **Use a word from each box to make a compound noun to match the definitions 1–8.**

baggage boarding check-in departure
green power public traffic

cut desk gate hall jam
pass spaces transport

**1** the place at an airport where passengers get on a plane
**2** a card that a passenger must have to get on a flight
**3** buses, trains, etc. that anyone can use
**4** a queue of cars, lorries, etc. that are moving slowly or not moving at all
**5** the place at an airport where you show your ticket and leave large suitcases
**6** a temporary problem when there isn't any electricity
**7** areas of grass, trees, etc. usually in a city, where people can walk, play sport and enjoy themselves.
**8** the place at an airport where you collect your suitcases after a flight

## GRAMMAR

**1** **Choose the correct word.**

**1** There isn't ________ crime in my neighbourhood.
**A** many **B** much **C** some
**2** My sister and I are having ________ arguments at the moment.
**A** a lot of **B** many **C** a little
**3** We did ________ sightseeing on holiday, but we mainly relaxed on the beach.
**A** a few **B** much **C** a little
**4** I'm taking out the rubbish. Have you got ________?
**A** any **B** a lot of **C** many
**5** I made ________ new friends at the party.
**A** any **B** a little **C** a few
**6** How ________ boarding passes have you got in your hand?
**A** a lot of **B** many **C** much
**7** There's ________ amazing graffiti under the bridge.
**A** some **B** any **C** a few
**8** There's ________ traffic on the roads this evening.
**A** a lot of **B** many **C** much
**9** There isn't much serious crime where I live, but there's ________ vandalism.
**A** a little **B** any **C** much

**2** **Complete the story. Use the past simple or past continuous form of the verbs.**

On a cold January morning, Flight 1549 [0] *was taking off* (take off) from a New York airport when it [1] ______ (hit) some birds. The engines [2] ______ (stop) almost immediately. Captain Sullenberger quickly realised that the plane [3] ______ (fall) very fast. There was only one place he could land the plane: on the Hudson River in the middle of New York!

Steven Day is a photographer. That morning he [4] ______ (work) on his computer when someone passed his desk. 'What's that?' they asked, pointing to something on the river. Steven [5] ______ (find) his camera. At first, he didn't know what he [6] ______ (take) pictures of. 'It [7] ______ (move) down the river, like a boat,' he said. When he looked closely, he [8] ______ (see) it was a plane. People [9] ______ (stand) on its wings in the middle of the river!

The next day Stephen's photograph [10] ______ (appear) in newspapers and on websites all over the world.

**3** **Complete the second sentence so that it means the same as the first. Use three or four words including the word in brackets.**

1 It isn't necessary to take your passport. (have)
You ______ take your passport.
2 What's your advice about splitting up with Francesca?
Do you think ______ with Francesca? (should)
3 It wasn't necessary for them to print their boarding passes.
They ______ print their boarding passes. (have)
4 Taxi drivers are only allowed to pick up passengers at the rank.
Taxi drivers ______ passengers at the rank. (must)
5 Is it a good idea for us to come round after dinner? (should)
______ after dinner?

**4** **Complete the sentences with the correct form of *be going to* or the present continuous.**

1 That woman near the bags is behaving oddly. I think she ______ (steal) something.
2 We ______ (get) together on Saturday. Are you free?
3 I ______ (go away) on holiday in the last two weeks of August.
4 You drive too fast. One day you ______ (get) a fine.
5 I've changed my plans. My friends ______ (not come round) this evening any more.
6 Mum and Dad ______ (find out) about this and there ______ (be) trouble.

**5** **Choose the correct words.**

1 One day I'm *asking* / *going to ask* you for a favour.
2 In my opinion, young people *have to* / *should* stay at school until they are 18.
3 We've got *a little* / *a few* time before we need to set off.
4 We *saw* / *were seeing* the crowds of people when we were leaving my apartment building.

**6** **Correct the mistake in each sentence.**

1 Last week we must do three tests.
2 When we travelled to Cambridge, the car broke down.
3 I think I going to visit your house.
4 When I was younger, I spent much money on sweets.

**7** **For each question, write the correct answer. Write one word for each gap.**

## How I met my best friend

A few years ago we moved to a new city, so I had to change schools. On the first day at my new school, I was really nervous. I find [1] ______ hard to make new friends and hardly said a word to anyone for hours. [2] ______ the morning break started, I went outside and stood on my own. I was feeling really lonely.

Towards the end of break, a girl walked up to me. She introduced [3] ______ as Monica and started chatting right away. She was also quite new at the school and we soon discovered we had a [4] ______ in common. We watched the same TV shows, listened to similar types of music, and we were both learning to play the guitar. Also, we lived just a [5] ______ minutes' walk from each other!

Monica and I have been really good friends since that day. Naturally we sometimes argue [6] ______ everyone does, but we're very close.

# 9 SHOP TILL YOU DROP

## ABOUT YOU

Do you get pocket money for helping at home?
How often do you go shopping? What do you like buying?

## VOCABULARY Money and shopping

**1** **Read the quiz questions. Match the words to photos A–H. Two words or phrases match one of the photos.** EP

# MONEY WIZARD OR MONEY WASTER?

**1** Do you **save up** for things?
- a Yes, I'm always saving up for something.
- b Sometimes, but not often.
- c No, I never save up for anything.

**2** Have you got a **bank account**?
- a Yes. I save my money in mine.
- b Yes, but I never use it.
- c No way. I'm not old enough!

**3** Do you always look at the **price** of things before buying them?
- a Of course.
- b I don't always check with small things like a drink.
- c Not really. If I want something, I buy it.

**4** Do you look for **special offers**?
- a All the time.
- b Sometimes. But if I really want something, I don't care.
- c Not really. Life is too short!

**5** Do you ever decide not to buy something while you're waiting at the **checkout**?
- a Often. I realise I don't need something and put it back.
- b Sometimes.
- c Not really.

**6** Do you always check your **change**?
- a Always. Shop assistants often make mistakes.
- b Sometimes.
- c Hardly ever.

**7** Do you keep **receipts** in case you need to **take something back**?
- a I keep everything.
- b Only for expensive things.
- c Never.

**8** What do you do with old clothes, DVDs and other stuff?
- a I throw them in the bin.
- b I usually **give** everything **away**.
- c I sell them to friends or online.

41 **2** **Listen to Gemma and Leo, and read the quiz again. Write *G* next to Gemma's answers for the quiz. Do you think Gemma is a Money Wizard or a Money Waster?**

**3** **Complete the sentences with words from the quiz.**

1 The assistant at the ________ gave me too much ________.
2 I want to open a ________ so that I can put money in there and ________ to buy a new phone.
3 Look! Those jumpers are on ________ this week – there's 25% off the normal ________!
4 I tried to ________ the shoes ________ to the shop, but I didn't have the ________, so they wouldn't accept them!
5 Why don't you ________ your old clothes ________ to a charity shop?

**4** » **Do the quiz and discuss your answers in pairs. Then read the key on page 122. Do you agree?**

# HELP! I just can't stop … SHOPPING!

42

***Have you ever bought something and then changed your mind? For Alison Jenson, 23, this used to happen several times a week. Alison was a shopaholic. She just couldn't stop shopping and she loved special offers.***

**Alison's bedroom is full of stuff.** 'I've been to every shop in Birmingham, I think,' says Alison. She picks up some trainers. The price tag is still on them. 'I paid £20 for these. They cost £40 originally, so they were half price,' she says. 'But I've never worn them.' Alison's problem wasn't just clothes. She bought jewellery, make-up and hundreds of other small things online. She hasn't used any of them!

**According to experts,** we all feel excited when we buy something new. For shopaholics, it's a little different. Soon after they buy something, they regret buying it and start to feel miserable. So they buy themselves something else to feel happier.

**Psychologists** first described the problems of shopaholics in 1915. However, there was very little research on the subject until recently. Now, doctors think thousands of people suffer from the problem, both men and women, and the situation is getting worse. There are also more teenage shopaholics now, although most young people don't have enough money to go shopping very regularly.

**Alison knew she had a problem.** 'I often bought something every day. It was usually something small, but I just needed to buy it,' she says. 'When I ran out of money, I started using credit cards. Unfortunately, I couldn't pay them back and the charges quickly became a problem. When I couldn't go shopping, I felt anxious. Then one day, my mum just looked at all the stuff in my room and said, "Alison, this is crazy!" She was right. I needed some big changes in my life.'

**Alison's parents helped** with her problem and she now feels she has changed. She no longer thinks she's a shopaholic. 'When I want to buy something in a shop, I ask myself two questions,' she says. 'Do I need it? Can I afford it? The answer to both questions is usually "no", so I walk away. It's great!'

## READING

**1** **Read the article quickly. Which statement is not true?**

1 Alison's parents know about her problem.
2 Alison's problem is a very modern one.
3 More people are shopaholics now than fifty years ago.

**2** **Read the article again. Choose the correct answers.**

1 What is the purpose of the article?
- A to persuade people to go shopping less
- B to encourage people to get help if they have a problem
- C to inform people about a problem
- D to warn people about the dangers of shopping

2 What did Alison especially like buying?
- A sneakers and other items of clothing
- B discounted items
- C anything she could take back to a local shop
- D things she could order on the internet

3 What do experts say about shopaholics?
- A They feel more excited than other people when they shop.
- B They soon feel unhappy after they have bought something.
- C Shopping is the only way they can feel happy.
- D They feel unhappy when they are paying for things.

4 What is Alison's attitude to shopping now?
- A She doesn't often want to buy things now.
- B She doesn't enjoy shopping now.
- C She still buys things she doesn't need.
- D She is in control of her shopping now.

5 What advice might Alison give to someone who has a problem with shopping?
- A Ask someone you are close to for help.
- B Never borrow money from friends or family.
- C Always look at the price carefully.
- D Avoid going to shops.

**3** **Match the highlighted verbs to their meanings.**

1 give someone the money that you borrowed from them
2 be able to buy or do something because you have enough money or time
3 feel sorry about a situation, especially something that you wish you had not done
4 finish, use or sell all of something so that there is none left
5 have an illness or other health problem

### TALKING POINTS

How do you feel when you buy something new?
What was the last thing you bought that you didn't need?
What advice can you give for saving money?

## GRAMMAR Present perfect

**1** **Read the examples and complete the rules with the words in the box.**

1 **I've been** to every shop in Birmingham.
2 She **hasn't used** any of them.
3 **I've never worn** them.
4 **Have** you **ever bought** something and then been unhappy with it?
Yes, I **have**. / No, I **haven't**.

| ever | -ed | past participle | never |
|---|---|---|---|

**a** We use the present perfect to talk about experiences in our life.
**b** The positive form is: *have* / *has* + ________.
**c** The negative form is: *have* / *has* + *not* or ________ + ________.
**d** We often use ________ in questions.
**e** Regular past participles end in ________ and are the same as the past simple form.

**2** **Write the infinitive of these regular and irregular past participles. Use the list of irregular verbs on page 158 to help you.**

| chosen | heard | lent | made |
|---|---|---|---|
| paid | read | travelled | tried |
| worn | written | | |

**3** **Complete the sentences with the present perfect form of the verbs.**

1 My sister ________ (win) lots of competitions.
2 My grandparents ________ (never / buy) anything online.
3 I ________ (never / use) a credit card. I'm not old enough!
4 My brother ________ (never / borrow) any money from me.
5 We ________ (visit) Ireland. My aunt lives there.
6 Tim and I ________ (never / have) an argument.
7 You ________ (not / meet) my brother.
8 I ________ (never / steal) anything in my life!

**4** » **Turn to page 122.**

### The past participle of *go*: *been* and *gone*

**5** **Match the examples to the meanings.**

1 My brother's **gone** to the shops.
2 My brother's **been** to the shops.

**a** My brother went to the shops earlier but he isn't there now.
**b** My brother is travelling to the shops or he's at the shops now.

» **GRAMMAR REFERENCE AND PRACTICE PAGE 146**

**6** **Complete the sentences with the correct present perfect form of *go*.**

1 ________ you ever ________ to London?
2 Sally isn't here. She ________ swimming.
3 Rob ________ home. He wasn't feeling well.
4 You're late! Where ________ you ________?
5 I ________ never ________ to Spain but I'd like to go.
6 Where ________ Dad ________? I can't find him anywhere.

## VOCABULARY Easily confused words: *pay*, *charge*, *cost*

**1** EP **Read the examples. Complete the definitions with *pay*, *charge* or *cost (of)*.**

1 I **paid** £10 for these.
2 These trainers **cost** £40 originally.
3 They **charge** £1.50 for a small bottle of water!
4 My brother enjoys his job but the **pay** is terrible.
5 The **cost of** repairing my phone was over £100.
6 The **charges** quickly became a problem.

**a** *Charge* is the amount of money that a business asks for something, especially a service.
**b** ________ is the amount of money someone receives for doing a job.
**c** The ________ something is the amount of money you pay for it.
**d** Products ________ an amount of money to buy.
**e** Sellers ________ an amount of money for a product or service.
**f** Customers ________ sellers an amount of money for a product or service.

**2** **Choose the correct word.**

1 How much do they *charge* / *cost* for delivery on that website?
2 I only *paid* / *charged* £20 for these trainers.
3 How much does it *pay* / *cost* to go by train?
4 The job is hard but the *cost* / *pay* isn't bad.
5 My parents couldn't believe the *charge* / *cost* of food on holiday. It was really expensive.
6 Students can visit the exhibition free of *charge* / *pay*.

**3** » **Work with a partner. Turn to page 122.**

# WRITING A story (2)

**1** Look at the pictures and read the first sentence of the story. What do you think happens in the story?

*I've never enjoyed shopping for clothes.*

**2** Read the first few sentences of Jamie's story and check your ideas.

I've never enjoyed shopping for clothes. It takes ages, and when I get home I always regret buying something, and then I have to take it back. So one day I decided to try doing it online.

I looked up the website of my favourite clothes shop and soon I had everything I needed. And there were lots of special offers too! While I was paying for everything, I noticed a competition. I could win the money I paid for my clothes. I've never been lucky, but I decided to enter.

A few days later the clothes arrived. Unfortunately, *nothing* fitted me apart from some socks. So I sent back everything … except for the socks.

A few weeks after that, I got an email. I was one of the winners in their competition. I got back everything I paid for the clothes online. And how much was that? £4.99!

**3** Read the *Prepare to write* box. Then read the story again. Does it have a clear beginning, middle and end?

## PREPARE TO WRITE

### A story (2)

**When you write a story:**

- make sure there is a beginning, middle and end
- use interesting verbs to describe the actions of the story
- use time adverbs and phrases to describe when things happened: *first, then, when, while, soon, a few days later, a few weeks after that, suddenly.*

**4** Match the highlighted verbs in the story to the meanings.

1 take part in a competition
2 found by looking on a computer
3 returned something to a shop by post
4 saw

**5** Find five time adverbs and phrases in the story. Then choose the correct time adverbs in the sentences.

1 I called my friend *as soon as* / *while* the accident happened.
2 About ten minutes *then* / *later*, I finally arrived home.
3 He discovered the truth *while* / *then* he was reading some old letters.
4 She *when* / *suddenly* had a brilliant idea!
5 I needed a new jacket. *Soon* / *First*, I tried looking online.
6 *When* / *While* I got to school, it was already nine o'clock.

**6** Read the task and plan your story.

Your English teacher has asked you to write a story.
Your story must begin with one of these sentences:

- *My dad handed me a big bag from a department store.*
- *While Chloe was looking at the website, she saw the special offer.*
- *While I was leaving the shop, the security guard stopped me.*

**7** Write your story.

- Use the tips in the *Prepare to write* box.
- Write about 100 words.
- Remember to check your spelling and grammar.

# 10 TASTE THIS!

## ABOUT YOU

06 **Watch the video and then answer the questions.**

What are your favourite types of food?

Is your diet healthy? Why?

What's the most unusual food you've ever tried?

Do you think it's good to try lots of different food and drink?

A

B

C

D

E

F

G

H

## VOCABULARY Food and drink adjectives

**1** Look at the photos. Which of the foods have you tried? Did you like them?

43 **2** Listen to the first part of a conversation. What is Isla asking Ali to do?

44 **3** Listen to the second part of the conversation. Number the photos in the order of the taste test.

45 **4** Match the adjectives to the foods in Isla's project. Then listen and check.

EP

| | |
|---|---|
| 1 juicy | a curry |
| 2 sour | b pineapple |
| 3 raw | c lemon juice |
| 4 spicy | d salmon |
| 5 bitter | e bread |
| 6 sweet | f vegetables |
| 7 frozen | g cake |
| 8 fresh | h coffee |

46 **5** Match the foods that Ali tasted to the adjectives he used to describe them. Then listen again and check.

EP

| delicious | disgusting | horrible | tasty |
|---|---|---|---|

1 pineapple
2 sushi
3 lemon juice
4 curry

**6** Discuss the questions.

1 What's the most delicious food you've ever eaten?
2 What's the most disgusting food you've ever tried?
3 What food do you eat raw?
4 What spicy food do you eat?
5 Do you often eat vegetarian meals?
6 Do you eat a lot of sweet things?

# OLLIE, DON'T EAT THAT!

**When Ollie James was one, his brother had a tiny pet turtle. One day, it disappeared. Then Ollie's mum noticed a turtle's leg, hanging out of Ollie's mouth! This was the beginning of Ollie's interest in very unusual types of food. And, don't worry, the turtle was fine! Now, aged 16, Ollie's eaten everything from ants to zebra. And for the last two years, he's written about them on his blog: 'Ollie, Don't Eat That!'**

47

**1** ........ Once my dad brought home some giant toasted ants from a business trip to Colombia. They tasted good, like salty meat. I described them on a website and I got a *lot* of replies! So I started looking for other unusual foods and I set up a blog to write about them. I've tried over a hundred different things since I started my blog.

**2** ........ The strangest is durian fruit, from South East Asia. It's actually illegal to carry them on public transport in some countries because they smell disgusting – like old fruit and rubbish. However, they taste incredible – sweet and creamy. I've also cooked with unusual ingredients. I found a recipe for an ostrich curry online, and last week I made that. An ostrich is a bird, but its meat is dark red. I expected a strong flavour, but it isn't as meaty as lamb. I got it from an ostrich farm in England.

**3** ........ That's definitely the cheeseburger in a can. A reader sent it to me from Germany. It tasted like a really low-quality vegetarian burger. It looked horrible and it tasted worse. I really couldn't finish it.

**4** ........ Oh, my favourite is miracle berries, from Africa. They taste bitter, and after you eat them anything that's sour tastes sweet! Lemon juice, for example, tastes like sweet lemonade!

**5** ........ Not once. I'm always careful that the food is safe. My parents check everything. They've tried lots of things too. They loved my ostrich curry!

## READING

**1 Read the interview quickly. Match questions a–e to spaces 1–5.**

**a** What's the most interesting thing you've ever eaten?
**b** Why did you start your website?
**c** Have you ever been ill because of something you've tried?
**d** And what about the most disgusting?
**e** What's the best food you've tried?

**2 Complete the sentences with one word in each space.**

1 Ollie started his blog ........ years ago.
2 Ollie's ........ gave him the toasted ants.
3 In some countries, it's against the law to ........ durian fruit on public transport
4 The smell of durian fruit is ........ .
5 Ollie recently made a curry with some ostrich ........ .
6 Ollie didn't eat all of the cheeseburger in a ........ .
7 Miracle berries make sour things taste ........ .
8 Ollie has never been ........ from eating foods for his blog.

**3 Find these words in the article. Then match them to their meanings.**

1 giant
  **a** very large
  **b** very small
2 recipe
  **a** instructions for cooking something
  **b** a book about food
3 flavour
  **a** how food or drink smells
  **b** how food or drink tastes
4 lamb
  **a** meat of a young sheep
  **b** a type of fruit
5 low-quality
  **a** something that's very good
  **b** something that isn't very good

### TALKING POINTS

What food or drink from your country would you like Ollie to try?
Do you think more people will eat insects in the future? Why? / Why not?

## GRAMMAR Present perfect and past simple

**1** **Read the examples. Then complete the rules with *present perfect* or *past simple*.**

1 Ollie's eaten everything from ants to zebra.
2 I made an ostrich curry last week.

**a** We use the ________ to ask or talk about experiences in our life.
**b** We use the ________ (often with a past time phrase) to ask or say exactly when something happened.
**c** We do not use past time phrases with the ________.

**2** **Choose the correct form of the verbs.**

1 We enjoyed the party, but there *hasn't been* / *wasn't* anything to eat.
2 Macy *had* / *'s had* an argument with her best friend yesterday.
3 We eat meat, but we *went* / *'ve been* to vegetarian restaurants lots of times.
4 *Did you ever cook* / *Have you ever cooked* a meal for your friends?
5 It was Mum's birthday on Sunday and we *went* / *'ve been* out to a restaurant.
6 I *never ordered* / *'ve never ordered* pizza online.

**3** **Ask and answer questions using the present perfect with *ever* and the past simple.**

0 go to a concert? – Who / see?
1 make anyone angry? – Who / be / it?
2 eat out with your friends? – Where / go?
3 win anything? – What / win?

**A:** *Have you ever been to a concert?*
**B:** *Yes, I have.*
**A:** *Who did you see?*
**B:** *I saw Calvin Harris last year.*

### How long? and for/since

**4** **Read the examples. Then complete the rules with the words in the examples.**

1 How long has Ollie had a blog? He's had a blog for two years.
2 He's tried over a hundred different things since he started his blog.

We use:
**a** ________ to ask a question in the present perfect about a period of time.
**b** ________ to say when something started.
**c** ________ to give the period of time something has continued.

» GRAMMAR REFERENCE AND PRACTICE PAGE 147

**5** **Write *for* or *since* for these time phrases.**

three weeks   this morning   a long time
2018   Monday   a few years
four o'clock   midday

**6** **Complete the sentences about you.**

0 I *'ve been* (be) at this school for three years
1 I ________ (not miss) a lesson since ________.
2 We ________ (be) in this classroom for ________.
3 I ________ (not eat) anything since ________.
4 Our teacher ________ (work) here for ________.
5 I ________ (not do) an exam since ________.
6 I ________ (live) in this town for ________.

**7** **Correct the mistake in each sentence.**

1 Yesterday I have left my phone at your house.
2 Hi! I didn't see you for a long time.
3 I know her since 2010.
4 On my last birthday I've got a lot of presents from my friends.
5 Have you ever visit London?
6 Two weeks ago I've watched a tennis match.

**8** **In pairs, ask questions with *How long …?* Answer them with *for* or *since*.**

0 you / know / your best friend?
1 you / have / your phone?
2 you / be / in this class?
3 you / live / in your home?

**A:** *How long have you known your best friend?*
**B:** *I've known my best friend for …*

## VOCABULARY look, taste, smell

**1** **Read the examples. What type of word can we use after the verbs *look*, *taste* and *smell*?**

EP

1 It looked horrible.
2 They taste bitter.
3 It smells disgusting.

**2** **Complete the sentences with the correct form of *look*, *taste* or *smell* and an adjective from the box.**

disgusting   clean   exhausted   bitter
delicious   upset   ~~new~~

0 Those trainers *look new*. When did you buy them?
1 What are you cooking? It ________!
2 My coffee ________. Did you put sugar in it?
3 These socks don't ________. Put them in the washing machine.
4 You all ________. Did you go to bed late last night?
5 Mum ________. You should apologise.
6 This burger ________. I'm not going to finish it.

**3** » **Work with a partner. Turn to page 122.**

# LISTENING

**1** **Have you ever made a meal for anyone? Who was it for? What did you make?**

**2** **You are going to listen to some short extracts. Read the questions and look at the pictures. What words might you hear in each extract?**

**1** What did the girl cook when she was young?

**2** Where does the boy get his recipes from?

**3** Who is a vegetarian?

**4** Which dish is only available today?

**5** Which food does Lizzie dislike?

**6** Which ingredient do they need to buy?

**7** What do the couple decide to have for dinner?

48 **3** **Listen and choose the correct picture A, B or C. Listen again and check.**

# SPEAKING Ordering food

**1** **Look at the menu below and answer the questions.**

**1** What do you think 'veggie' means?
**2** How much is a spicy beef pizza with olives?
**3** Why are there two prices for cola?

49 **2** **Listen to the conversation. What does Emma order? How much is her meal?**

49 **3** **Read the *Prepare to speak* box. Then listen again. Which phrases do Emma and the server use?**

## PREPARE TO SPEAK

### Ordering food

| Phrases the server uses | Phrases the customer uses |
|---|---|
| What can I get you? | Could I have … , please? |
| What would you like? | I'll have … , please. |
| And to drink? | I'd like … , please. |
| Anything else? | Have you got any … ? |
| Eat in or take out? | Here you are. |
| Here's your change. | |

**4** **Look at the menu again and decide what you would like to order. In pairs, practise ordering food. Use phrases from the *Prepare to speak* box.**

**5** **Act out your conversation for the class.**

**Sandwiches / Panini**

| | |
|---|---|
| Cheese | £3.50 |
| Tuna | £4.00 |
| Chicken | £4.00 |
| Roast beef | £4.75 |

**Pizza**

| | |
|---|---|
| Margherita | £6.50 |
| Veggie – peppers, onions, olives | £8.00 |
| Spicy beef – beef, red peppers, onion, chilli | £8.50 |

*Extras (50p each): mushrooms, chilli, olives, etc.*

**Salads**

| | |
|---|---|
| Green salad | £3.00 |
| Mixed salad | £4.00 |
| Tuna salad | £5.50 |
| Grilled chicken | £6.00 |

**Drinks**

| | |
|---|---|
| Tea | £2.00 |
| Coffee | £2.50 |
| Fresh orange juice | £2.50 |
| Still/sparkling water | £1.50 |
| Cola | £1.50/£2.00 |

# CULTURE

## BRITISH FOOD

**1** Answer the questions.

1 What do you think British people eat in a typical day?
2 What do you know about traditional British dishes?
3 Do you think British food is very different from food in your country?

**2** Read the text quickly. Match the underlined food to photos A–G.

## Discover British food

50

**Many tourists are quite surprised by all the delicious food they can find in the UK. In the past, many visitors had a bad opinion of British cooking, but that was often because they ate in cheap restaurants that only served food for tourists. Fortunately, things have changed in recent years and now tourists can find many types of good quality food all over the country.**

### Typical favourites

You can find excellent traditional British food in the thousands of cafés, restaurants and takeaways around the UK. A typical café dish, and perhaps the best-known abroad, is the 'full English breakfast'. That's eggs, sausage, tomatoes, beans and fried bread. If you want something hot for lunch in a café, try the meat or vegetarian pies on offer.

A classic summer dish is ploughman's lunch, which is a cold dish of bread, butter, cheese, pickled onion and salad. On Sundays, it's typical to have a roast dinner with friends and family. Roast beef, lamb or chicken is served with potatoes and boiled vegetables such as carrots and broccoli, and gravy is poured on top. Gravy is a thick, brown sauce and it's delicious!

Takeaways are really popular in the UK. These are small shops that sell hot food that customers take home or eat on the street. Fish and chips has been a British takeaway favourite for a long time. They fry the fish in batter (a mixture of flour and water) and it's often served with peas, and, of course, lots of chips!

### Local dishes

Many places in the UK have local specialities. In Scotland, Cullen skink is a creamy soup with fish, potatoes, onions, and milk. In Wales, one of the most popular dishes is called Welsh rarebit. It's hot cheese on toast. And for dessert you can try some bara brith. It's a sweet bread with fruit and spices.

### International options

Since the 1950s, many immigrants have come to Britain from all over the world and they have brought lots of international dishes with them: curry from India and Pakistan, pizza and pasta from Italy, along with dishes from China, Japan, Egypt, Mexico and many other places. Curry, in particular, has become so popular that it is often called a 'national dish' of the UK.

With all of these choices, tourists nowadays won't have any problems eating in the UK. Their biggest challenge will be deciding what to eat!

**3** **Are the sentences true or false? Correct the false sentences.**

1. At the moment, British food hasn't got much variety.
2. Nowadays, British people don't eat roast dinners.
3. People usually cook fish and chips at home.
4. Cullen skink is an English dish that has fish and potatoes.
5. Welsh rarebit is a recipe that hasn't got any meat or fish.
6. British food has become more varied because of immigration.

**4** **Match the highlighted words in the text to the meanings.**

1. kept in vinegar or salty water
2. famous dishes
3. a place that cooks and sells food for people to eat somewhere else
4. maybe, possibly
5. something difficult

51 **5** **Listen to Emily and her cousin Andrew, who is from the USA. Answer the questions.**

1. Where are Emily and Andrew now?
2. What decision are they trying to make?
3. What historical event does Emily talk about?

51 **6** **Listen again. Complete the sentences with one or two words.**

1. At first, Andrew suggests they have ________ for lunch.
2. Emily thinks some ________ tikka masala would be good.
3. Andrew says he isn't a big fan of ________ dishes.
4. Bangers and mash are ________ with mashed ________.
5. Emily says that cottage pie isn't a ________.
6. Trifle is made with ________, ________ jelly and cream.

**7** **Read the *Useful language* phrases. Complete them with ideas about food in your country.**

## USEFUL LANGUAGE

**Discussing possibilities**

1. A famous dish in our country would be …
2. A popular local speciality might be …
3. Visitors could perhaps try …
4. A popular fast food here would be …
5. Some tourists might not like …
6. People who like desserts might want to try …

F

G

## PROJECT *A food guide*

**Write a food guide for tourists who visit your town or city. Use the questions below to help you.**

- What food is popular in your country?
- What are the local specialities where you live?
- Which restaurants should tourists try in your area?
- What fast food is popular where you live?
- What desserts or sweets should visitors have?
- What other food might people want to try?

**Present your guide to the class. Then post your work at school where other people can see it.**

07 NOW WATCH THE CULTURE VIDEO

# 11 A HEALTHY FUTURE

## ABOUT YOU

08 Watch the video and then answer the questions.

Are you generally quite healthy?

Have you ever broken an arm or a leg? What happened?

Do you think most people would like to live to be 1,000 years old? Why? / Why not?

## VOCABULARY Body and health

52 **1** **Match the words to the parts of the body A–N. Then listen and check.** EP

ankle back cheek chest chin
elbow finger forehead knee
neck shoulder throat thumb toe

**2** **Complete the table with the words from Exercise 1. Add more parts of the body you can see in the photo.**

| | |
|---|---|
| head | *chin, …* |
| body | *back, …* |
| leg | *ankle, …* |
| arm | *elbow, …* |

53 **3** **Listen to three conversations. Match the speakers to the sentences.**

Sam Kelly Josh

**a** ________ might be ill.
**b** ________ had an accident and is injured.
**c** ________ has sore legs and arms after doing sport.

**4** **Discuss the illnesses and injuries. What parts of the body do they affect?** EP

aches broken (a) cold (a) cough
(a) cut earache (a) fever flu
sore stomach ache toothache

53 **5** **Complete the sentences with words from Exercise 4. There is one word you don't need. Listen again and check.**

1 Sam played tennis yesterday and now she's got **(a)** ________ in her arms, legs and back.
2 Kelly's got a headache, and she has a **(b)** ________ inside her mouth. She says her cheek's **(c)** ________. She needs to go to the dentist because she has **(d)** ________. The other girl hurt her thumb, but it wasn't **(e)** ________.
3 Josh feels very hot, so he thinks he's got a **(f)** ________. Dora thinks that Josh might be getting a **(g)** ________. Josh has a sore throat and a **(h)** ________. Last night he had **(i)** ________, too. He hopes he hasn't got **(j)** ________.

**6** **In pairs, compare the illnesses and injuries you've had.**

**A:** *I've had a fever.*
**B:** *Me too. I had a high temperature last year.*

HOME | UK NEWS | WORLD NEWS | OPINION | VIDEO | PICTURES

# We will live for **1,000 years**

54

**How long do you expect to live? One hundred years ago, people died at the age of about 50. These days, people often live for 90 years or more, and doctors predict that most teenagers alive today will live to be over 100. But one scientist, Dr Aubrey de Grey, thinks that medicine will soon allow people to live to the age of 1,000.**

Dr de Grey says that most people die from old age, or rather from a disease that old people's bodies are unable to fight. But, he says: 'I think we're close to keeping people so healthy that at the age of 90, they'll wake up every day in the same physical state as they were at the age of 30.' Dr de Grey believes that doctors can look after the human body in the same way that we look after things like old cars. Scientists have invented drugs that can completely repair old or damaged parts of our bodies. Their research suggests that people who take these drugs aren't going to get old or die from common diseases. Their bodies are going to stay healthy – and young. De Grey's plans mean there might be a lot more people on the planet, but de Grey says that doesn't matter, because our priority should be health not population. 'We still need to give people the best healthcare that we can,' and de Grey is going to continue to do exactly that through his research. However, Dr de Grey warns that people won't live for ever. Although people won't die from the diseases of old age, they'll still have accidents, such as car crashes.

Many scientists disagree. All through history, scientists have predicted that we will live for ever, says Professor S. Jay Olshansky. A Chinese scientist, Ko Hung, said 1,700 years ago that eating very little would help people to live for ever, but he died at the age of 60. The English scientist Roger Bacon thought we could live for ever by eating gold, but he died aged 78. There's a long list of promises, says Professor Olshansky, but there's no evidence that people will ever live for 1,000 years.

## Comments (43)

I don't believe this. Anyway, who wants to live that long? Life will become very boring after a few hundred years!
***Simone, Peterborough, UK***

People love the idea of living for ever, but I think it's impossible. I'm going to look after my own health, and forget about Dr de Grey.
***Hannah, Sydney, Australia***

Dr de Grey is probably right. I think I'll find out more about these drugs! But millions of people die every year from cancer, for instance, and we can't even cure that yet. Let's cure cancer first!
***Damian, London, UK***

## READING

**1** **Read the news report and the comments quickly. Who agrees with Dr de Grey?**

**2** **Match the highlighted words in the article to the meanings.**

**1** medicines
**2** an illness
**3** broken, hurt
**4** the opposite of *dead*
**5** say something will happen

**3** **Read the news report again and answer the questions.**

**1** How has the length of human lives changed in the past 100 years?
**2** How does Dr de Grey think the length of human lives will change in the future?
**3** What do most people die from today?
**4** Why does Dr de Grey compare human bodies with cars?
**5** How might Dr de Grey's ideas affect the human population?
**6** What will people die from if they don't die from disease?
**7** What do Ko Hung and Roger Bacon have in common?
**8** What is Simone's opinion about living for ever?
**9** What would Damian prefer scientists to work on?

### TALKING POINTS

What do you think of Dr de Grey's ideas? Do you agree or disagree with Professor Olshansky? Why? / Why not? Would you like to live to be 1,000? Why? / Why not?

## GRAMMAR *will* and *be going to*

**1 Match the examples to the rules.**

1 Medicine **will allow** people to live to the age of 1,000.
2 Their research suggests that people **aren't going to die** from common diseases.
3 De Grey **is going to continue** to do exactly that.
4 I think **I'll find out** more about these drugs.

We use *will* …
**a** to predict the future generally.
**b** when we decide to do something while we are speaking.

We use *be going to* …
**c** to talk about something we have already decided to do.
**d** to predict the future based on something we can see or know now.

» GRAMMAR REFERENCE AND PRACTICE PAGE 148

**2 Choose the correct verb form.**

1 I'm glad you *'ll visit* / *'re going to visit* in June.
2 Let's have a snack. I *'m going to get* / *'ll get* us some popcorn.
3 No, I don't want to come out, thanks. I *'ll have* / *'m going to have* an early night.
4 There isn't a cloud in the sky. It *won't rain* / *isn't going to rain*!
5 I *'ll go* / *'m going to go* and visit my cousins in the summer. We've already bought the tickets.
6 In my opinion, scientists *are going to find* / *will find* a cure for all cancers soon.
7 You should watch this film. I think you *'ll like* / *'re going to like* it.
8 Speak clearly or the children *won't understand* / *aren't going to understand* you.

**3 Complete the sentences. Use the *will* or *be going to* future form of the verb in brackets.**

1 Hey, I ________ (help) you pick up these books.
2 Do you think we ________ (find) life on other planets?
3 I've decided about the party. I ________ (not come). I have to study this evening.
4 Oh, no, look at those cyclists. They ________ (crash)!
5 Don't worry about me. I ________ (see) the doctor tomorrow.
6 It's late, I think I ________ (go) home now.

**4 Read the questions and prepare your answers. Then ask and answer the questions.**

1 Is it going to rain later?
2 What are you going to do at the weekend?
3 Do you think you'll go to university?
4 What kind of job do you think you'll do?
5 Where will you live when you're older?

## VOCABULARY Illnesses and injuries: verbs

**1 How many verbs can you match with 1–3?**

EP

break catch cut feel get
have hurt injure be

1 a cold 2 sick 3 your leg

**2 Choose the two correct answers.**

0 I was quite ill yesterday, but I'm __ better now.
 A catching (B) feeling (C) getting
1 Ouch! My throat __.
 A injures B feels sore C hurts
2 My sister __ ill last night.
 A was B caught C felt
3 He's never __ flu.
 A caught B had C felt
4 I've __ my ankle.
 A broken B caught C injured
5 Be careful. Don't __ your thumb.
 A cut B get C hurt
6 My uncle __ his shoulder last week.
 A got B broke C hurt

55
**3 Complete the conversations with the correct form of the verbs. Then listen and check.**

break hurt injure

**Doctor:** What seems to be the problem?
**Zac:** My finger really [1] ________. I [2] ________ it last night when I was playing football.
**Doctor:** Let me see. Can you move it at all?
**Zac:** Yes, a bit.
**Doctor:** OK, so you haven't [3] ________ it. But we need to …

catch feel have (got) have (got)

**Niall:** What are you going to do this weekend?
**Anna:** Not much! I [4] ________ flu. I started to [5] ________ ill on Thursday, and now I'm exhausted. I [6] ________ a fever at the moment, and aches in my arms and legs.
**Niall:** Is anyone else in your family ill?
**Anna:** No, but my sister was ill last week, so maybe I [7] ________ it from her.

**4** » Work with a partner. Student A turn to page 123. Student B turn to page 126.

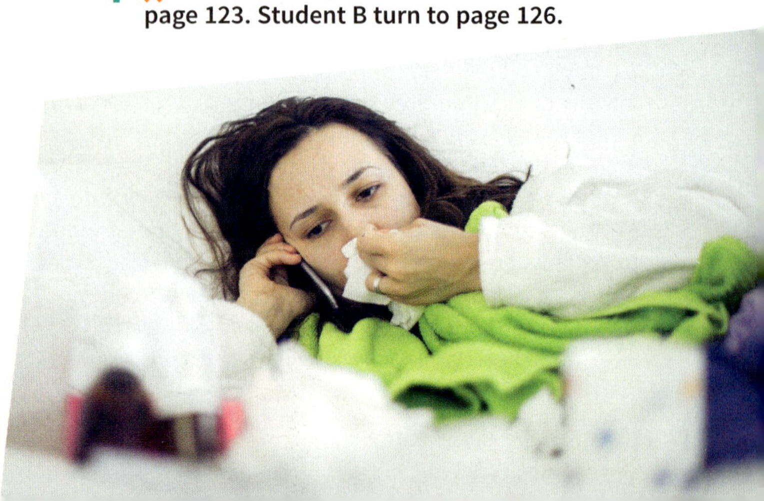

# WRITING An article (1)

**1** What do you do to keep fit during the summer holidays?

**2** Read the notice. What should your article include? What suggestions would you make?

You see the following notice in a magazine.

> **ARTICLES WANTED!**
>
> Doing sport is healthy, but routines can be hard to follow. Why is sport important? What sports are you going to do this holiday? How will you make sure you do them regularly?
>
> **Write an article answering these questions. We will publish the most interesting articles in our magazine.**

**3** Read the article that a student has written. (It is not in the correct order.) Does it include any of your suggestions?

**A** I find it's a good idea to have a goal, like a race, because a goal gives you a reason to do sports regularly.

**B** People know that doing sport is healthy, but they often say they don't have time to do it.

**C** Doing sports is a great way to keep fit. It's good for your heart and it makes your body strong and healthy. There's a triathlon in my town at the end of the holiday, and I'm going to compete in it! A triathlon is a race where you have to swim, then cycle, and then run. So this holiday I'm going to train for the triathlon. I'm going to train with a group of friends. That way we will be able to encourage each other to carry on.

**4** Read the *Prepare to write* box. Match the parts of the article 1–3 below with paragraphs A–C in Exercise 3.

> **PREPARE TO WRITE**
>
> **An article (1)**
>
> **Organise your article into paragraphs:**
>
> **1** Introduction
> **2** Main article: answer each question from the exam task
> **3** Conclusion
>
> **Then write a title that will help readers to understand the *whole* article.**

**5** Read the article in the correct order. Then choose the best title.

**1** Encourage your friends
**2** How to stay fit and healthy
**3** You should do a triathlon

**6** Read the notice. What should your article include? Make notes of your suggestions.

You see this notice in a health and fitness magazine.

> **ARTICLES WANTED!**
>
> We know we should avoid fast food and sweets, but it can be hard to do. What should a healthy diet include? How healthy is your diet? How can you avoid unhealthy food?
>
> **Write an article answering these three questions. We will publish the most interesting articles in our magazine.**

**7** Write your article.

- Use your notes from Exercise 6.
- Follow the structure and instructions in the *Prepare to write* box.
- Use *be going to* and *will* to explain your decisions and predictions.
- Use language for giving advice: *It's a good idea to, Remember to, You should*
- Write about 100 words.
- Remember to check your spelling and grammar.

# 12 INCREDIBLE WILDLIFE

## ABOUT YOU

What is your favourite animal? Why?
Which of these animals have you seen? Where?
Which of them can you see in your country?

## VOCABULARY Animals

56 **1** Look at the quiz. Match the animals to the photos. Then listen and check. EP

| ant | bat | bee | butterfly | deer | donkey | eagle |
|---|---|---|---|---|---|---|
| fly | fox | frog | mosquito | shark | wolf | worm |

57 **2** Do the quiz. Then listen and check.

**3** Describe an animal without saying its name. Can your partner guess what it is?

## The CREATURES Quiz

### Guess which animal …

1. **can grow mushrooms.**
   A ant B bee C parrot D worm
2. **kills the most humans every year.**
   A mosquito B shark C snake D tiger
3. **uses sound to find food.**
   A ant B bat C donkey D frog
4. **loves the smell of toothpaste.**
   A bear B deer C fox D parrot
5. **communicates by dancing.**
   A butterfly B bee C eagle D kangaroo
6. **can't recognise itself in a mirror.**
   A dog B dolphin C elephant D monkey
7. **doesn't drink much water.**
   A camel B donkey C giraffe D wolf
8. **usually lives alone.**
   A bat B bee C fly D whale
9. **is not frightened of lions.**
   A cat B dog C donkey D rat
10. **can't fly.**
   A ant B bat C parrot D penguin

# Weird animals

58

**Animals** > wild **weird** wonderful

**A** ........ They think that at least 80% of animal and plant life on Earth could still be unknown. And of the known animals, there are some pretty unbelievable species.

**B** ........ The **blobfish** could be the world's ugliest animal. Out of the water, it has a face like an old man because its body is soft and full of fat. It looks more like a 'normal' fish 1,000m underwater because the water pressure pushes its body into shape. The **lamprey** looks like it might be something out of a horror film! Actually, it's a fish, and in this picture its mouth is open. To eat, the lamprey bites another fish and drinks the blood – like a vampire. As its name suggests, the **star-nosed mole** looks like it has a star on its face! In fact, those are tentacles around its nose. It lives under the ground and is almost blind. It moves slowly and uses its tentacles to feel for worms in the dark. Once its tentacles find a worm, it can eat it in 0.25 seconds!

**C** ........ Sometimes harmless-looking animals can be extremely dangerous as well. The **slow loris** has a sweet face and huge eyes, but be careful – it might bite you, and there's poison in its mouth. The **golden poison dart frog** looks beautiful, but you mustn't touch it. There's enough poison on the back of this frog to kill 10 people! The **pufferfish** can kill people even when it's dead. In Japan, pufferfish (or *fugu*) is a rare and expensive dish. It must be absolutely delicious because people who eat it are taking a big risk. Parts of its body contain poison. Eating the wrong part can cause death, and only special chefs are allowed to prepare it. Still, around 100 people die every year from eating *fugu*.

## READING

**1** **In pairs, discuss the animals in the photos.**

1 What kinds of animal are they?
2 Where do they live?
3 What is interesting about them?

**2** **Read the paragraphs quickly and check your answers to Exercise 1. Then match the bold animal names with the photos.**

**3** **Match the sentences to spaces A–C.**

1 What animals do you think are the most dangerous – a snake, a spider, perhaps a shark?
2 There are some very funny-looking animals out there.
3 Scientists discover hundreds of new and unusual animals every year.

**4** **Match the highlighted words in the article to the meanings.**

1 not dangerous
2 a substance that can kill you if you eat it
3 unable to see
4 quite, but not completely or extremely
5 the surface of the earth
6 the physical form of something

**5** **Discuss the questions in pairs. Read the article again and check.**

1 Why does the blobfish look less ugly 1,000 m underwater?
2 Why is the lamprey similar to a vampire?
3 Why does the star-nosed mole need tentacles?
4 How can the slow loris hurt people?
5 How can the golden poison dart frog kill people?
6 Why do people eat pufferfish?

### TALKING POINTS

Why have we discovered only 20% of the world's animals and plants?
What other weird-looking or dangerous animals can you think of?

## GRAMMAR Modals of probability

**1** **Look at the photo and read the conversation. Then complete the rules with the bold verbs.**

**A:** This looks like it **might** be a plant.
**B:** Or it **could** be a stick.
**A:** No, wait. It **can't** be a stick. It's got eyes.
**B:** Yes, and antennas.
**A:** And it's got six legs, so it **must** be some sort of insect.

**a** We use ________ / ________ + infinitive to talk about things that are possible.
**b** We use ________ + infinitive to talk about things that we think are certain.
**c** We use ________ + infinitive to talk about things that are impossible.

» GRAMMAR REFERENCE AND PRACTICE PAGE 149

**2** **Choose the correct option.**

1 That bird *could* / *can't* be a penguin. It flew onto the roof.
2 Our dog hasn't moved all day. He *could* / *can't* be ill.
3 Be careful. I can hear a mosquito. It *might* / *must* bite you.
4 Something is eating food from the bins. There aren't any wolves around here, but it *can't* / *could* be a fox.
5 It's big and it's got brown fur. It *can't* / *might* be a bear.
6 The cat's asleep. She *can't* / *must* be sleepy today.
7 It's got four legs, so it *could* / *can't* be a snake.
8 I can hear a voice speaking, but there's nobody here. It *must* / *can't* be that parrot!

59 **3** **Listen to sounds 1–8. In groups, discuss what the sounds *can't*, *might* or *must* be.**

**4** **Look at the photos and discuss what animals they *can't*, *might* or *must be*.**

**A:** *It has some red on it, so it can't be a tiger.*
**B:** *It could be a bird …*
**A:** *Oh, I know. It must be a … !*

## VOCABULARY Adverbs of probability

**1** **Read the examples. Complete the diagram with the bold adverbs.**

EP

1 It has fur. It's **definitely** an animal of some kind.
2 It isn't in water, so it's **definitely not** a fish.
3 It's very small, so it's **probably** an insect.
4 I'm not sure what it is. **Perhaps** it's a bird of some kind.

NO ⟵⟶ YES

1 ________ *probably not* 2 ________ / *maybe* 3 ________ 4 ________

**2** **Look at the photos and discuss what they might be. They both have a connection to this unit. Use adverbs of probability. Check your ideas on page 123.**

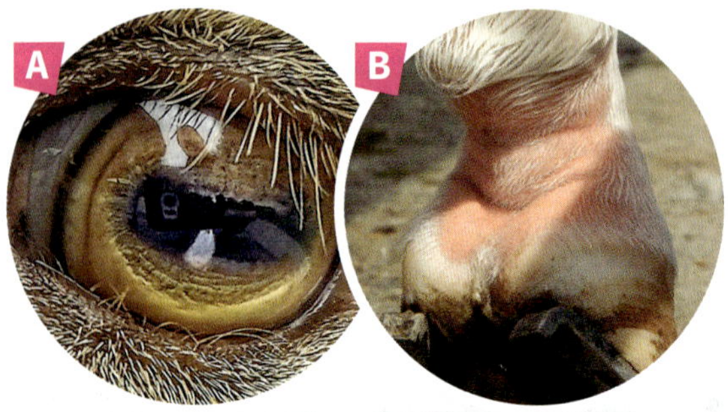


**3** **» Work with a partner. Student A turn to page 123. Student B turn to page 127.**

## LISTENING

**1** **Read the TV guide and look at the photos. In pairs, discuss how the animals might help people.**

### ANIMALS at work

We're always hearing stories in the news about how we need to save the planet's wildlife. But sometimes humans need help too. In today's show we look at how clever creatures can help people to live normal lives – for example, people who are blind, or wheelchair users – as well as how animals help the emergency services and army to keep us safe.

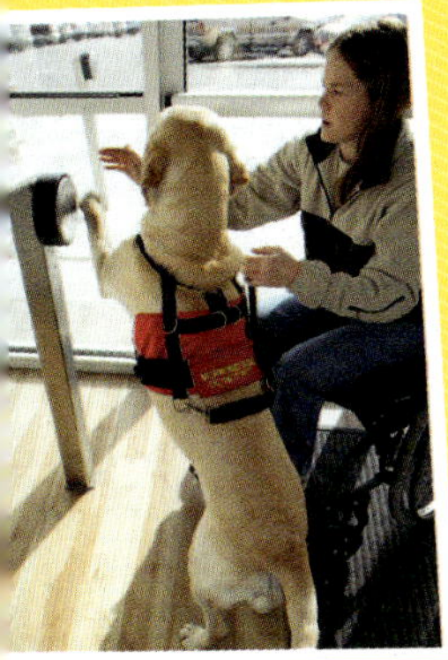

60 **2** **Listen to the show. Which three animals do they talk about?**

60 **3** **Listen again. Complete the sentences with *Dogs*, *Rats* or *Bees*.**

1 ________ avoid a problem because they aren't as heavy as humans.
2 ________ can bring things to people.
3 ________ can help find dangerous chemicals.
4 ________ can help find bombs that are under the ground.
5 ________ can help with buying things.
6 ________ are cheaper to train than other animals.

**4** **Discuss the questions.**

1 In what ways do you think Riley has improved Donna's life?
2 In what other ways can animals improve people's lives?
3 Is it fair to use animals to help us in dangerous situations? Why? / Why not?

## SPEAKING Describing a photo (1)

**1** **Look at the photo. What do you think is happening?**

61 **2** **Listen to someone describing the photo and check your ideas.**

### PREPARE TO SPEAK
**Describing a photo (1)**

| **Saying what you can see** | **Guessing what's happening** |
|---|---|
| I can see … | Perhaps … |
| There's … | Maybe … |
| On the left/right, … | It's probably … |
| In the middle … | They might be … |

61 **3** **Read the *Prepare to speak* box. Then complete the sentences about the photo using words from the box. Listen again and check.**

1 The dog is ________ a rescue dog.
2 On the ________, one person is digging down into the snow.
3 ________ they're looking for someone.
4 The other person's on the ________.
5 He ________ be the dog's trainer.
6 ________ the dog has found the person.

**4** **Work with a partner. Take turns to describe the photo in Exercise 1. Use phrases from the *Prepare to speak* box.**

**5** » **Work with a partner. Turn to page 124.**

# LIFE SKILLS SOCIAL RESPONSIBILITY

## RESPECTING THE ENVIRONMENT

### LIFE SKILLS

**Respecting the environment**

The environment is the natural world around us. It includes the land, water and air where plants and animals live. People also need the environment to live, so we must work together to protect and care for our natural home.

**1** **Ask and answer the questions with a partner.**

1. How often do you use public transport?
2. Does your family recycle at home?
3. Do you like spending time in natural areas?

**2** **Read the text quickly. What are the three Rs?**

## Caring for our world

**Many countries have programmes to care for the environment, but ordinary people can also help in everyday ways. For example, we can follow the three Rs: reduce, reuse and recycle. We can also care for natural areas and teach others about environmental protection to keep our world clean, beautiful and healthy.**

### Reduce, reuse, recycle

The first way to help the environment is to ***reduce*** any resources that you use. For example, you can turn off the water while brushing your teeth, and have a short shower instead of a long one.

Turning off lights and other electrical items when they aren't needed also saves energy. And eating less meat eat can help the environment too - it takes ten times more energy to produce beef compared with vegetables.

Perhaps the biggest change we can make is reducing how much plastic we use. Try to buy food that is not wrapped in plastic and buy a reusable bottle for water instead of buying water in plastic bottles.

We must also ***reuse*** things more often. For example, when we're going to go to the supermarket, we can take reusable bags. If we do that, we won't need plastic bags, which usually end up in the rubbish. Other things can also be reusable, such as batteries. If we use rechargeable batteries, we won't need new ones all the time. We can also sell or give away things that we don't want, like old clothes or books, so other people can reuse them.

The third rule is to ***recycle*** as much as possible. If we recycle paper and cardboard, we won't need to cut down so many trees. Many sorts of plastic, metal and glass are also recyclable. If we recycle those old materials, it will save resources and use less energy than creating new materials. Look out for recycling bins in your neighbourhood and separate materials correctly when you recycle.

### Protect and teach

In addition to the three Rs, we need to care for natural spaces, such as parks. We should always throw paper, plastic and other litter into the correct rubbish bins. When we go camping, we mustn't feed any wild animals, such as ducks. We don't want them to follow people around for food. And if we make a fire to cook our food, we must be careful so we don't start any forest fires.

We can also inform other people about the need for environmental protection. We can make presentations at school and collect money for environmental organisations. Finally, we can celebrate special occasions about nature, such as Earth Day on 22nd April.

## 3 Complete the sentences with one or two words from the text.

1 There are many ________ to protect the environment.
2 People need to ________ the natural resources that they are using.
3 It's better to take ________ bags when you go to the supermarket.
4 It takes less ________ to recycle materials than to make new ones.
5 We should throw litter into ________ to keep our nature parks clean.
6 If campers aren't careful when they cook, they can start ________.

## 4 Match the highlighted words in the text to the meanings.

1 types or kinds of things
2 tell people about something
3 paper and other things that people drop in the street
4 normal, not special or unusual
5 things from nature that we can use

63
## 5 Listen to a podcast about an environmental campaign. What are the two main problems in the park?

63
## 6 Listen again. Are the sentences true or false?

1 Hannah works for an organisation that protects the environment.
2 The students have finished making their video.
3 Lots of young people go hiking in the nature park.
4 Some people are burning the trees in the park.
5 The main characters of the film are superheroes.
6 They're only going to show the film at school.

## 7 Complete the *Useful language* phrases with the words in the box.

could else idea possible
sure think

# USEFUL LANGUAGE

**Brainstorming ideas**

1 I think we ________ make a poster.
2 What do you ________ we should do?
3 Do you think that's ________?
4 I'm not ________ about that.
5 What ________ can we do?
6 That's a great ________.

# PROJECT

***An environmental campaign***

**Work in groups. Brainstorm ideas for an environmental campaign and then make a presentation or video. Use the questions below to help you think.**

- What environmental topics interest you?
- Are there any environmental issues in your area?
- Do the people in your area recycle enough?
- What sorts of campaign would be fun to do?
- Are you good at taking photos or making videos?
- Could you create a computer presentation?

**Share your presentation or video with the class. Then vote on the best idea.**

# REVIEW 3 UNITS 9–12

## VOCABULARY

**1 Complete the crossword.**

Across
1 keep money until you have enough to buy something (4, 2)
4 You might do this to something when you don't want it any more. (4, 2, 4)
5 the place where you pay in a supermarket (8)
8 something that is cheaper for a period of time (7, 5)
9 You might do this when you buy something and then decide you don't like it. (4, 2, 4)

Down
2 the amount of money something costs (5)
3 a place where you put your money to keep it safe (4, 7)
6 a piece of paper that a shop assistant gives you when you buy something (7)
7 the money you get back at the 5 (6)

**2 Match four words in the box to each topic.**

| | | | | |
|---|---|---|---|---|
| bitter | chin | cough | cut | deer |
| flu | forehead | fresh | mosquitoes | |
| raw | shoulder | sour | stomach ache | |
| toe | eagles | wolves | | |

1 Describing food and taste: ________, ________, ________, ________
2 The body: ________, ________, ________, ________
3 Health: ________, ________, ________, ________
4 Animals: ________, ________, ________, ________

**3 Complete the sentences with the words in Exercise 2. Use two words from each topic.**

1 I've had a ________ for over a week. It's really making my throat sore.
2 This chocolate isn't very nice. It's too ________.
3 Unlike most other birds, female ________ are larger than the males.
4 Can you feel my ________? I think I've got a temperature.
5 ________ are the most dangerous insects in the world.
6 I don't buy fruit here. It isn't ________ enough.
7 You haven't got a cold. You've caught ________.
8 I was carrying a heavy bag today and now my ________ really hurts.

## GRAMMAR

**1 Complete the conversations. Use the past simple or present perfect form of the verbs.**

1 **A:** ________ you ever ________ (see) a shark?
**B:** No, I haven't. But last year I ________ (swim) with dolphins on holiday.
2 **A:** How long ________ Ruth ________ (have) stomach ache?
**B:** It started yesterday. She ________ (not eat) anything since then.
3 **A:** We ________ (go) to a Japanese restaurant last weekend.
**B:** I ________ never ________ (try) Japanese food.
4 **A:** James and Tom ________ (be) over 20 minutes late this morning.
**B:** ________ they ever ________ (arrive) at school on time? They're always late!

**2 Choose the correct verbs.**

1 **A:** Don't buy those trainers now. I think they *'ll* / *'re going to* have lots of special offers soon.
**B:** I know, but mine are really uncomfortable. I *'ll* / *'m going to* buy these ones now.
2 **A:** Is Paul interested in coming? Tell him we *'ll* / *'re going to* leave in ten minutes.
**B:** I don't think he *'ll* / *'s going to* want to watch that film. But I'll ask.
3 **A:** Our teacher *will* / *is going to* have a baby in June. She told us today.
**B:** Really? That's nice news. I *'ll* / *'m going to* send her a card.
4 **A:** I *'ll* / *'m going to* take my new jacket back to the shop today. It's too small.
**B:** I *'ll* / *'m going to* come with you! I've got nothing else to do today.

**3** **Write a sentence that means the same as the second sentence. Use the verb in brackets.**

1. He can't move his arm. *Perhaps it's broken.* (might)
2. It tastes disgusting. *I'm sure it isn't fresh.* (can't)
3. He's got a cough and a sore throat. *Perhaps he has a cold.* (could)
4. My brother often goes to that café. *I'm sure he knows your sister.* (must)
5. It looks bigger than a mouse. *Perhaps it's a rat.* (might)

**4** **Choose the correct words.**

1. This summer I *'ll go* / *'m going* to England with my friends.
2. Sorry, *I* / *have I* met you before?
3. I'm not sure at the moment, but I *can* / *might* be a bit late tomorrow.
4. I've known him *for* / *since* a long time.

**5** **Correct the mistake in each sentence.**

1. This change mustn't be correct. You've given me more money than I gave you!
2. We are friends since I was six.
3. I think you like it when you see it.
4. You have heard about the concert?

**6** **Read the text and choose the correct word for each space. For each question, choose A, B, C or D.**

# Eating when you're feeling ill

Sometimes the last thing you want to think about when you're not feeling well is food. You aren't hungry and nothing tastes good. But your body still needs energy, so it's important to eat. Soup is an excellent food at this time. It's simple to prepare and easy to eat. Plain yoghurt without any [1] ________ added is also good. If you've got a cold, [2] ________ dishes, such as curry or anything with chilli, will help. But avoid them if you're [3] ________ from stomach ache. Always drink plenty of water, and stay away from juices if you have a [4] ________ throat.

Finally, think about the times when you [5] ________ ill as a young child. What food did your parents prepare for you then? Some scientists advise eating the same food. The positive [6] ________ from your childhood can actually help you to get better.

| | A | B | C | D |
|---|---|---|---|---|
| **1** | **A** flavour | **B** recipe | **C** change | **D** sour |
| **2** | **A** juicy | **B** spicy | **C** raw | **D** frozen |
| **3** | **A** supporting | **B** experiencing | **C** complaining | **D** suffering |
| **4** | **A** cut | **B** broken | **C** sore | **D** hurt |
| **5** | **A** fell | **B** went | **C** had | **D** caught |
| **6** | **A** records | **B** memories | **C** rules | **D** minds |

# 13 MIXED FEELINGS

## ABOUT YOU

09 **Watch the video and then answer the questions.**

Are you usually in a good mood?

What kind of things put you in a bad mood?

## VOCABULARY Adjectives: moods and feelings

**1** **Read the social media posts and choose the correct adjectives.**

**2** **Match the adjectives you didn't choose in Exercise 1 with the definitions.**

- **a** feeling or showing thanks
- **b** unhappy because something was not as good as you hoped
- **c** very surprised
- **d** very tired
- **e** worried and not able to relax
- **f** showing no fear of dangerous situations

64 EP **3** **Complete the sentences with the adjectives in the box. Then listen to the conversations and check.**

amazed brave confused disappointed
embarrassed exhausted grateful hopeful
proud relaxed scared stressed

1. Ben's mum feels really ______ because he got to the final of the tennis competition. Tom is ______ because he didn't win.
2. Vicky is feeling ______ because she had football training all afternoon. However, she agrees to go to the shop for her dad and he is very ______.
3. Freddy is ______ that Sadie designed the rugby poster. It looks so professional. But he's also ______. He doesn't understand why Sadie is interested in rugby.
4. Anna is feeling ______ because she's got an exam tomorrow. Harry thinks she'll work better if she's ______.
5. Lucas feels ______ because he made some stupid mistakes in his exam. He's still ______ that he has passed.
6. Dan is ______ to tell his sister that he broke her phone. His mum tells him to be ______ and tell her now.

**4** **Complete the sentences. Then compare them with your partner's.**

1. I get embarrassed when …
2. On Friday afternoons, I usually feel …
3. At the weekend, I sometimes feel …
4. I get stressed when …
5. I feel a bit disappointed when …
6. I'm scared of …

**Ellen Gardner**

165 friends

### Your friends' recent activity

7 minutes ago

**Alfie Dale**

is feeling [1] *scared / grateful.*

I'm at home by myself. Maybe this wasn't the night to watch a horror film!

22 minutes ago

**Evie Turner**

is feeling [2] *proud / brave.*

Incredible game, Brighton ! Next week Chelsea!

1 hour ago

**Lily Gates**

is feeling [3] *stressed / relaxed.*

Sunday night is film night in our house. I'm on the sofa with some snacks!

1 hour ago

**Ollie Parks**

is feeling [4] *confused / amazed.*

OK. Does anyone want to explain the ending of Sherlock to me? I didn't understand it at all!

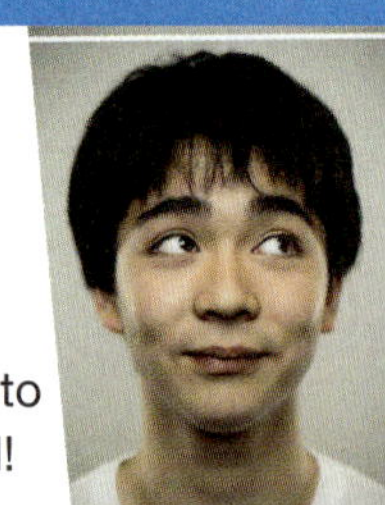

2 hours ago

**Jack Forrest**

is feeling [5] *exhausted / embarrassed.*

I thought that Sydney was the capital of Australia! Oops!

2 hours ago

**Grace Buxton**

is feeling [6] *disappointed / hopeful.*

I scored 92% in the practice maths test! I'm feeling pretty good about the real exam now.

# The WORST day of the week

65

**Ask someone who goes to school from Monday to Friday for the worst day of their week and many people will say Monday. On Mondays the fun of the weekend has just finished and the week has just begun. [1] ________**

However, two maths professors in the USA have just completed research that tells us more about the worst day of our week. Peter Dodds and Christopher Danforth analysed 10 million sentences on social networking websites like Facebook and Twitter. [2] ________ Then, the professors came up with a system of scores for words, between 1 and 9. They gave positive words like 'hopeful' and 'relaxed' high scores. Negative words, like 'stressed' and 'exhausted', got low scores. [3] ________

Their results could change your life – or at least your week! According to the professors, Sunday is the happiest day of the week. [4] ________ Monday is actually the second happiest day of the week. People haven't forgotten about their weekends yet. And the worst day of the week for most people is … Wednesday! [5] ________ As a result, their memory of the previous weekend has gone, and there are two more days before the next one.

The research found another surprising fact: people between 45 and 60 are the happiest people online, but the most miserable group is … teenagers!

## Comments

| | |
|---|---|
| **Ryan**, *Cambridge* | Sunday evening is definitely the worst evening of my week. I always put off starting my homework until then and I have to work until midnight. |
| **Omar**, *Riyadh* | It's different here. Our schools are closed on Friday and Saturday. So I think my worst day is probably Tuesday. |
| **Anna**, *Kraków* | I agree with this research. I always feel dreadful on Wednesday mornings. |

## READING

**1** **What's your worst day of the week? And the best? Read the article quickly and see if your answers agree with the research.**

**2** **Read the article again. Five sentences have been removed from the text. For each space choose the correct sentence. There are three extra sentences which you do not need to use.**

**A** On that day, people think and write about the fun things they did the day before – on Saturday.
**B** That's why it's most people's favourite day.
**C** Finally, they used these numbers to decide how happy people were on each day.
**D** All of these included the phrase 'I feel' or 'I'm feeling'.
**E** It was the result of four years' work.
**F** Most people have already been at school or work for two days.
**G** Everyone is back at school, or work, and the next weekend is in five days' time.
**H** There is just one more day before the weekend.

**3** **Match the highlighted words in the article to the meanings.**

1 thought of (an idea or plan)
2 examined the details of something carefully
3 not expected
4 decide to do something at a later time
5 terrible
6 as said by someone

### TALKING POINTS

Would it be a good idea to have two separate days off every week, instead of a weekend? Why? / Why not?

What's your worst day of the week? Why?

# GRAMMAR *just, already* and *yet*

**1** **Read the examples. Then complete the rules with *just, already* and *yet*.**

1 On Mondays the week has just begun.
2 People haven't forgotten about their weekends yet.
3 Most people have already been at school or work for two days.
4 Have you finished your homework yet?

We often use *just, already* and *yet* with the present perfect to talk about recent actions.
**a** ........ means that something happened before now or sooner than expected.
**b** ........ means a short time ago.
**c** ........ means that the speaker expected something to happen before now.

**2** **Choose the correct words.**

1 **A:** Have you told your parents *just* / *yet*?
**B:** No. I wasn't feeling brave enough last night.
2 **A:** I'm so proud of you. I've *already* / *yet* told everyone at my work.
**B:** Dad! I'm getting embarrassed!
3 **A:** You look relaxed.
**B:** Yes. I've *yet* / *just* been for a swim.
4 **A:** I'm confused about question 6.
**B:** Hold on! I haven't finished question 5 *yet* / *already.*

**3** **Look at the examples in Exercise 1 again and complete the rules.**

We use [1] ........ and [2] ........ in positive sentences. They come after *have* and before the past participle.
We use [3] ........ in negative sentences and questions. It comes at the end of the sentence.

» GRAMMAR REFERENCE AND PRACTICE PAGE 150

**4** **Make sentences using the present perfect and *just*, *already* and *yet*.**

1 We / hear / some amazing news. (just)
2 I / put off / my dentist's appointment once. I can't do it again. (already)
3 Ella isn't stressed! It's eleven o'clock and she / not / get up (yet)
4 Do I have to come? I / sit down and I'm absolutely exhausted. (just)
5 you / try / Jack's cake? (yet)
6 My phone was fully charged this morning and it / run out / of battery. (already)

**5** **Correct the mistake in each sentence.**

1 We just see your advertisement.
2 I haven't already bought a new book.
3 Did I tell you about my holiday yet?
4 I already asked a friend of mine.
5 He just has moved to a new house.
6 I haven't been yet there.

**6** **Kate is getting ready for a party. Look at the picture. Say what Kate *has already done* and what she *hasn't done yet*. Use the words in the box.**

| | |
|---|---|
| have a shower | write the birthday card |
| wrap the present | iron her clothes |
| tidy her room | wash her hair |

# VOCABULARY Adjectives: *-ed* or *-ing*

**1** EP **Look at the picture and the examples. Complete the rules with *-ed* or *-ing*.**

**a** Adjectives with ........ describe how a person feels about something.
**b** Adjectives with ........ describe the things, person, or situation that causes the person's feeling.

**2** **Complete the adjectives with *-ed* or *-ing*.**

1 I'm tidying my room and I'm bor........ .
2 Are you feeling relax........ after your holiday?
3 I want to go to bed. I've had a really tir........ day.
4 I think my brother's failed his driving test. He looks really disappoint........ .
5 That's really annoy........ . I've just bought that game and now it's 50% off.
6 When my mum sings, it's really embarrass........ .

**3** » Turn to page 123.

# WRITING An article (2)

**1** You see this notice on an English-language website. What's *your* favourite day of the week?

## ARTICLES WANTED!

Everyone has a favourite day of the week. What day of the week do you like the best? What do you do on this day that makes it your favourite day of the week? How do you feel?

Tell us what you think!

**Write an article answering these questions and we will publish the most interesting on our site.**

**2** Read the article. Write notes of the answers to the questions in the notice in Exercise 1.

### Friday? Saturday? No, it's …

Are you one of those people who looks forward to weekends? I am. And I absolutely love Sundays.

A typical Sunday starts around nine-thirty in my house. When I wake up, I feel excited and full of energy. I'm really into making stuff at the moment. I look online for ideas for projects.

My dad and I have just joined a climbing centre, so we go there on Sunday afternoons. I think it's a challenging sport, but it's also really exciting. Then, in the early evening, my aunt, uncle and cousins come round for a meal. After they leave, we watch a film together as a family. In my view, it's a perfectly relaxing end to my favourite day.

**3** Read the *Prepare to write* box. Find the phrases used in the article.

### PREPARE TO WRITE
**An article (2)**

**Ask questions to get the reader's attention:**

Do you … ?
Have you ever …?
Are you one of those people who …?
Can you imagine …?

**Make your article interesting:**

I **absolutely love** Sundays.
When I wake up, I feel excited and **full of energy.**
It's a **perfectly relaxing** end to my favourite day.

**Give your own opinion:**

I think …    For me, …    I would say that …

**4** Read these notices (1–3) and match them to the beginnings of students' articles (A–C).

## ARTICLES WANTED!

**1 Bored!**
We all get bored sometimes. It's part of life. What kinds of things do you find boring? Do you ever get bored in your spare time? Do you think being bored can ever be good for you?

**2 An amazing person**
We all know someone amazing. Perhaps it's an incredible musician, a talented sportsperson, or even a member of your family. Who do you think is amazing? Why do you think this? Have you ever told this person what you think about him or her?

**3 Your week**
According to experts, teenagers nowadays are busier than ever. Do you find your school week tiring? Which day is the worst? What do you do to relax out of school?

**A** Are you one of those people who jump out of bed in the morning, full of energy? I am definitely not.

**B** Can you imagine spending six hours in a car without anyone to talk to? I did this every day for a week last summer.

**C** Do you ever think about all the things your parents do for you? It's easy to forget sometimes.

**5** Which article 1–3 in Exercise 4 could each of these sentences be from? Match two possible sentences to each article.

**a** I'm incredibly grateful to her for all her help and she knows that.
**b** By the weekend, I am absolutely exhausted.
**c** As soon as that show starts, I switch off the TV.
**d** I would say that Thursdays are my toughest days.
**e** I don't think people should have to go to museums until they're an adult.
**f** For me, this person is my mum.

**6** Write an article. Use one of the notices in Exercise 1 or 4.

- Organise your article into paragraphs (see *Prepare to write* page 67).
- Use phrases from the *Prepare to write* box.
- Write about 100 words.
- Remember to check your spelling and grammar.

# 14 ON SCREEN

## ABOUT YOU

What films have you seen recently?
What are your favourite TV shows?

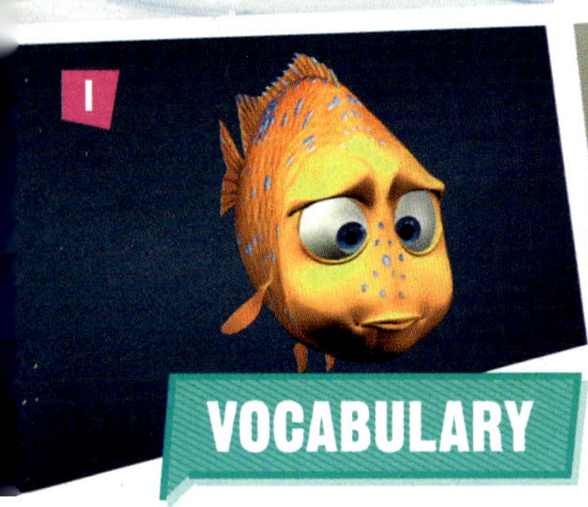

## VOCABULARY TV and film

**1** **Match the photos to the TV and film genres in the box.**

EP

| | | | |
|---|---|---|---|
| action thriller | animation | chat show | comedy |
| crime drama | documentary | horror film | period drama |
| reality show | science fiction | soap opera | the news |

*A – action thriller*

66 **2** **Listen and check your answers to Exercise 1.**

**3** **Are the genres in Exercise 1 a TV show, a film, or both?**

**4** **Complete the definitions with genres from Exercise 1. Then, in pairs, write one-line definitions of the other seven genres.**

**1** A ________ is a film or TV show that gives information about a subject.
**2** A ________ is a TV drama series about people's daily lives.
**3** A show or film about the future is called ________.
**4** A ________ is a show or film with a story that takes place in the past.
**5** A ________ is a TV show where someone interviews guests on various topics.

**5** **In pairs, think of one example for each of the genres from Exercise 1.**

The *Toy Story* films are animations.

Yes, and so are the *Despicable Me* films.

**6** **Complete the sentences with the genres that you like and dislike. Compare your opinions in groups.**

**1** I'm a big fan of …
**2** I can't stand …
**3** I love …
**4** I'm not a big fan of …
**5** I'm really into …
**6** I'm not into …

## READING

1 Discuss how you think people can get their first role in a film.

2 Read the text quickly. Did you think of the three ways that Kameron suggests?

# SO YOU WANT TO BE IN A FILM?

67

## HERE'S HOW ANYONE CAN DO IT ...

My best friend and I have just appeared in a film! It sounds unbelievable, but the truth is: it was easy. We were extras, and anyone can be an extra. Extras act in films or TV shows, but they aren't the main actors. They might be people who are chatting in a restaurant, walking down a street or playing sports. Sometimes, with smaller films, people are happy to work for free as extras. Although you don't get paid, you get to hang out with cool people, learn about film making and support a local director. Also, film companies provide great lunches!

BY KAMERON BADGERS

### There are three ways to get hired as an extra:

**1 JOIN A CASTING WEBSITE** I found a national website which producers and directors look through to find extras. It was free to join. I just had to send a photo and fill in a questionnaire about my skills and abilities, for example sports I'm good at, musical instruments I can play, and whether I have a motorcycle licence. A director is the person who is in charge of filming. A producer is responsible for the team that makes the film. Producers are interested in anyone, from babies to grandparents. Hopefully, you'll get something cool like a part in a reality show or a period drama!

**2 CONTACT YOUR LOCAL FILM BOARD** Film boards help local companies with things like money and the contacts they need to make a film. They'll also send you information about directors who are filming in your area.

**3 TAKE ACTING CLASSES** Drama schools are often the first place where producers look.

**FINALLY, A FEW WORDS OF WARNING!**

- Be prepared for long waits: you'll spend more time doing nothing than appearing in a scene.
- Forget advertisements that say they'll make you famous. They probably won't!
- Remember: this isn't your 'big chance' to become a star. Extras are there to do a job, not because they hope to 'show what they can do'.

3 Complete the sentences with the correct form of the highlighted words from the text.

1 The teacher gave her a .......... about being late.
2 Do you want to .......... in a video that I'm making?
3 The football team is going to .......... a new coach.
4 I'd like to talk to the person who's .......... here.
5 My brother played the .......... of a rock singer in a short film.
6 It's hard preparing for exams, but my teachers .......... me in various ways.

4 Read the text again and answer the questions.

1 How did Kameron appear in a film?
2 What do extras do?
3 Why do volunteers like helping smaller film productions?
4 What's the difference between a producer and a director?
5 How can film boards help people who want to start acting?
6 Why should you take acting classes?
7 Why might it be boring to be an extra?

**TALKING POINTS**

Would you like to be an extra or even an actor? Why? / Why not?

What films or shows would you like to appear in?

## GRAMMAR Relative clauses

**1 Read the examples. Then complete the rules with the words in the box.**

1 They'll send you information about directors **who** are filming in your area.
2 I found a national website **which** producers and directors look through.
3 A producer is responsible for the team **that** makes a film.
4 Local drama schools are often the first place **where** producers look.
5 Forget advertisements **that** say they'll make you famous.

| ~~that~~ | that | where | which | who |
|---|---|---|---|---|

We use relative clauses to explain who, what or where we are talking about. We use:
**a** *that* and ________ to talk about things.
**b** ________ and ________ to talk about people.
**c** ________ talk about places.

» GRAMMAR REFERENCE AND PRACTICE PAGE 151

**2 Read the text and choose the correct words.**

**Frankenstein** is a classic science fiction story. There are a lot of film versions, but *Frankenstein* was originally a novel [1] *that / who* was published in 1818. Many people think Frankenstein is a monster, but in fact the main character is a crazy scientist [2] *which / who* is called Dr Frankenstein. He's got a laboratory [3] *where / who* he is trying to create a beautiful, new kind of creature. Eventually, he makes a monster [4] *that / where* is huge – and ugly. Frankenstein's monster has got yellow and green skin, and a face [5] *where / which* is very frightening.

Boris Karloff played the part of the monster in a 1931 film version of the book. Karloff's monster had a big, square head with a white face and a metal bolt [6] *where / that* went through its neck. This 1931 film created the image of Frankenstein's monster [7] *that / who* most modern audiences are familiar with.

**3 Complete the sentences with *who*, *which* or *where*. Then tick (✓) the ones where *that* is also correct.**

0 This is a film about a weak boy *who* turns into a strong man. ✓
1 The Font Café is a quiet place ________ you can study.
2 Have you ever met anyone ________ can speak five languages?
3 My mum has a new car ________ I love.
4 I met a girl at the youth club ________ knows you.
5 Are there any places around here ________ I can charge my phone?

**4 Connect the sentences with relative pronouns.**

0 Mary Shelley was a British author. She wrote *Frankenstein* in 1818.
*Mary Shelley was a British author who wrote Frankenstein in 1818.*
1 *Stranger Things* is a brilliant series. I started watching it last week.
2 The *Fantastic Beasts* series was filmed in New York. It stars Eddie Redmayne and Katherine Waterston.
3 There's a new bookshop in the mall. You can buy English-language DVDs there.
4 Jennifer Lawrence is a Hollywood star. She has appeared in lots of great films.
5 Steven Spielberg is an incredible director. He has won three Oscars.
6 Cortlandt Alley is a tiny street in New York. They have filmed dozens of film scenes there.

## VOCABULARY Talking about films and shows

**1 Match the sentence halves.**

1 A **character** is
2 A **clip** is
3 A **plot** is
4 A **review** is
5 A **series** is
6 A **soundtrack** is
7 A **trailer** is

a a small part taken from a longer film or show.
b a report with an opinion of a film or show.
c the story in a film or show.
d a short video advertising a new film or show.
e a part which an actor plays.
f the music used in a film or show.
g individual programmes that use the same characters in different situations.

**2 Complete the sentences with words from Exercise 1.**

1 Homer is my favourite ________ in *The Simpsons*.
2 There's a new comedy ________ on tonight that I haven't watched, but there are ________ of the funniest scenes online.
3 Nothing happens in this film. The ________ is really boring.
4 Have you read any ________ of the new Marvel film? – No, but I've watched a ________ for it. It looks amazing.
5 The ________ has some great songs on it.

**3 Discuss the questions.**

1 Who's your favourite film or TV show character?
2 Do you read reviews before you choose a film to watch? Where?

**4** » **Work with a partner.** **Turn to page 123.**

# LISTENING

68 **1** **Look at the list of film and TV genres. Listen to six conversations and write the conversation number next to the genre. (There is one genre that you don't need.)**

**a** ____ comedy
**b** ____ documentary
**c** __1__ horror film
**d** ____ period drama
**e** ____ reality show
**f** ____ the news
**g** ____ science fiction

**2** **Read the questions and possible answers in the exam task in Exercise 3. Underline the key words.**

68 **3** **Listen to the six conversations again. For each question, choose the correct answer.**

**1** You will hear two friends talking about a film. What do they say about it?
**A** The reviews of it are rather negative.
**B** They are too young to see it.
**C** Someone they know found it hard to follow.

**2** You will hear two friends talking about reality shows. What annoys the girl about reality TV stars?
**A** They get paid too much.
**B** They behave badly in public.
**C** They are boring to listen to.

**3** You will hear two friends talking about taking part in a short film. The boy is unlikely to appear in the film because
**A** he didn't see the information about it.
**B** he doesn't want to go to the meeting about it.
**C** the producer won't pay people who appear in it.

**4** You will hear two friends talking about a sci-fi film they've seen. They agree that
**A** the creature was scary.
**B** the film was too long.
**C** the soundtrack was excellent.

**5** You will hear two friends talking about the news. They agree that
**A** there's too much politics in the news.
**B** they should stop watching the news.
**C** their attitudes to the news have changed.

**6** You will hear two friends talking about going to the cinema. What does the boy suggest?
**A** asking someone to get their tickets
**B** reading about the film before they set off
**C** seeing the last showing of the day

# SPEAKING Reaching agreement

**1** **You are going to watch a film with friends. Look at the menu. Which one would you like to watch? Why?**

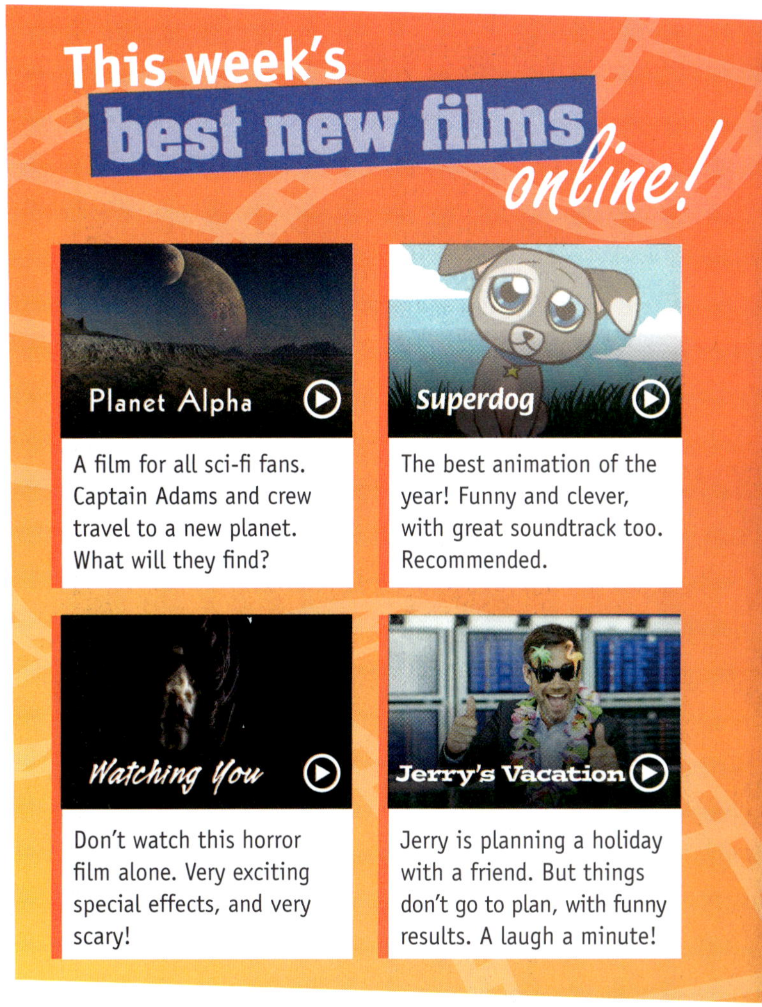


69 **2** **You will hear two friends talking about which film to watch. Which one do they choose?**

69 **3** **Read the *Prepare to speak* box. Then listen again. Which phrases do you hear?**

## PREPARE TO SPEAK
### Reaching agreement

| Giving reasons | Reaching agreement |
|---|---|
| because … | Let's decide. |
| It's too … | Yes, that's a good choice. |
| It looks/sounds … | I think we're both happy with that. |

**4** **Follow the instructions to reach agreement about watching a film or show.**

**1** Look at the films and shows on page 80. In pairs, make a list of three that you would like to watch.
**2** Discuss the films/shows, and reach agreement on which one to watch. Use phrases from the *Prepare to speak* box.

# CULTURE

## THE FILM INDUSTRY

**1** Ask and answer the questions with a partner.

1 What's your favourite film?
2 What are some famous films from your country?
3 Who is the most famous film director from your country?

**2** Do the film quiz.

# FILM quiz

**1** **The Lumière brothers made the first ever film. What was the year?**
A 1895 B 1905 C 1959

**2** **The first full-length film was *The Story of the Kelly Gang*. Where did they make it?**
A the UK B the USA C Australia

**3** **The earliest films were silent. When was the first film with dialogue and music?**
A 1927 B 1957 C 1987

**4** **Which famous fictional character has appeared in the most films?**
A Mickey Mouse
B Sherlock Holmes
C James Bond

**5** **In which country do people go to the cinema most frequently?**
A Iceland B the USA C Poland

70 **3** Listen and check your answers.

**4** Read the *World film facts* on page 85. Complete the sentences with the names of the countries.

1 .................. makes the most films every year.
2 .................. has got the most cinema screens.
3 .................. celebrates the BAFTA awards.
4 .................. makes the most money in tickets.
5 .................. made Godzilla films popular.

**5** Answer the questions about the text.

1 Which of the countries has the fewest screens?
2 Why do Hollywood studios make films in Canada?
3 What were Chinese films usually about in the past?
4 When did Japanese samurai films become popular?
5 Why are Bollywood films called *masala films*?
6 What type of film is *Sense and Sensibility*?

**6** Match the highlighted words in the text to the meanings.

1 great, amazing
2 something that becomes popular
3 famous
4 formal celebrations
5 extremely large
6 plant products used to give food a special taste

71 **7** Listen to Jack's presentation of the Japanese film *The Hidden Fortress*. Which characters in the box does Jack talk about?

| doctors | farmers | general | king |
|---|---|---|---|
| monsters | princess | queen | samurai |

71 **8** Listen again. Are the sentences true or false? Correct the false sentences.

1 *The Hidden Fortress* was filmed in 1954.
2 All of the locations in the film are in Japan.
3 The story takes place about 200 years ago.
4 General Rokurota protects Princess Yuki.
5 The two farmers are quite serious characters.
6 At first, the film wasn't very popular in Japan.

1 **The USA**
**40,000**
Cinema screens
approximately
**$10 billion**
Ticket sales / year

2 **China**
**41,000**
Cinema screens
approximately
**$6.6 billion**
Ticket sales / year

3 **Japan**
**3,500**
Cinema screens
approximately
**$2.0 billion**
Ticket sales / year

4 **India**
**10,000**
Cinema screens
approximately
**$1.9 billion**
Ticket sales / year

5 **The UK**
**4,200**
Cinema screens
approximately
**$1.7 billion**
Ticket sales / year

# World film facts: THE BIG FIVE

72

## The USA

The biggest films studios in the USA are in Hollywood, California. However, many studios make their films in other states, like New York and Louisiana. Canadian locations, like Vancouver and Toronto, are also popular because it's cheaper to work there. The most renowned film awards in the USA are the Golden Globes and the Oscars. Both ceremonies take place in Los Angeles, California.

**Big hits:** *Black Panther, Jurassic World*

## China

Chinese audiences watch many films from the USA, but they have a dynamic national industry too. In the past, Chinese films were often about serious, historical topics, but now studios also make horror films, thrillers, comedies and romances, with Chinese stars, of course! One of the most famous actresses is Yang Mi. She's also a pop singer and fashion model.

**Big hits:** *Monster Hunt, The Great Wall*

## Japan

In the 1950s, Japan became famous for action-adventure films about martial arts, like *Seven Samurai* or *The Hidden Fortress*. In 1954, there was also a very popular film about a giant monster, called *Godzilla*. Audiences loved the film and it started a new trend. In more recent years, animated films, called anime, have become popular, as well as scary horror films about ghosts and other monsters.

**Big hits:** *Princess Mononoke, The Ring*

## India

India makes more films than any other country per year. Many are Bollywood films, which combine love, drama, comedy and action with Indian music and dancing. Indians call them *masala films* because they have so many ingredients, like the masala spices that Indians use for cooking. Bollywood actors usually speak and sing in Hindi, but they often use English phrases too.

**Big hits:** *Sultan, Chennai Express*

## The UK

Britain has made some of the world's most popular films, like the James Bond and Harry Potter series. They also make lots of historical films about famous novels, like *Sense and Sensibility* or *Jane Eyre*. If you like detective and crime stories, the Sherlock Holmes films are also terrific. The biggest prizes for British cinema are the BAFTA awards, which take place every year in London.

**Big hits:** *Casino Royale, Fantastic Beasts and Where to Find Them*

**9** **Read the *Useful language* phrases. Complete them with information about *The Hidden Fortress*.**

### USEFUL LANGUAGE

**Talking about films**

1 It's a film from …
2 The director's name is …
3 It was filmed in …
4 The story takes place …
5 The main characters are …
6 The film won (the award for) …

## PROJECT

***A presentation about a film***

**Plan a presentation about a famous film that you like. Go online and find information about it. If possible, find photos and music from the film.**

1 Where is it from? What type of film is it?
2 Who directed the film? Where was it filmed?
3 Where and when does the story take place?
4 Who are the main characters in the film?
5 Has the film won any important awards?
6 What do you like the most about the film?

**Present your film to the class.**

10 NOW WATCH THE CULTURE VIDEO

# 15 DIGITAL LIFE

**ABOUT YOU**

What do you use your phone or computer for? Make a list of things.

## VOCABULARY Computer phrases

**1** (73) Match the beginnings and ends of the quiz questions. Then listen and check. EP

**2** (74) Listen to Jack's answers to the quiz. Alex asks follow-up questions to get more details. Complete the questions.

1 What did *you do* ?
2 How did you ______ ?
3 How do you ______ ?
4 What kind of things ______ ?
5 What did ______ ?
6 Which apps do you use ______ ?
7 How many do you ______ ?
8 Which ones do you ______ the most?

**3** (74) Complete the sentences about Jack with words from Exercise 1. Then listen again and check.

1 Jack *deleted* a school project, but his dad helped him to get it back.
2 He got a ______ when he installed a game.
3 He uses a different ______ for each website.
4 He often ______ to funny videos or photos.
5 He has ______ for his name and found it in some football reports.
6 He ______ a lot of ______ and mainly uses Instagram.
7 He has ______ about ten ______ this week and has over 200 altogether.
8 He sometimes ______ and his favourites are the ones about science.

**4** In pairs, take turns to answer the quiz questions in Exercise 1. If you can, use the follow-up questions in Exercise 2 to find out more information.

**5** Tell the class something interesting you found out about your partner.

> Sara got a virus on her dad's computer and they had to buy a new one.

1 Have you ever **deleted** an
2 Have you ever **had**
3 Do you have a
4 Do you often **share**
5 Have you ever **done**
6 Do you **upload**
7 How many new **apps** have you
8 Do you ever **download**

a **photos or videos** to the internet to share with friends?
b different **password** for each website you use?
c important **file** by mistake?
d **podcasts**?
e **a search** for your own name online?
f **a virus** on your computer?
g **installed** on your phone this week?
h **links** to interesting websites with friends?

## READING

**1** **Emre wants an app to help him with learning English. Read about Emre and notice the key underlined information a–c.**

**1** Emre often [a] finds language apps easy and wants some difficult practice. He [b] would like to improve his listening skills and he [c] intends to use the app on his short bus journey to and from school.

**2** **Read the descriptions of the first three apps (A–C). Find two apps that do these things:**

1. mention difficult practice *B, C*
2. practise listening skills
3. are suitable for use on short journeys

**Which app is best for Emre?**

**3** **Read about four more teenagers who want apps to help them with learning English. Underline three key pieces of information about each person.**

**2** Anna enjoys all subjects but she needs more help with English vocabulary and grammar. She is bored of doing traditional exercises and is looking for an app with activities that are quick to complete.

**3** Luis would like to get better at understanding movies and TV shows in English. He expects apps to look good and is prepared to spend money on the right one.

**4** Evie's interested in developing and revising her vocabulary. She likes fun activities and she really enjoys competing against friends.

**5** Filipe is an advanced level student and he would like an app to help him revise grammar. He doesn't want to pay for an app.

**4** **Read the descriptions of the apps (A–H). Decide which app would be the most suitable for each teenager in Exercise 3. There are three apps you don't need.**

# APPS FOR LEARNING ENGLISH

75

**A** **WordPowr** is all about learning words – nouns, verbs, everything. There are eight games, which are very enjoyable, but the best part is that you can also play online against other users. At less than the price of a coffee, the app is great value for money. Games last just a few minutes, so it's perfect for a bus ride. Turn down the annoying music, though!

**B** Although **EnglishScene** is expensive, the app is often given awesome reviews by its users. As soon as you use it, you can understand why. Everything about this app is professional, from the high-quality and interesting video stories, with challenging activities to support students in understanding them, to the simple, but attractive design.

**C** **Newscast** is a professional-looking app that helps you understand the news in English. You listen to and read stories, do some typical exercises about new words, even a little grammar, and then answer the questions. Each activity takes between five and ten minutes and is surprisingly hard.

**D** Practise the 3000 most frequent words in English with **PassWords3000**. This app is for low-level students working by themselves and includes a very common range of activity types. It's free, so sometimes you have to watch video advertisements to continue using it. New questions are added every month.

**E** **LanguageLab** costs nothing, but will be of limited interest to anyone except high-level language learners. The grammar reference for each topic is full of important details but the practice that follows is fairly typical. The app also allows you to compare your progress with friends on social networks.

**F** The design of **VidEnglish** isn't always clear and it seems to be mainly links to very high-level video clips from documentaries. The clips aren't downloaded with the app, so it's best to use when you have free wi-fi. There is a basic dictionary and the app is completely free, with no advertisements.

**G** The first thing you notice with **GrammarWise** is its professional-looking design. Everything about this app is easy to use. There are fun, animated grammar presentations and a huge choice of practice activities, with over 50 different grammar topics per level. You can try one topic for free but it costs to get access to the whole app.

**H** **Themez** is a fresh and unusual app. It uses games to teach grammar and vocabulary through topics like science and history. The app is perfect for when you only have a few minutes to practise, but at the moment you can only play by yourself.

### TALKING POINTS

What apps do you use to help you with studying?
Do you mind paying for apps?

# GRAMMAR Present simple passive

**1** **Read the examples. Then complete the rules with the words in the box.**

1. The app **is** often **given** awesome reviews **by** its users.
2. New questions **are added** every month.
3. The clips **aren't downloaded** with the app.
4. What **is** the app **called**?

| be | by | past participle |
|---|---|---|

**a** We use the passive when the person or thing that causes the action is unknown or unimportant.
**b** We form the present simple passive with the correct form of ______ and the ______ of the verb.
**c** When we include who or what did the action, we use ______.

» GRAMMAR REFERENCE AND PRACTICE PAGE 152

**2** **Complete the text about Instagram. Use the present simple passive form of the verbs.**

**Instagram** is an online photo and video sharing app and [1] ______ (own) by Facebook.

The app is extremely popular and [2] ______ (use) by over 500 million people daily.

Over 95 million photos and videos [3] ______ (share) every day and a word or phrase [4] ______ (add) to the photo, called a 'tag'. Thousands of products [5] ______ (advertise) by companies on the app too. Users click a heart icon next to the photos they like the most. Around 50,000 'likes' [6] ______ (give) to photos and videos every *second* on Instagram!

**3** » **Complete the questions with the present simple passive form of the verb. Then answer the questions with your own ideas. Turn to page 124 to check.**

1. Which type of program ______ (download) from the internet the most often?
2. Which password ______ (use) by people most often online?
3. Which celebrities ______ (search) for online the most often?
4. How much ______ (spend) on buying apps every year?
5. Which countries ______ most smartphones ______ (make) in?

**4** **Correct the mistake in each sentence.**

1. My best friend called Luis.
2. This computer it's used by everyone in my family.
3. More computers need in our school.
4. My favourite game calls FIFA and costs about £50.
5. This phone is recommend for older people.
6. The virus was deleted some important files.

# VOCABULARY Phrasal verbs: technology

**1** **Complete the phrasal verbs.**

EP

| look | plug | shut | switch |
|---|---|---|---|
| switch | take | turn | turn |

1. ______ down
2. ______ in
3. turn on / ______ on
4. ______ up
5. turn off / ______ off
6. ______ out
7. ______ down
8. ______ up

**2** **Complete the sentences with the correct form of the phrasal verbs in Exercise 1.**

0. Please *turn off / switch off* your mobile phones. The film is starting soon.
1. This TV isn't working. Can you check it is ______?
2. This app makes it easy to ______ the train times.
3. ______ that music! It's too loud!
4. Is there a problem? Try ______ the computer. Wait ten seconds, then ______ the computer again.
5. Don't forget to ______ your SIM card before you sell your phone.
6. Can you ______ the sound on the TV? I can't hear what they're saying.

**3** » **Work with a partner. Turn to page 124.**

## WRITING An informal email (3)

**1** **Read this email that Paul receives from his friend Abbie. Why is Abbie looking for new apps and podcasts?**

From: Abbie
Subject: Good apps?
Reply Forward

Hi Paul,

*Great* — I'm going on a road trip with my family next week. We're visiting relatives in Scotland for a few days. It's going to be a long journey!

*Recommend …* — I need some new games for my phone. What's your favourite at the moment?

*Explain* — Why do you like it?

*Tell Abbie …* — Also, have you heard any good podcasts recently?

Thanks!
Abbie

**2** **Read Paul's reply. Does he answer all of Abbie's questions?**

Hey Abbie,

Your road trip sounds fun! Yes, it's long, but if you have a few good games and podcasts, I think you'll be fine.

My favourite game on my phone at the moment is *Rollercoaster Tycoon*. You should try it. You have to design your own theme park, build rollercoasters and encourage as many visitors as possible. I love this game because I can play for hours and never get bored. I would say it's perfect for long journeys.

For podcasts, I'd recommend *Reply All*. It's a show about anything on the internet, and in my opinion, the stories are really original. Everyone in your family will enjoy it.

Have a great time!

Paul

**3** **Which game and which podcast does Paul mention? What phrases does he use to recommend them to Abbie?**

**4** **Read the *Prepare to write* box. Find three phrases that Paul uses to give his opinion.**

### PREPARE TO WRITE

**An informal email (3)**

**In an informal email:**

- use phrases to give your opinion:
  *I (really) think …*
  *I don't think …*
  *For me, …*
  *In my opinion, …*
  *I would say …*
- use phrases to make suggestions and recommendations:
  *You should … I recommend …*
- remember to answer any questions
- remember to use an informal phrase to begin and end the email.

**5** **Complete the sentences with your opinions about game apps and podcasts. Compare your opinions with a partner. Do you agree with your partner's opinions?**

**1** In my opinion, …
**2** I really think …
**3** I would say …

**6** **What informal phrases does Paul use to begin and end his email?**

**7** **Read Abbie's email again and plan your reply. Use all Paul's notes in Exercise 1.**

**8** **Write your email to Abbie.**

- Use the phrases and tips in the *Prepare to write box*.
- Write about 100 words.
- Remember to check your spelling and grammar.

# 16 AMAZING SCIENCE

## EXPERIMENTS YOU CAN TRY AT HOME

### MOVING A CAN WITHOUT TOUCHING IT

**YOU WILL NEED:**

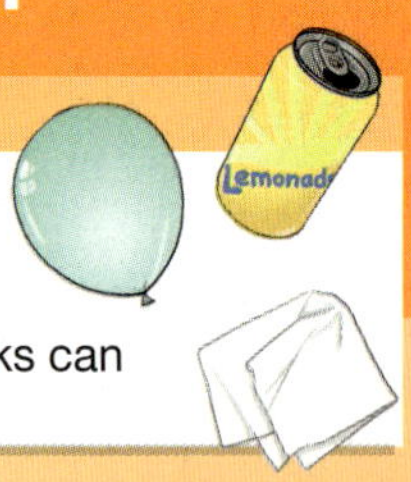


- ✔ a balloon
- ✔ a tissue
- ✔ an empty drinks can

| blow | rub | tie |
|---|---|---|

- ★ **a** ________ air into the balloon and **b** ________ the end.
- ★ **c** ________ the filled balloon on your hair or on a tissue.
- ★ Put the can on the floor and hold the balloon near it.
- ★ **Pull the balloon away from the can slowly, and the can will move towards the balloon!**

**HOW IT WORKS**

The can moves towards the balloon because when you rub the balloon, it gets a negative [1] *electricity / electrical* charge. When you put the balloon near the can, the [2] *electricity / metal* in the can gets a small positive charge. The result is that the static [3] *electricity / air* in the balloon attracts the can.

### KEEPING LIQUIDS APART

**YOU WILL NEED:**

- ✔ two glasses
- ✔ salt
- ✔ food colouring
- ✔ a small piece of thin, hard plastic or cardboard

| cover | fill | stir |
|---|---|---|

- ★ **d** ________ the glasses with water.
- ★ Put two large spoons of salt into the first glass and **e** ________ it.
- ★ Add a few drops of food colouring into the other glass.
- ★ **f** ________ the glass of coloured water with the cardboard/plastic. Turn it upside down and put it on top of the glass of salt water. Pull the cardboard/plastic out from between the glasses.
- ★ **The coloured water and the salty water won't mix!**

**HOW IT WORKS**

The coloured water and the salty water stay apart because salt water is heavier than [4] *normal / warm* water. The [5] *heavier / lighter* salt water stays at the bottom of the glass and the [6] *heavier / lighter* coloured water floats at the top.

### GETTING AN EGG INTO A BOTTLE

**YOU WILL NEED:**

- ✔ an egg
- ✔ a towel
- ✔ a glass bottle with a 25–30 mm lid
- ✔ some hot water

| boil | pour | shake | wrap |
|---|---|---|---|

- ★ **g** ________ the egg for 4 minutes, until the white of the egg is hard but the yolk is soft. Let it cool. Then peel it.
- ★ **h** ________ the hot water into the bottle. Put on the lid, **i** ________ it in a towel and **j** ________ it well.
- ★ Take off the lid and pour out the water.
- ★ Put the egg in the opening of the warm bottle.
- ★ **After a few minutes the egg is pulled into the bottle.**

**HOW IT WORKS**

The egg is pulled into the bottle because the hot water in the bottle makes the bottle [7] *smaller / warm*, and the air in the bottle gets warm too. Hot air expands: it gets bigger and takes up more space than [8] *cold / hot* air. Cold air contracts, in other words it gets smaller and takes up less space than warm air. So as the air in the bottle goes back to room temperature, it gets [9] *smaller / warmer*, and so it pulls the egg into the bottle.

### ? ABOUT YOU

Are you more into science or arts? Why?
What scientific experiments have you done at school?

## VOCABULARY Doing experiments

EP **1** Look at the instructions for three experiments and complete a–j in the sentences with the words in each box.

76 **2** Choose the correct words to complete the *How it works* explanation for each experiment. Then listen and check.

**3** In pairs, discuss the questions. Use one or more verbs from Exercise 1 in your answers.

**0** How do you make a candle go out? *You blow it.*
**1** How do you make coffee?
**2** What do you do when you add sugar to coffee?
**3** How can you keep flies off your food?
**4** How can you say no without speaking?
**5** How can you keep your hands warm in cold weather?
**6** What do people with long hair often need to do?
**7** What can you do if your glass is empty?
**8** What do you do with a present before giving it to someone?

# READING

**1** **Discuss the questions.**

1 What is the Nobel Prize?
2 Do you know the names of anyone who has won a Nobel Prize?

**2** **Look at the title of the article and the photos. What do you think people have done to win the Ig Nobel Prize? Read the text quickly and check.**

# The *Ig* Nobel Prize

77

**Science tries to answer the biggest questions of our time: 'If we explore nearby galaxies, will we find other forms of life?' or 'What will happen to the planet if we don't stop climate change?' The greatest scientific achievements are awarded a Nobel Prize: Alexander Fleming (penicillin), Marie Curie (radioactivity) and Albert Einstein ($E=mc^2$) are all Nobel Prize-winners. Science is serious, but scientists are only human and sometimes they want answers to questions like: 'Why do shower curtains blow towards you when you have a shower?' And so the Ig Nobel Prize was born, with the aim of making people smile first, and then think about science.**

## *Here's a selection of scientific ideas that have won an Ig Nobel Prize*

**If a cow has a name, it produces more milk!** Farmers have always known this, but now there's proof. Cows *without* names produce about 13,000 litres a year, but cows *with* names produce 13,500 litres. This is probably because the cows with names feel more loved by farmers.

**When you drop a slice of toast, it falls to the ground with the buttered side down 80% of the time,** according to experiments. This is because it usually falls from table height and only has time to turn over once before it reaches the floor.

**Mosquitoes love the smell of feet.** They'll bite your feet if you take off your shoes! But Limberger cheese smells like feet and is even more attractive to mosquitoes, so they bite you less when there's Limberger nearby. This is a good example of how a silly discovery can be important. 'Cheesy' mosquito traps now help in the fight against malaria, a disease that is carried by mosquitoes. Malaria kills 500,000 people per year.

Only one person has won both an Ig Nobel and a Nobel Prize: Andre Geim made the headlines in 1997 for his 'flying frog' experiment, in which he made a frog float in the air! Then in 2010 he discovered graphene, a form of carbon that is one *atom* thick. Graphene is the thinnest and strongest substance known to man. There are no prizes for guessing which experiment won an Ig Nobel!

**3** **Answer the questions.**

1 What's the difference between a Nobel Prize and an Ig Nobel Prize?
2 Why do cows without names produce less milk?
3 Why does toast fall with the buttered side down?
4 Why are some mosquitoes dangerous?
5 Which of Andre Geim's experiments do you think won a Nobel Prize? Why?

**4** **Match the highlighted words in the article to the meanings.**

1 stay in the air without support
2 the reason for doing something
3 something for catching animals
4 information to show that something is true
5 allow something to fall
6 something difficult that you succeed in doing

### TALKING POINTS

What 'problem' would you like the Ig Nobel Prize to solve?
What do you think are the biggest questions of our time? Why?

# GRAMMAR Zero and first conditional

**1 Read the examples and complete the rules.**

1 **If** a cow **has** a name, it **produces** more milk.
2 Mosquitoes **bite** you less **when** there**'s** cheese nearby.

**Zero conditional**
**a** We use the zero conditional for things that are *true* / *probable* or always happen.
**b** We use the present simple in *the first* / *both* clauses.
**c** The *If* or *When* clause can come first or second. The meaning is *different* / *the same*.

**2 Complete the zero conditional sentences.**

1 Water ............ (boil) when you ............ (heat) it to 100°C.
2 If you ............ (not add) sugar to this coffee, it ............ (taste) very bitter.
3 If you ............ (press) 'play', the music ............ (start).
4 When a player ............ (score) a goal, the fans ............ (go) crazy.
5 My journey to school ............ (be) quicker if I ............ (take) the bus.

**3 Read the examples. Then choose the correct words to complete the rules.**

1 What **will happen** to the planet **if** we **don't stop** climate change?
2 Mosquitoes **will bite** your feet **if** you **take off** your shoes.

**First conditional**
**a** We use the first conditional to talk about possible or probable *future* / *past* events.
**b** We use *if* + *present simple* / *past simple*, and *will* + infinitive.

**4 Choose the correct words to make first conditional sentences.**

1 If I light the candles, everyone *sing* / *will sing* 'Happy Birthday'.
2 What *will* / *do* you do if you get lost?
3 You *make up* / *will make up* if you shake hands.
4 Where will you go if it *will rain* / *rains* later?
5 The gift will look lovely if we *wrap* / *will wrap* it in some pretty paper.

**5 Read the rule and choose the sentence that means the same.**

Life will end **unless we stop** climate change. =
**a** Life will end **if we don't stop** climate change.
**b** Life will end **if we stop** climate change.

**First conditional: *if* and *unless***
We can use *unless* instead of *if*. *Unless* means *if not*.

» GRAMMAR REFERENCE AND PRACTICE PAGE 153

**6 Complete the sentences with *if* or *unless*.**

1 ............ you fill the bottle, the experiment will work.
The experiment won't work ............ you fill the bottle.
2 The computer won't turn on ............ you enter the password.
............ you enter the password, the computer will turn on.
3 I won't cover the picnic ............ the rain gets worse.
I'll cover the picnic ............ the rain gets worse.
4 I hate soap operas. I'll watch TV with you ............ you turn to another channel.
............ you turn to another channel, I won't watch TV with you.

**7 Correct the mistake in each sentence.**

1 You want to start a fire, blow the flame gently at first.
2 Dad won't cook a pizza for you unless you'll text him later.
3 When it's OK with you, I'll come to your place after school.
4 Unless we'll meet before 8 pm, we won't have time to buy tickets.
5 Wrap yourself in a blanket you have a fever.

# VOCABULARY Phrasal verbs: science

**1 Match the sentence halves.**

EP
1 We're trying to **add**
2 To do this experiment, **cut**
3 First, you need to **carry**
4 I can't **work**
5 If you have 1 trillion and you **take**
6 Be careful. Don't **blow**

**a** **away** 1 million, you get …
**b** **up** a sheet of paper into 1 cm strips.
**c** **up** the whole school!
**d** **out** the answer to this problem.
**e** **out** some experiments in a lab.
**f** **up** the number of atoms in this molecule.

**2 Complete the sentences with the verbs above.**

1 I can't ............ how to design this experiment.
2 If you ............ the units and divide by two, you get the answer.
3 We'll ............ the pizza into six slices.
4 We ............ lots of experiments last year.
5 This potassium won't ............ unless you get water on it.
6 If you have seventy-five and ............ ten, it leaves sixty-five.

**3** » **Work with a partner. Turn to page 125.**

# LISTENING

78 **1** **You are going to hear a conversation about a teenage inventor. Look at the pictures and discuss what you think he has invented. Listen and check.**

78 **2** **For each question, choose the correct answer. Then listen again and check that the other two options are wrong.**

**1** How did Lauren Phillips first discover Taylor Wilson?
  **A** She made a show about him.
  **B** She watched a video about him.
  **C** She met him online.

**2** Taylor's neighbours left their houses because
  **A** everyone wanted to see his experiment.
  **B** they were frightened by the noise.
  **C** Taylor blew up his house.

**3** Taylor went to a special school
  **A** where Mark Zuckerberg and Lady Gaga studied.
  **B** which had a fantastic nuclear physics department.
  **C** which allowed its students to visit a nearby university.

**4** What does 'a star in a jar' refer to?
  **A** a famous person who went to a special school
  **B** a nuclear fusion reaction inside a reactor
  **C** a machine that detects bombs

**5** Taylor met President Obama because he
  **A** invented some important security equipment.
  **B** was the 42nd person to make a nuclear fusion reaction.
  **C** is a brilliant public speaker and video presenter.

**6** Lauren Phillips thinks that Taylor should
  **A** carry on sharing his excitement about science.
  **B** make more security equipment for the government.
  **C** consider becoming an actor.

**3** **In pairs, think of five questions you would like to ask Taylor Wilson. Find the answers online if possible, then discuss your findings in groups.**

# SPEAKING Describing a photo (2)

**1** **Look at the photo. Where do you think the people are? What do you think is happening?**

79 **2** **Listen to someone describing the photo. Compare your ideas.**

79 **3** **Read the *Prepare to speak* box. Then listen again. Which phrase do you not hear?**

## PREPARE TO SPEAK

### Describing a photo (2)

**When you aren't sure**
It looks like …
It looks like a kind of / some sort of
It could/might be …
They seem very …
I'm not really sure, but …

**When you don't know the word**
I don't know what it's called.

**4** **Look at another photo. Where do you think the people are? What do you think is happening? Take turns to describe it. Use phrases from the *Prepare to speak* box.**

# LIFE SKILLS ICT LITERACY

## STAYING SAFE ONLINE

### LIFE SKILLS

**Staying safe online**

We use the internet for many things, such as studying, communicating with friends and having fun online. The internet is a normal part of modern life, but we must use it carefully in order to stay safe and prevent problems.

**1** **Ask and answer the questions with a partner.**

1 How many hours do you spend on the internet on a typical day?
   **A** less than 1 **B** 1 to 2 **C** 3 to 4 **D** more than 4
2 What electronic device do you use most often for going online?
   **A** smartphone **B** a tablet **C** a laptop **D** other
3 How much do you think you know about internet safety?
   **A** nothing **B** a little **C** quite a lot **D** a lot

**2** **Read the text quickly. Match photos A–D to four of the rules. How well do you follow these rules?**

80

A

## INTERNET SAFETY

**The internet is useful and it can also be a lot of fun, as long as people use it responsibly.**

**Here are some basic rules that you should always follow to stay safe on the internet:**

**1** When you're online, you should protect information like your real name, address, phone number and date of birth. This information is too personal to share with everyone.

**2** Don't accept any friend or chat requests from strangers on social media apps or websites. All your online contacts should be people that you already know and trust.

**3** Be cautious about websites and apps that tell people your location. You don't want strangers to know where you are going or when you aren't home!

**4** If you really want to meet a new online friend, you should always tell your parents first. They should know where you're going, and they may want to accompany you the first time.

**5** Think very carefully before you share any personal photos or videos online. Just pause for a moment and ask yourself, 'Do I really want everyone in the world to see this?'

**6** Don't share any photos or videos of your friends and other people unless you have their permission. Be polite and respect other people's privacy online.

**7** Keep your passwords secret, so strangers can't access your email or other accounts. And don't choose an obvious password, like 123456. Choose something that people can't guess.

**8** If you use social media, you shouldn't write nasty comments about people or the things they post online. Respect their feelings and don't be mean. You wouldn't want someone to say those things about you!

**9** If you have any problems with other people online, ask an adult for help. It's better to talk with someone as soon as possible. Don't keep the problem a secret!

B

C

D

**3** **Match the highlighted words in the text to the meanings.**

1 easy to guess
2 stop or wait
3 unkind or nasty
4 keep someone or something safe
5 where someone or something is

**4** **Answer the questions. Use ideas from the text.**

1 What type of information should you keep personal?
2 What must you do if you want to meet a new online friend?
3 Why shouldn't you tell other people your password?
4 What can happen if you share silly photos of yourself online?
5 When can you safely accept friendship requests online?
6 Why shouldn't you write bad things about other people?

**5** **Read the comments. Are these people using the internet safely? Why? / Why not?**

**Angela says**
I love posting photos of my friends online. Sometimes they get angry with me, but I think it's funny.
posted 2h ago

**Daniel says**
I don't like it when strangers send me friend requests. I never answer, and I block them when I can.
posted 2h ago

**Kelly says**
I use a phone app that shows people where I am, but only my parents can see that information.
posted 2h ago

**Samuel says**
When people insult me online, I always insult them back. Sometimes it gets really nasty.
posted 2h ago

81 **6** **Listen to Melissa, Justin, Laura and David. Choose the correct answers.**

1 A boy posted comments about *Justin* / *David* on a social network.
2 Girls were making fun of *Laura* / *Melissa* because she looks different.
3 A boy was writing nasty emails about *Melissa* / *Laura* last year.
4 *David* / *Justin* always receives lots of emails from strangers.

81 **7** **Listen again and write the correct names: *Justin*, *David*, *Laura* or *Melissa*.**

1 ______ didn't tell her parents about the cyberbullying.
2 ______ changed the privacy settings on his profile.
3 ______ has closed his email account five times already.
4 ______ got a new phone. Now she blocks messages from strangers.

**8** **Complete the *Useful language* phrases with the words in the box.**

| best | important | need |
|---|---|---|
| opinion | tell | should |

## USEFUL LANGUAGE

**Giving advice**

1 You ______ tell your parents right away.
2 I think people ______ to be more careful.
3 I'd ______ my friends not to be mean.
4 In my ______ , people should be nicer.
5 The ______ thing to do is ask for permission.
6 It's ______ to keep your password secret.

## PROJECT

***A poster about internet safety***

**Make a poster about cyberbullying and the dangers of internet use. Give practical advice.**

- What type of things do cyberbullies do?
- Why shouldn't people do these things?
- What can people do if they're being cyberbullied?
- Why is it important to talk about cyberbullying?
- Where could people find more information about this problem?

**Present your poster to the class. Then display it at school.**

# REVIEW 4 UNITS 13–16

## VOCABULARY

**1** **Find the words (→ ↓ ↘) and complete the lists. You have got the first letter of each word.**

| | | | | | | | | | | | |
|---|---|---|---|---|---|---|---|---|---|---|---|
| d | o | c | u | m | e | n | t | a | r | y | s |
| m | i | d | g | w | r | a | p | n | e | p | e |
| b | d | s | p | r | a | b | l | i | s | r | m |
| o | o | r | a | i | a | s | r | m | l | o | b |
| c | w | e | s | p | y | t | h | a | i | u | a |
| o | n | s | s | y | p | n | e | a | n | d | r |
| m | l | o | w | u | r | o | s | f | k | t | r |
| e | o | c | o | v | e | r | i | o | u | e | a |
| d | a | r | r | w | e | e | h | n | r | l | s |
| y | d | a | d | v | i | r | u | s | t | e | s |
| b | l | o | w | t | o | r | n | c | h | e | e |
| e | a | c | h | a | t | s | h | o | w | r | d |
| p | t | p | a | n | i | m | a | t | i | o | n |

**Adjectives: feelings**
d........ e........
g........ p........

**Computer words**
p........ l........
v........ d........

**TV and film**
a........ c........
c........ d........

**Doing experiments**
b........ c........
s........ w........

**2** **Complete the sentences with the words in the box.**

blow up characters confused deleted exhausted plot plug in search soap opera soundtrack stressed turn off work out

1 I did a ........ for a cheap ticket online, but there weren't any.
2 This ........ is on TV five times a week.
3 I've just run 15 km. I'm ........!
4 She's upset because she ........ her homework by mistake.
5 I'm ........ . I can't ........ how to answer this question.
6 I'm feeling very ........ this evening. I need to sit down and relax.
7 Can you ........ this HDMI cable to the back of the screen?
8 Have you heard the ........ from the new *Star Wars* film?
9 ........ the machine, quickly. This experiment's going to ........!
10 The ........ of *Stranger Things* is great; it always keeps you guessing what will happen next. I love the main ........ too.

## GRAMMAR

**1** **Complete the sentences. Use the correct form of the verbs.**

1 .... you ........ this book yet? (read)
2 When I switch off the lights, it ........ always very dark in here. (be)
3 This table ........ of wood. (not make)
4 He never ........ much homework when he's in his room. (do)
5 Look! The teacher .... just ........ . (arrive)
6 Breakfast ........ every day between 7 and 10 am. (serve)
7 Don't worry. I'll remind her if she ........ . (forget)
8 I'm not hungry. I .... already ........ lunch. (have)
9 If you click 'yes', the film usually ........ quite quickly. (download)
10 Unless he arrives soon, we ........ leave without him. (have to)

**2** **Make sentences.**

1 you / upload / your film / yet?
........
2 this film / not translate / into Spanish
........
3 Jon / just / shut down / his computer
........
4 if / I / fill / the kettle, / you / make / the coffee?
........
5 the app / open / when you / enter / your password
........
6 the British actors / not mention / in the reviews
........
7 the rubber ring / not float / unless / you / fill / it with air
........
8 Sonia / already / wrap / your present
........

**3** **Complete the second sentence so that it means the same as the first sentence. Use no more than three words.**

1 They produce most Indian films in Bollywood.
Most Indian films ______ in Bollywood.
2 If you don't come to the cinema, you'll be really bored tonight.
______ be bored tonight if you come to the cinema.
3 This laptop doesn't install updates automatically.
Updates ______ automatically on this laptop.
4 I finished watching the documentary a few minutes ago.
I've ______ watching the documentary.
5 She's the new actress. She plays Juliet.
She's the new ______ Juliet.
6 Do you sell DVDs here?
Are ______ here?
7 This is a really funny comedy. You should watch it.
This is a really funny ______ should watch.
8 Unless someone can remember the password, we can't use the computer.
We ______ the computer if someone can remember the password.

**4** **Choose the correct words.**

1 My friend hasn't arrived *already* / *yet.*
2 You *have* / *'ll have* fun if you come with us.
3 This is the computer game *that* / *who* I bought a few weeks ago.
4 I've been watching a series that *called* / *'s called Stranger Things*.

**5** **Correct the mistake in each sentence.**

1 I've just spend some money on lunch.
2 You'll like the pizza restaurant where is near my house.
3 My closest friend calls Simone.
4 If you'll have a problem, I'll help you.

**6** **For each question, write the correct answer. Write one word for each gap.**

## PRIZES FOR YOUNG ENGINEERS

Any student between the ages of 12 and 19 can enter the *Young Engineers for Britain* competition. This is an annual event in which students [1] ______ challenged to be creative in developing their own idea. The aim of the competition is to design [2] ______ useful item that can eventually be produced and sold.

Ruth Amos won the prize a [3] ______ years ago for her invention, the 'StairSteady', which helps old people to go up and down stairs. It is [4] ______ from a strong metal and is very safe, as well as being simple to use. Ruth [5] ______ sold over 1,000 StairSteadys all around the country.

More recently, Matthew Hunter developed a product to charge a mobile phone [6] ______ will fit on a bicycle. He won the *Young Engineers' Duke of York Award* and received prize money of £1,000 for his invention.

# 17 TALENTED

## ABOUT YOU

▶ 11 **Watch the video and then answer the questions.**

Have you ever tried creating art, playing music or performing on stage?

Do you know anyone who is young and talented?

## VOCABULARY Arts and entertainment

**1** Look at the photos. What can you see? What are these places?

82 **2** Listen to three conversations. Do they mention any of your ideas?

**3** Which words are related to which profession? Add the words to the table. Some words match more than one profession. Can you add any other words to the lists?

audience biography director gallery novel painter painting poet poetry sculpture studio writer

| | |
|---|---|
| Actor | *audience,* |
| Artist | |
| Author | |

**4** Complete the articles with words in Exercise 3.

### YOUNG TALENT

There's an exhibition of new [0] *artists* called Young Talent at the university [1] ______ this month. It's mainly [2] ______ and drawings, but there are a few huge outdoor [3] ______ in the park next to it.

### Secrets told

The best-selling [4] ______ Jenny Lee has written dozens of books over the years. Now it's time for us to read all about the secrets of Dr Lee's life in a new 600-page [5] ______ of the writer. It tells her life story, from her childhood in Singapore right up to the present day, and discusses in detail how she thought of ideas for her series of crime [6] ______, *What We See.*

### Hollywood hopes

There's trouble in Hollywood this week for the *Project Z* movie. The main [7] ______ in the film won't work because they're unhappy with their pay and with the conditions in the [8] ______. However, time is money in show business, so the [9] ______, Frankie Jones, needs to show that he's in charge and end this argument quickly.

**5** Discuss the quiz questions.

### What's the difference between ...

1 a studio and a gallery?
2 an artist and a painter?
3 a novel and a biography?
4 an author and a poet?
5 a sculpture and a painting?

READING

# WHO ARE THE REAL ARTISTS?

83

## THE SONGWRITERS

When you hear a new song, you probably don't think about who wrote it. And although certain **performers** like Lady Gaga always write their own songs, hundreds of others **perform** songs written for them by songwriters. Sia is a famous singer who has **toured** the world several times and sold millions of her own albums. She's also a successful songwriter, who has written hits for Rihanna and other big stars. Next time you hear a song you love, why not look it up online and see who actually wrote it?

## THE GHOSTWRITERS

Kylie Jenner and her sister Kendall were teenagers when they wrote their first science fiction novel, *Rebels: City of Indra*. But the Jenner sisters grew up as reality show stars, so how did they manage to write a book? The truth is, they didn't write it on their own. They had lots of ideas for the story, but they asked an author called Maya Sloan to write it with them. Sloan is also a ghostwriter who writes celebrities' books for them. Celebrities often use ghostwriters, either because they don't have time, or because they aren't natural writers. **Publishers** usually order ghostwriters not to talk about the books they've written for celebrities, but the Jenner sisters didn't mind anyone knowing about Maya Sloan.

## THE STUNT DOUBLES

Daniel Craig has an action-hero reputation thanks to his performances as James Bond. But does the actor appear in all the dangerous scenes himself? Not always. Instead, a **stunt double** does lots of them. Ben Cooke was competing in a martial arts tournament when a producer saw him and advised him to become a stunt double. Ben Cooke looks a bit like Daniel Craig, so he became Craig's double. He's won a lot of prizes, including one for an incredible jump in *Casino Royale*.

## THE SECRET PAINTERS

Damien Hirst produces hundreds of paintings every year. How does one man produce [1] ________ many? Like da Vinci and Michelangelo before him, he employs assistants in a studio. He usually tells them [2] ________ do the easy jobs, but they often do whole paintings [3] ________. Rachel Howard was 22 when she started working [4] ________ Hirst. According to Hirst, he only ever made five 'spot' paintings himself and the best spot painting is one painted [5] ________ Rachel! Nowadays, Rachel Howard doesn't work for Hirst. She is a well-known artist [6] ________ work fills galleries all around the world.

**1** **Look at the photos. Who or what can you see?**

**2** **Read the article quickly. What do these people have in common?**

Ben Cooke    Maya Sloan    Rachel Howard    Sia

**3** **Choose the correct answers. Read the article again and check.**

1 Sia has written songs for ________ and ________.
  A herself  B Lady Gaga  C Rihanna
2 Maya Sloan is ________ and ________.
  A a ghostwriter  B a reality show star  C an author
3 ________ and ________ acted in *Casino Royale*.
  A James Bond  B Daniel Craig  C Ben Cooke
4 Painters like ________ and ________ had assistants.
  A Rachel Howard  B Michelangelo  C Damien Hirst

**4** **Now read 'The secret painters' again and think of the word which best fits each gap. Use only one word in each gap.**

**5** **Match the highlighted words in the article to the meanings.**

1 travelled around, playing in concerts or appearing at events
2 people who entertain others by acting, singing, dancing or playing music
3 act in a film or a play
4 somebody who does the difficult or dangerous scenes for an actor
5 a company, or the people, that produce books

### TALKING POINTS

Do you think it's fair that famous people get others to do things for them? Why? / Why not?
Whose book would you most like to ghostwrite? Why?

## GRAMMAR Reported commands

**1 Read the examples and choose the correct commands, a or b.**

1 The Jenner sisters **asked** a ghostwriter **to write** a novel with them.
  a 'Please write a book with us!'
  b 'Don't write our book, thanks.'
2 Publishers usually **order** ghostwriters **not to talk** about the books they've written.
  a 'You mustn't discuss these books with anyone!'
  b 'Feel free to talk about the books you've written.'
3 A film-maker **advised him to be** a stunt double.
  a 'You shouldn't be a stunt double!'
  b 'You should be a stunt double!'
4 He usually **tells them to do** the easy jobs.
  a 'Don't do the easy jobs.'
  b 'Do the easy jobs, please.'

**2 Complete the rules with *to* or *not*.**

We report:
a positive commands using a reporting verb + object pronoun + ____ infinitive.
*The teacher* ***ordered us to be*** *quiet.*
b negative commands using a reporting verb + object pronoun + ____ + *to* infinitive.
*The teacher* ***reminded us not to talk.***

» GRAMMAR REFERENCE AND PRACTICE PAGE 154

**3 Choose the correct option.**

1 Why don't you *ask* / *tell* Tina to go to cinema with you?
2 I persuaded Lou *to not read* / *not to read* her poems!
3 I was crying, so my friend *said to me* / *told me* to calm down.
4 Go to the teacher and *tell to* / *ask* her for help.
5 The gallery attendant *told* / *said* us to be quiet.
6 Don't tell us what *do* / *to do*!
7 Dad *reminded* / *remembered* us to study for the test.
8 Who advised you *not print* / *not to print* your tickets?

**4 Complete the reported commands. Use the reporting verbs in brackets.**

0 **Mum:** '**Help** in the kitchen, please.'
  Mum *asked* them *to help* in the kitchen.' (ask)
1 **Karen:** 'You mustn't **touch** my things!'
  Karen ________ me ________ her things. (warn)
2 **Police officer:** '**Stop**!'
  A police officer ________ us ________. (order)
3 **Anna:** 'You must **be** more careful.'
  Anna ________ him ________ more careful. (tell)
4 **Sara:** 'You should**n't worry** so much.'
  Sara ________ her ________ so much. (advise)
5 **Diane:** 'Come on! It's time to **go**!'
  Diane ________ us ________. (persuade)
6 **Mrs Holt:** '**Don't hand in** the work late.'
  Mrs Holt ________ us ________ the work late. (remind)

**5 Read the example and notice how *your* changes to *their*. Then report the commands. Use the reporting verbs in brackets and change the pronouns if necessary.**

0 A teacher to her students: 'Remember to finish your homework before Friday.' (remind)
  *The teacher reminded her students to finish their homework before Friday.*
1 A father to his child: 'Don't run!' (tell)
2 A boy to his sister: 'Pass the salt, please.' (ask)
3 A girl to her brother: 'Get out of my room!' (order)
4 A woman to her daughter: 'Don't be late.' (warn)
5 A taxi driver to his passenger: 'Don't get out at the traffic lights.' (advise)
6 A boy to his friend: 'Watch the match with me! Go on, it'll be fun!' (persuade)

## VOCABULARY Adjectives: *-al* and *-ful*

**1 Read the examples and answer questions a and b.**

EP
1 She's also a **successful** songwriter.
2 They aren't **natural** writers.
3 We were watching a **historical** drama.

a Which part of speech (verbs or nouns) do we use to make adjectives with *-al* and *-ful*?
b What spelling changes do you notice in examples 2 and 3?

**2 Complete the sentences with adjectives formed from the nouns in brackets.**

1 This exhibition is very ________. (colour)
2 I love the countryside. It's so ________. (peace)
3 That's a really ________ idea. (origin)
4 Ouch! My leg is still ________. (pain)
5 My brother's always smiling. He's very ________. (cheer)
6 The articles aren't at all ________. (politics)
7 I have three exams next week. It's very ________. (stress)
8 Is your apartment ________? (centre)

**3 » Work with a partner. Student A turn to page 125. Student B turn to page 127.**

## WRITING A biography

**1** Look at the photo. What do you know about Taylor Swift? Read the biography and check your ideas.

# TAYLOR SWIFT

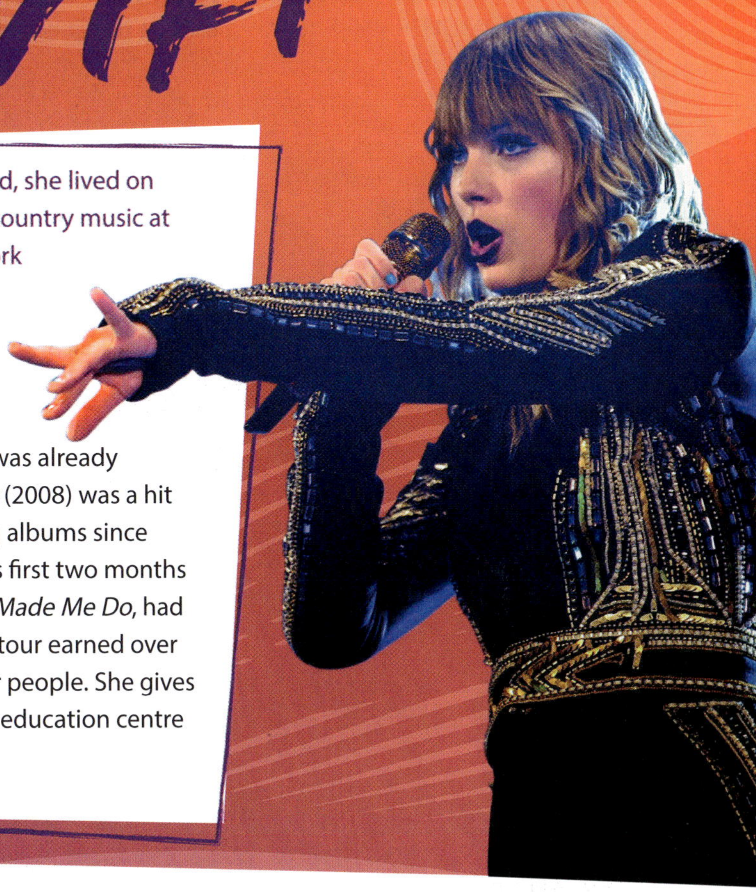

Taylor Swift was born in 1989 in Pennsylvania. As a child, she lived on her family's Christmas tree farm. She fell in love with country music at the age of nine, and often travelled 200 km to New York for singing lessons. Then, as soon as she learnt to play the guitar, people started noticing her talent. She was only 12!

In 2004, her family moved to Nashville, the centre of country music, because they wanted to help her career. By the time Swift was 16, her first album *Taylor Swift* (2006) was already popular with country music fans. Her second album *Fearless* (2008) was a hit with both country *and* pop fans. She's had many best-selling albums since then – her 2017 album *Reputation* sold 2 million copies in its first two months on sale. A video for a single from the album, *Look What You Made Me Do*, had over 40 million views in 24 hours, and the *Reputation* world tour earned over $400 million! Nowadays, Swift uses her success to help other people. She gives lots of money to charity, and she once paid $4 million for an education centre in Nashville.

**2** Read the *Prepare to write* box, then read the biography again. What interesting facts do you learn about Taylor Swift?

### PREPARE TO WRITE

**A biography**

**When you write a biography, include:**

- interesting or unusual facts about the person
- important dates from the person's life
- information about what the person did at different ages:
  *As a child, …*
  *At the age of …*
  *As soon as he/she …*
  *By the time he/she was …*
  *Nowadays, …*

**3** How many important dates are mentioned in the biography? What happened in each year?

**4** Write one word in each space. Use language from the biography in Exercise 1.

1 He left home ______ the age of 14.
2 She got married ______ soon ______ she was 21.
3 He started playing football ______ a young child.
4 ______, she's a well-known guitarist.
5 ______ the ______ he started at college, he was already in two bands.

**5** You are going to write a biography. Choose a famous person or someone you know. Plan your biography and make some notes. Here are some ideas to help you.

- When was he/she born?
- What are the important dates in his/her life?
- What are his/her main achievements?
- What interesting facts do you know about him/her?

**6** Write your biography.

- Use the tips in the *Prepare to write* box.
- Write about 150 words.
- Remember to check your spelling and grammar.

# 18 THE WORLD OF WORK

## ABOUT YOU

12 **Watch the video and then answer the questions.**

What jobs do people you know do?

What job might you want to do? Why?

## VOCABULARY Jobs

84 **1 Label the photos with the jobs in the box. Then listen and check.**

EP

| architect | babysitter | builder | coach | firefighter |
|---|---|---|---|---|
| hairdresser | journalist | lawyer | pharmacist | |
| politician | presenter | vet | | |

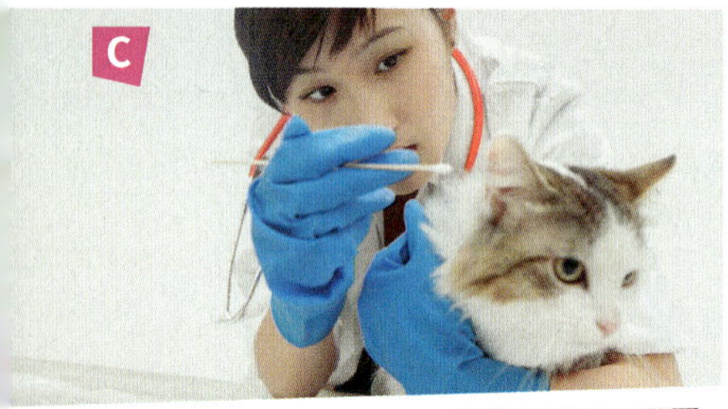

85 **2 Listen to six people describing their jobs. What are their jobs?**

**3 Answer the questions, using the jobs you didn't use in Exercise 2.**

Who …

1 explains the law to people and gives them advice?
2 designs buildings?
3 works in government?
4 introduces a TV or radio show?
5 gives people medicine?
6 writes news stories or articles for publications, radio or TV?

**4 Discuss the questions.**

Which jobs …

1 do you usually need to get a degree for?
2 are paid the highest?
3 do people mainly do in an office?
4 often mean working weekends?
5 would be the most interesting/boring?

## READING

**1** Read the introduction and look at the photos. What jobs do you think the three young people did? Read the article quickly and check.

86

**If you could do any job for a day, what would it be? A famous actor? An amazing sports star? A well-known musician? *Takeover Challenge* offers thousands of young people this opportunity. Read more to find out how it works and hear about the experiences of Sophie, Simon and Alexandra.**

# I'M IN CHARGE

***Takeover Challenge* is an annual event in English schools and about 50,000 young people 'take over' from adults and have a go at their jobs. They're in charge for just one day! Of course, it's difficult to make someone into a film or music celebrity. However, *Takeover Challenge* has offered young people the chance to be TV presenters, sports coaches, journalists, teachers and even politicians.**

**The event has two aims. Firstly, it gives young people experience in a wide range of jobs. Secondly, adults can learn from young people's opinions and fresh ideas.**

**Sophie Cameron,** 15, became the headteacher of her school. 'I'd go mad if I were a headteacher permanently,' she said. 'There were so many meetings and some of them went on for ages!' Sophie thinks she learned a lot. 'My favourite part of the day was meeting the school chef and approving the school menus for the week. It was a great opportunity to tell her what we really like eating!'

**Simon Evans** spent the day at Coventry Football Club. He became coach of the football team. 'Training with professional players was exhausting. They're really fit,' said Simon. 'I would do this job every day if I could. It was an unforgettable experience.'

**Alexandra Shaw** spent the day with a politician. She even went to a meeting with the prime minister! Alexandra thought that if everyone did a politician's job for a day, they'd be amazed. 'It isn't a nine-to-five job,' she said. 'It's 24/7. There isn't even any time for lunch!'

**2** Read the article again. Answer the questions.

1 How often does *Takeover Challenge* happen?
2 Who does the day help? How?
3 What did Sophie dislike about her day?
4 What part of being a coach was difficult for Simon?
5 What surprised Alexandra about a politician's work?
6 What jobs does the article mention?

**3** Match the highlighted words in the article to the meanings.

1 a lot of different types
2 opportunity
3 a long time
4 new and different
5 exciting and impossible to forget
6 the leader of a government

### TALKING POINTS

Is *Takeover Challenge* a good idea? Why? / Why not?
What job would you like to 'take over' for a day?

## GRAMMAR Second conditional

**1 Read the examples. Then complete the rules with the correct words.**

1 **If** everyone **did** a politician's job for a day, they**'d** be amazed.
2 **If** you **could** do any job for a day, what **would** it be?
3 I **would** do this job every day **if** I **could**.
4 I**'d** go mad **if** I **were** a head teacher permanently.

We use the second conditional to talk about an unlikely or impossible situation in the present or future, and its results.

**a** We form the second conditional with: *If* + __________, and __________ + infinitive
**b** The short form of *would* is __________.
**c** We can use *I* __________ instead of *I was* in the *if* clause of the second conditional.
**d** The *if* clause can come first or second in the sentence.

» GRAMMAR REFERENCE AND PRACTICE PAGE 155

**2 Match the sentence halves and choose the correct verbs.**

1 You probably *didn't* / *wouldn't* earn much money
2 I *get* / *'d get* paid a lot of money
3 *Did* / *Would* you be worried
4 If I *were* / *would be* the headteacher of my school,
5 If I *wanted* / *would want* to be a vet,
6 If Dad *worked* / *would work* nine-to-five in an office,

**a** if your dad *was* / *would be* a firefighter?
**b** he *got* / *'d get* very bored.
**c** if you *became* / *would become* a musician.
**d** what subjects *did* / *would* I have to study?
**e** if I *became* / *'d become* a lawyer.
**f** lessons *started* / *would start* at 10 am.

**3 Complete the second conditional sentences.**

1 You __________ (sleep) better if you __________ (do) more exercise.
2 If you __________ (fail) the end-of-year exam, what __________ your parents __________ (say)?
3 If my brother __________ (not take) my things, we __________ (not have) so many arguments.
4 You __________ (finish) your homework before dinner if you __________ (not waste) so much time on the internet.
5 If I __________ (can) live anywhere in the world, I __________ (choose) somewhere hot.
6 __________ you __________ (be) upset if your best friend __________ (not give) you a birthday present?

**4 Correct the mistake in each sentence.**

1 If I were you, I'll get a job as a babysitter.
2 Would you be a football coach if you would have the chance?
3 If you met her, you will really like her.
4 It will be fun if you came with me.
5 I would leave if I would find my job stressful.
6 If I would see them again, I could identify them.

**5 Complete the sentences with your own ideas. In pairs, compare your answers.**

1 If I were a journalist, *I'd write about fashion.*
2 If I could do any job for a day, …
3 If I had €100,000 to spend on equipment for my school, …
4 I wouldn't ever be bored again if …
5 If I were in charge of my school, …
6 My parents wouldn't be pleased if …
7 If I could be the coach of any team, …
8 If I were prime minister of my country, …

**6 Tell the class about your partner's answers in Exercise 5.**

If Luca could do any job for a day, he'd be a photographer.

## VOCABULARY Suffixes: *-er*, *-or*, *-ist*, *-ian*

**1 Read the examples. Then make nouns for people from the words in the box.**

EP

1 He spent the day with a **politician**.
2 It isn't easy being a **teacher**.
3 Would you like to be a **journalist**?
4 I'd love to be a **film director** for a day!

| ~~act~~ | art | clean | music |
|---|---|---|---|
| reception | run | visit | |

*actor*

**2 Complete the words with the correct suffix and match them to the definitions.**

1 A blogg*er*
2 A competit…
3 A scient…
4 A football support…
5 A vegetar…
6 A guitar…
7 A novel…
8 A comed…
9 A goalkeep…

**a** competes in a competition.
**b** is an expert who studies or works in one of the sciences.
**c** is the player who stands in the goal.
**d** writes a blog.
**e** writes novels.
**f** plays the guitar.
**g** doesn't eat meat or fish.
**h** tells jokes.
**i** likes a particular football team and wants them to win.

**3** » **Work with a partner.** **Turn to page 125.**

## LISTENING

87 **1** Listen to two conversations about problems and complete the table.

| | Conversation 1: Allie | Conversation 2: Evan |
|---|---|---|
| What is his/her problem? | | |
| Who is he/she asking for advice? | | |

87 **2** Listen again. Are the sentences true or false?

Conversation 1

1. Ben has already got a weekend job.
2. Allie's parents said she is allowed to get a weekend job.
3. Ben thinks Allie might be able to earn some money at home.
4. Allie wants to avoid asking her parents about a weekend job.

Conversation 2

5. Evan knows what he wants to study at university.
6. Evan has already done some research online.
7. Mrs Shaw thinks Evan should choose a wide range of subjects.
8. Mrs Shaw thinks that ten subjects might be too many for Evan.

## SPEAKING Discussing options

**1** Look at the picture. Nicole is thinking about getting a weekend job. Which jobs is she thinking about?

88 **2** Listen to two friends discussing the jobs that Nicole could do. Which one do they agree would be best for Nicole?

88 **3** Read the *Prepare to speak* box. Then listen again. Which phrases do you hear?

**4** Work with a partner. Talk together for three minutes about the different jobs Nicole could do and decide which would be best. Use the phrases in the *Prepare to speak* box.

**5** In pairs, discuss the questions.

1. Would you like to have a weekend job?
2. Which job would you choose? Why?
3. Do you think students should have weekend jobs? Why? / Why not?

### PREPARE TO SPEAK

**Discussing options**

**Making suggestions**
What about …?
I think … might be a good idea
What do you think about …?
If I were you/him/her, …

**Agreeing**
Yes, you're right.
That's true.
Maybe you're right.
I see what you mean.

**Disagreeing**
No, I don't agree.
I'm not so sure.
The problem with … is …
… might be better.
But don't you think …?

**Reaching agreement**
Yes, that's a good choice.

# CULTURE

## SPECIAL TRAINING

**1** **Ask and answer the questions with a partner.**

1 What activities do you enjoy in art class?

2 What after-school activities do you enjoy?

**2** **Read the article. Complete it with the words in the box.**

acrobatics | companies | dancers | fashion | regular | training

# SCHOOLS FOR THE ARTS

**Most schools offer a variety of subjects and activities for students, but some schools offer additional training in certain areas, such as the performing and visual arts. In this way, schools can help students develop their artistic talents from an early age and have greater success in their future profession.**

89

### THE ROYAL BALLET SCHOOL

For ballet dancers, one of the best training centres in the world is The Royal Ballet School, in London, England. The school only accepts the most talented [1] ............, who must complete eight years of full-time training. There are 225 students, aged 11–19, and most of them live together in boarding houses. On school days, they start at 8.30 am and finish at 4.00 pm. They have two hours of ballet classes and four hours of [2] ............ subjects. Students also have ballet practice after school and on Saturdays. It's a lot of work, but the results are incredible.

### IDYLLWILD ARTS ACADEMY

Located in the mountains about 100 miles from Los Angeles, the Idyllwild Arts Academy is a boarding school for young artists. It offers [3] ............ in visual arts, like drawing, painting, sculpture, photography and cinema, along with programmes for the performing arts, like music, dance and theatre. There is even a special department for young [4] ............ designers. Every year, more than 300 students from about 25 countries attend Idyllwild, and it has become one of the most famous arts schools in North America. The school's quiet, rural location also makes it a very peaceful and beautiful place to learn.

### THE NATIONAL CIRCUS SCHOOL

If you'd like to join the circus, you should apply to the National Circus School in Montreal, Canada. Since it was founded in 1981, the school has offered training in [5] ............, theatre, dance, juggling and other circus arts. About 150 people study there every year and 30 of them are teen students in the high school programme. In a typical week, they have twenty hours of circus classes and twenty hours of regular classes. After finishing the programme, many students find work in circus [6] ............, such as the Cirque du Soleil. That's the dream of every circus artist!

## 3 Are the sentences true or false? Correct the false sentences.

1 Any students who like dance can attend The Royal Ballet School.
2 Royal Ballet School students must also practise at the weekend.
3 The Idyllwild Arts Academy isn't in the centre of Los Angeles.
4 Idyllwild only offers programmes for visual arts students.
5 The National Circus School has about 150 high school students.
6 Everyone who does the circus programme joins the Cirque du Soleil.

## 4 Match the highlighted words in the text to the meanings.

1 ask for permission, usually in writing
2 be present or go to a place or event
3 agrees to take someone or something
4 work or job that someone chooses
5 a school where students live and study
6 very good, surprising

## 90 5 Listen to an interview with Carolina Woods. Answer the questions.

1 What is Carolina's special talent?
2 Where did she start studying when she was 11?
3 Where did she decide to study when she was 15?

## 90 6 Listen again and complete the sentences.

1 Carolina didn't like her first ballet class, but then her parents …
2 Her first week at The Royal Ballet School was hard because …
3 The advantages of studying in Russia are …
4 The disadvantages of studying in Russia are …

## 7 Read the *Useful language* phrases. Complete them with information about your own school.

### USEFUL LANGUAGE

**Describing schools**

1 The school is located in …
2 There are about … students.
3 The school offers classes in …
4 Students can also … after school.
5 On a typical day, students …
6 The advantages/disadvantages are …

## PROJECT Research a training school

**Find information about an unusual training school in your country or anywhere in the world. Make a presentation about the school and its programmes.**

1 Where is the school located?
2 How many students attend the school?
3 What can young people study there?
4 What do students do on a typical day?
5 What are the advantages and disadvantages?

**Make your presentation to the class.**

13 NOW WATCH THE CULTURE VIDEO

# 19 THE WRITTEN WORD

## ABOUT YOU

Do you like reading? What do you read?
Do you prefer printed magazines or digital ones? Why?

## VOCABULARY Things that you read

**1** Match the words with the photos. Then listen and check. (91) (EP)

advert article brochure e-book graphic novel note notice paper poster sticker

**2** Listen to four short conversations. What things that you read are they talking about? (92)

**3** Complete the sentences.

1 I don't want to carry the novel I'm reading around the whole time, so I read ________.
2 I read an interesting ________ in this magazine all about how to relax before exams.
3 My dad buys a ________ six days a week, even though the news is at least a day old.
4 There's a big ________ in the corridor all about World Book Day.
5 Your parcel was posted in the States. Look, there's a customs ________ stuck on it.
6 I like looking at the ________ in magazines, but they don't persuade me to buy anything.

**4** Where can you see the following? Include things that you can read from Exercises 1 and 2 as well as other words you know.

1 an advert
2 an article
3 instructions
4 poetry
5 a review

**5** Discuss the questions.

1 How often do you read each of the things from Exercise 1?
2 Is most of what you read printed or digital?
3 What are the advantages and disadvantages of reading printed material as opposed to digital?

# READING

**1** Look at the texts 0–5 below. What kind is each one? In pairs, discuss where you think you might see them.

**0** *email – on your tablet or laptop*

**2** Look at the example (0) again and answer these questions.

1 Underline the part of the email where Paula offers to help Jon.
2 Who is going to write Jon's CV?
3 What did Paula discuss with the bike shop manager?

93

**3** Look at texts 1–5 again. What does each one say? Choose the correct answer, A, B or C.

**0**

To: Jon
Subject: bike shop job advert
Reply Forward

I called the bike shop about the job advert. The manager said he wanted people to send a CV. We should discuss what qualifications and experience you can include when you write yours.
Paula

**1**

**STAFF ONLY**
Students are not permitted in the staff room. Please knock on the door if you need to speak to a teacher.

**2**

Don't worry, Deb, everyone makes mistakes. Mum and Dad told me they wouldn't get angry, but you have to come home to talk about everything. Love you, sister!

**3**

Soph,
Mum said she could take us to the cinema later. Why don't we get together after school and walk to mine? Mum said she was working till 6.30. She can drive us to the cinema after that.
Georgia

**4**

Children under the age of 16 must be accompanied by an adult.

**5**

**Win a trip to Barcelona!**

**We've hidden the football in this photo. Put a 'X' where you think the ball was and win a holiday!**

Includes tickets to see an FC Barcelona match. To enter, complete your details and send us the picture.

Name ........................
Address ........................
........................
Email ........................

**0** Paula is offering to
- **A** help Jon with his CV.
- **B** write Jon's CV.
- **C** introduce Jon to the manager.

**1**
- **A** Students can only go into the staff room with a teacher.
- **B** Students can speak to teachers outside the staff room.
- **C** Students can't speak to members of staff.

**2**
- **A** Deb has done something wrong.
- **B** Deb's parents miss her.
- **C** Deb's sister is in trouble.

**3**
- **A** Georgia and Soph are going to walk to the cinema.
- **B** Georgia is going to meet Soph and her mum at the cinema.
- **C** Georgia and Soph are going to watch a film after school.

**4** At this pool
- **A** you must be at least 16 to swim alone.
- **B** you have to be 16 or younger.
- **C** children can't swim at the same time as adults.

**5** You can win a competition
- **A** to go on tour with FC Barcelona.
- **B** by finding the location of a ball.
- **C** by emailing a picture.

## TALKING POINTS

What qualifications and experience could you put on your CV?
Have you ever entered a competition? What for? Did you win?

## GRAMMAR Reported speech

**1 Match the speech bubbles to the examples.**

**a** I **can** take you later.

**b** We **won't get** angry.

**c** I **want** people to send a CV.

**d** I'**m working** till 6.30.

1 The manager said he **wanted** people to send a CV.
2 They told me they **wouldn't get** angry.
3 Mum said she **was working** till 6.30.
4 Mum said she **could** take us to the cinema later.

**2 Match the examples 1–4 in Exercise 1 to the tense changes a–d in the box.**

We use reported speech to repeat what someone said earlier. We change the tense in reported speech.

| **Direct speech** → | **Reported speech** |
| --- | --- |
| **a** present simple | past simple |
| **b** present continuous | past continuous |
| **c** *can* | *could* |
| **d** *will* | *would* |

We also often change pronouns:
*'I make films.'* → *He said* ***he*** *made films.*
Remember: *say* + ~~object~~; *tell* + object.
*He said* ~~*me*~~ *he made films.* → *He told* ***me*** *he made films.*

» GRAMMAR REFERENCE AND PRACTICE PAGE 156

**3 Choose the correct options.**

1 Katy *says* / *said* she liked reading graphic novels.
2 Dexter *told* / *told us* he would leave us a note.
3 Adam told me he *is reading* / *was reading* an e-book.
4 Tatum *said me* / *said* she couldn't read my handwriting.
5 Sally *told* / *said* me there were some adverts online.
6 Cosmo said the noticeboard *will* / *would* be full soon.
7 Jude *said* / *told* he was coming to the party.
8 Caz said *I* / *she* was getting some stickers.

**4 Complete the second sentence so that it has the same meaning as the first. Use one, two or three words.**

0 **Clare:** 'I love writing about fashion.'
Clare said that *she loved writing* about fashion.
1 **Ewan:** 'I don't want to write about sport!'
Ewan told me he ______ to write about sport.
2 **Anita:** 'My article will be really funny.'
Anita said her article ______ really funny.
3 **Paul:** 'I'm writing about the cafeteria.'
Paul told us that he ______ about the cafeteria.
4 **James:** 'The story can't be true.'
James said the story ______ true.
5 **Sophie:** 'The photos look amazing.'
Sophie told me the photos ______ amazing.
6 **Dan:** 'You'll enjoy the movie.'
Dan told me that I ______ the movie.
7 **Sarah:** 'There won't be any more shows in that series.'
Sarah said there ______ any more shows in that series.
8 **Chris:** 'I'm not listening to a word you say!'
Chris said that he ______ to a word she said.

**5 Report what the people said.**

I don't read print magazines very often. I prefer reading online. It's free and I can choose from thousands of websites. I'll start my own website one day.

*Louisa said she didn't read print magazines very often. …*

Sandra can help us put up some posters. She does it every day, and she knows all the best places. She'll be a graphic designer one day!

*Pavel said that Sandra could …*

## VOCABULARY *say, speak, talk* and *tell*

**1 Read the examples. Then match the verbs to the uses.**

EP Can you **speak** Turkish?
I **said**, 'Hello.'
I've **told** you the answer.
I'm **talking** about blogs.

| | |
| --- | --- |
| 1 speak | a someone something |
| 2 say | b about something or to someone |
| 3 tell | c something |
| 4 talk | d a language |

**2 Choose the correct verbs.**

1 What did you *tell* / *say*?
2 I can *say* / *speak* English.
3 I *spoke* / *told* him my phone number.
4 She was *talking* / *telling* about you.
5 Nobody *told* / *said* anything.
6 Did you *talk* / *tell* to Mr Marsh?
7 Can anyone here *speak* / *say* German?
8 Please *tell* / *say* us the truth.

**3** » **Work with a partner. Student A turn to page 125. Student B turn to page 127.**

## WRITING An online book review

**1** Do you read reviews of books or films online? Do you ever write reviews?

**2** Read the review quickly. Tick (✓) the information that Sachin includes.

1 the title of the book
2 the author's name
3 information about the author
4 the name of the main character
5 the story of the whole book
6 a description of part of the story
7 details about how the story ends
8 his own opinion of the book

REVIEW
# Crocodile Tears
### by Anthony Horowitz

I've just read *Crocodile Tears* by Anthony Horowitz. It's a great book! The main character is a teenager called Alex Rider. He's a spy for the British government. Alex visits a farm in England that belongs to a criminal. The criminal is called Desmond McCain and he's creating a new type of crop that can kill people. He's planning to cause lots of problems around the world using the crops. Suddenly, McCain catches Alex! I think it's a very exciting story, but I won't write more in case you read the book!

**Sachin Patel**

**3** Read the *Prepare to write* box and find features a–d in Sachin's review.

### PREPARE TO WRITE
**An online book review**

**In an online book review:**

a include the title of the book and the author
b include the name of the main character(s)
c give your opinion of the book
d include some details of the story, but avoid 'spoilers' – and don't say how the book ends!

**4** Read an online review of *Artemis Fowl*. What is the writer's opinion of the book? Complete the review with the words in the box.

| author | character | incredible |
|---|---|---|
| thought | written | |

# Artemis Fowl
### by Eoin Colfer

I've just read a really good fantasy novel called *Artemis Fowl*. It was [1] ________ by Eoin Colfer, an Irish [2] ________. The main [3] ________ is a teenage boy called Artemis Fowl II. He comes from a family of criminals and he does all sorts of awful things to make his family richer. He isn't a very nice person, but that doesn't matter because the story is [4] ________. It was the first in a series of eight books. I [5] ________ it was a really exciting story, and I'll definitely read the rest of the series.

RATING: ★★★★☆

**5** You are going to write an online book review. Think about a book that you like and plan your review. Use the notes to help you.

- What is the title of the book?
- Who is the author?
- Who is the main character?
- What happens in the story?
- What is your opinion of it?

**6** Write your online book review.

- Use the tips in the *Prepare to write* box.
- Write about 100 words.
- Remember to check your spelling and grammar.

# 20 SEEING IS BELIEVING

## ABOUT YOU

Look at the pictures on this page. Have you ever seen any of these pictures before?
Do you know the name for these types of pictures?
What other examples have you seen?

A

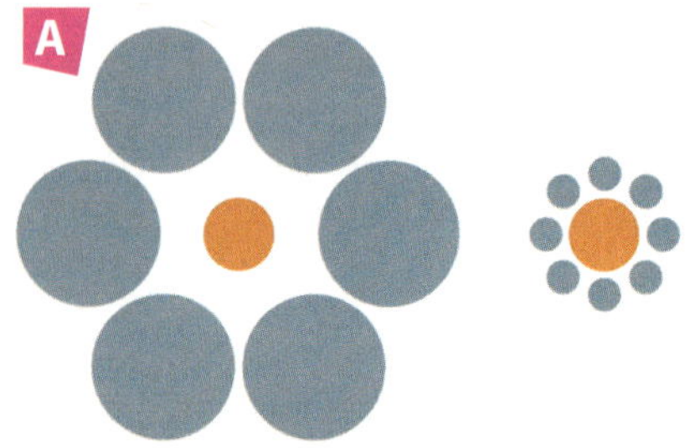

Which orange circle is larger?

B

Is the woman in the picture young or old?

C

What animals can you see?

D

How many 3s can you see?

E

blue green yellow
pink red orange
purple black grey
white brown

Can you say the colours of each word without saying the word itself?

## VOCABULARY Collocations: thinking

**1** Work in pairs. Look at the pictures and answer the questions.

94 **2** Listen to five short conversations. Match them to the pictures.

94 **3** Match the sentence halves. Then listen again and check.

EP
1 I lost
2 Can you give me
3 It didn't cross
4 I've just had a
5 I'm having
6 Make up
7 You have to use

a second thoughts now.
b your imagination to see the second person.
c your mind!
d concentration!
e a hint?
f thought.
g my mind to look there.

**4** Complete the sentences with the correct form of the collocations in Exercise 3.

0 I've just *had a thought*. Why don't you get some work as a babysitter?
1 It's time to ........... . Are you coming or not?
2 I wanted to watch that new comedy show. But now I've read the reviews I'm ........... .
3 As soon as I fell in the water, the thought of sharks ........... .
4 Question ten is impossible and Mrs Thomas wouldn't even ........... .
5 I can't do my homework while I watch TV. I ........... .
6 I find it hard to write stories because I'm not good at ........... .

**5** In pairs, ask and answer the questions.

1 Do you find it difficult to make up your mind about things? Or are you good at making decisions?
2 What causes you to lose concentration while you are studying at home or at school?
3 When was the last time you had second thoughts about something?
4 What school subjects allow you to use your imagination? Do you use your imagination out of school?

# READING

**1** **Read the article quickly. Choose the main topic of the article.**

**A** The ways optical illusions are used
**B** How optical illusions work
**C** Optical illusions in nature

**2** **Read the article again. Are the sentences true or false?**

1. Scientists can't fully explain optical illusions.
2. Akiyoshi Kitaoka designed his optical illusion for a car advertisement.
3. Alexander McQueen only made one of his striped 'optical illusion' dresses.
4. Animals use optical illusion to hunt for food.
5. The road safety illusions have been successful.
6. The plate illusion means it is probably healthier to use larger plates instead of smaller ones.

# Illusions everywhere

**Optical illusions often use light, colour and patterns to trick our brains into seeing something that isn't there. The Ancient Greeks studied them over 2,000 years ago, yet scientists still don't completely understand how they work. One explanation is that our brains are trying to understand so much information that they have to make guesses about some of it. Optical illusions happen when these guesses are wrong.**

**They might seem like only fun puzzles, but optical illusions have practical uses too. Here are some everyday examples – from advertising and nature to restaurants and on the roads.**

In advertising, optical illusions are useful to get people to pay attention. Look at this picture by Akiyoshi Kitaoka, a Japanese professor of Psychology. Kitaoka created it while he was making a New Year's card for his family and friends. The picture was later used in a car advertisement. Can you guess why?

On roads, several countries have used optical illusions to encourage people to drive more safely. For instance, these pedestrian crossings were painted on roads in China. From a distance, they look 3D and the research shows that this causes drivers to go more slowly near the crossings.

In fashion, optical illusions are used to change our appearance. This dress was designed by the famous fashion designer, Alexander McQueen. But it wasn't designed just to look good. The narrow black and white lines create an illusion, and the person appears slimmer than they are. Several celebrities bought one.

In the natural world, some animals need optical illusions to stay alive. Many butterflies, snakes and spiders are a similar colour to the place where they live. They don't want their enemies to see them – and eat them. They can also use their colour to catch other animals themselves. Can you see the animal hiding in this picture? What is it?

Researchers have found that one simple illusion could help us to eat, and also waste, less food. In experiments, the same amount of food was served on two plates: one small and one large. When people were asked to estimate the amount of food on each plate, they usually said the same thing: there was more food on the smaller plate. Restaurants sometimes use this trick too – if we think we are getting more food, then a meal looks better value for money.

**3** **Match the highlighted words in the text to the meanings.**

| | |
|---|---|
| 1 trick | a stop something or someone from escaping |
| 2 appears | b seems |
| 3 catch | c make someone more likely to do something |
| 4 encourage | d watch, listen to or think about something carefully |
| 5 pay attention (to something) | e make someone believe something that is not true |

## TALKING POINTS

What practical uses of optical illusions have you seen?
What are your favourite optical illusions from the unit so far?

# GRAMMAR Past simple passive

**1** **Match the examples to the passive forms.**

1. The picture **was used** in a car advertisement.
2. In fashion, optical illusions **are used** to change our appearance.
3. This dress **wasn't** just **designed** to look good.

a present simple positive
b past simple positive
c past simple negative

**2** **Look at the examples and complete the rules.**

**ACTIVE:**
A Japanese professor **created** the picture.
**PASSIVE:**
The picture **was created by** a Japanese professor.

In the past simple passive:
a we use *was* / ________ + (not) + ________ participle.
b if we want to say the person/thing that did the action, we use ________.

» **GRAMMAR REFERENCE AND PRACTICE PAGE 157**

**3** **Read the first part of an article and choose the correct forms of the verb.**

Street painting first [1] *appeared / was appeared* in the 16th century in Italy. The painters [2] *called / were called* 'madonnari' and they [3] *painted / were painted* pictures of well-known characters on the pavement.

In 1984, 3D pavement art [4] *invented / was invented* by the American, Kurt Venner. When you look at 3D pavement art from a certain place, it looks like it is 3D! A few years later, a TV documentary [5] *made / was made* Kurt and his work famous. He [6] *asked / was asked* to make 3D art for adverts, festivals and museums. This 3D pavement art [7] *didn't do / wasn't done* by Kurt, but by Julian Beever, a British pavement artist.

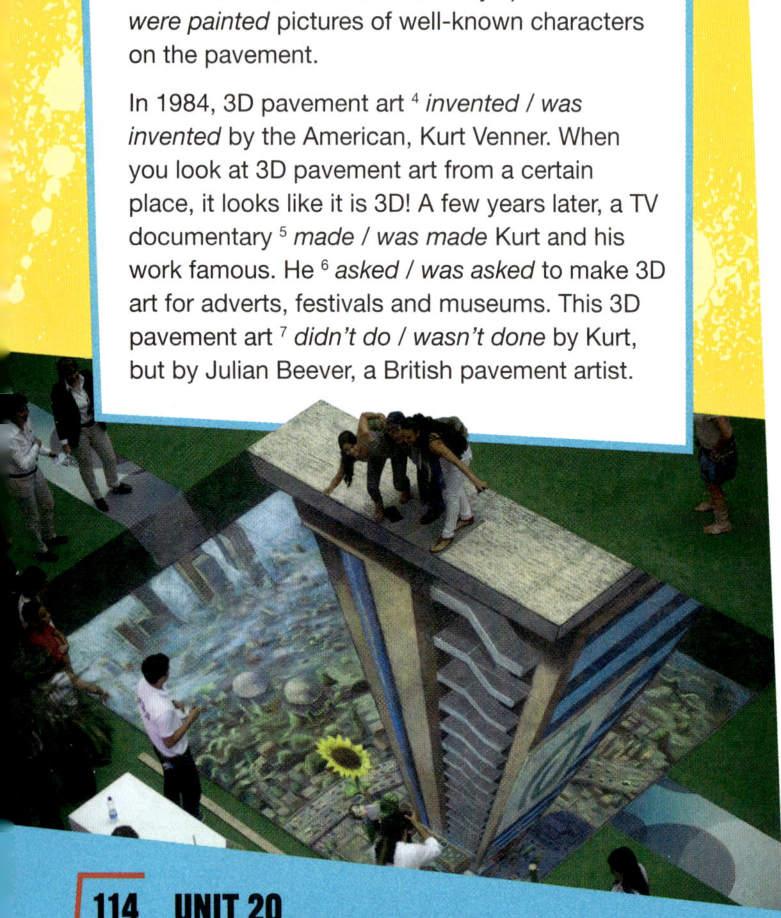

**4** **Complete the second part of the article. Use the past simple active or passive form of the verbs.**

Between 1790 and 1820, over 150 kilometres of canals [1] ________ (build) in London to help transport materials. Nowadays, cyclists and pedestrians share the path next to these canals, but some cyclists ride too fast. Recently, 3D pavement art [2] ________ (use) to make the path safer. A large 3D hole [3] ________ (paint) on it by two local artists. As cyclists approached the painting, it [4] ________ (look) like there was a huge hole in the path. Many cyclists stopped or [5] ________ (start) to ride more slowly. Then they [6] ________ (give) information about safer cycling!

**5** **Correct the mistake in each sentence.**

1. He born in Paris and he died in London.
2. This house it's built in the 16th century.
3. Yesterday we were met to have lunch together.
4. The medicine was tasted terrible.
5. The film we saw yesterday called *Now You See It*.
6. We were allow to eat in the classroom.

# VOCABULARY *look (at), see, watch*

**1** **Read the examples. Match the verbs *look (at)*, *see* and *watch* to their meanings.** EP

1. **Look at** this picture by Akiyoshi Kitaoka.
2. They don't want their enemies to **see** them.
3. I wanted to **watch** that new comedy show.

a ________: notice people or things with your eyes
b ________: pay attention to something, usually for a short time and especially something that isn't moving.
c ________: pay attention to something, usually for a longer time and especially something that is moving.

**2** **Complete the sentences with the correct form of *look (at)*, *see* and *watch*.**

1. Did you ________ that white van? It was going really fast.
2. ________ the whiteboard and copy the words.
3. It crossed my mind today that I haven't ________ your brother for ages.
4. ________ my hands carefully and I'll show you how the trick was done.
5. ________! That guy is shoplifting!
6. I'm exhausted. I was ________ films all night.
7. The World Cup final was ________ by over a billion people around the world.

**3** » **Work with a partner. Turn to page 125.**

# LISTENING

**1** **In pairs, discuss the questions.**

1 Do you know the names of any famous magicians?
2 What are the best magic tricks you've seen?
3 Can you do any magic tricks?

**2** **Read the description of the podcast. In pairs, write five questions that you think the presenter might ask.**

## The University Podcast

LATEST EPISODE:
33 Mysteries of the mind

Play    More episodes …

This week's show is all about mysteries of the mind. And we start with an interview with Amelia Rogers, a first-year French and Spanish student at the university. Amelia is also a member of the University Magic Club, whose recent show was reviewed very well by this podcast in episode 31.

96 **3** **Listen to the podcast. Did the presenter ask any of the questions you wrote in Exercise 2?**

96 **4** **Listen to the interview again. For each question, choose the correct answer.**

1 Amelia became interested in magic because
  A her older brother used to enjoy it.
  B she was told she was naturally good at it.
  C she was given a magic set on her birthday.
2 Amelia's favourite performances have been
  A at children's parties.
  B in competitions she won.
  C during her time at university.
3 Amelia thinks creating your own tricks is
  A less important than how you perform them.
  B impossible for people with her level of experience.
  C necessary if you want to become famous.
4 What does Amelia say about practising tricks?
  A She does it in lots of different places.
  B Her friends aren't interested in helping.
  C It's something she prefers doing alone.
5 What does Amelia say about explaining to other people how she does tricks?
  A She thinks it's a bad idea because people can't keep secrets.
  B She sometimes does it with her closest friends.
  C She only ever does it with other magicians.
6 What are Amelia's plans for the future?
  A She wants to be a professional magician.
  B She wants to concentrate on her studies.
  C She wants to work abroad.

# SPEAKING
## Expressing surprise and disbelief

**1** **Look at the photo. How would you feel if you saw someone do this?**

97 **2** **Listen and decide which sentence is true.**

a Mark doesn't believe Lucy.
b Lucy doesn't believe Mark.

97 **3** **Read the *Prepare to speak* box. Then listen again. Which phrases do Mark and Lucy use?**

### PREPARE TO SPEAK
**Expressing surprise and disbelief**

You won't believe this, but …
I find that hard to believe.
You're joking!
Are you serious?
No way!
I can't/couldn't believe my eyes.
That just isn't possible.

**4** **Work in pairs. Discuss the quiz questions together. Use the language in the *Prepare to speak* box.**

## The No Way! quiz

**1** **Which two events happened in the same year?**
A The Eiffel Tower in Paris was finished.
B Contact lenses were invented.
C The Japanese company Nintendo was started.

**2** **Which law is true in parts of Australia?**
A You are only allowed to own a pet rabbit if you are a magician.
B Cats aren't allowed to make a noise after 9 pm.
C You must attend classes before you can own a dog.

**3** **When the *Mona Lisa* was stolen in 1911, who did the police think the thief was?**
A a French poet
B a museum guard
C Picasso

**4** **How thick would a piece of paper be if you folded it in half 42 times?**
A It would be about 2 metres thick.
B It would be as tall as a house.
C It would be thick enough to reach the moon.

**5** **Which two people were born in the same year?**
A Marilyn Monroe, the film actress
B Queen Elizabeth II
C Pelé, the Brazilian footballer

**5** » **Turn to page 127 and check your answers to the quiz. Which answers surprised you the most?**

# LIFE SKILLS CRITICAL THINKING

## IDENTIFYING RELIABLE NEWS

### LIFE SKILLS

**Identifying reliable news**

We can get news from many sources. We can ask people we know and we can turn on the radio or TV. We can also use the internet to find out what's happening. However, we can't trust everything we see or hear. We need to identify reliable sources that we can believe and trust.

**1 Ask and answer the questions with a partner.**

What sources of information help you stay up to date?

- my parents
- teachers and other adults
- my friends at school
- newspapers and magazines
- news on the radio or TV
- internet websites and apps
- other sources

Which sources of information above do you believe the most? Why do you think they are better than other sources?

**2 Read the text quickly. Match the questions (a–e) to the expert's answers.**

**a** Why do people create fake news?
**b** How can we avoid or identify fake news?
**c** Is fake news only a recent problem?
**d** What other negative effects can fake news have?
**e** What does the phrase 'fake news' mean?

**3 Match the sentences to similar ideas in the introduction and paragraphs 1–5.**

1. New technology, like the internet, makes it easier to share fake news.
2. You should always check the facts if a news story sounds false.
3. We can get information about the news from lots of places.
4. Fake news stories can change opinions about people and companies.
5. A fake story can become famous if lots of people share it online.
6. Some websites use fake news to get more visitors and make money.

**4 Match the highlighted words in the text to the meanings.**

1. funny stories that people tell
2. give or supply something
3. notice or understand something
4. topic or subject
5. very new and up-to-date
6. have a bad effect on something

98 **5 Match the photos (A–D) to the topics (1–4). Then listen to four people talking about fake news. Which topics do they discuss?**

1. a food that sounds disgusting
2. stories about health and medicine
3. celebrities and their private lives
4. something surprising in space

98 **6 Listen again and answer the questions.**

**1 A** In the astronomy article, what did scientists see on Mars?
**B** Why might NASA want to keep the story secret?
**2 A** Who did the article say the actor had married?
**B** Why was it impossible for them to be married?
**3 A** Why didn't the company like the phrase 'strange pink liquid'?
**B** What happened after the report was shown on TV?
**4 A** What health products are fake stories often about?
**B** What are the fake news writers really trying to do?

**7 Complete the *Useful language* phrases with the words in the box.**

| cases | discuss | issue | serious |
|---|---|---|---|
| share | solution | | |

### USEFUL LANGUAGE

**Discussing a problem**

1. It can be a ________ problem.
2. There have been many ________ of this.
3. It's quite an important ________.
4. We need a ________ to this problem.
5. People shouldn't ________ fake news.
6. It'd be good to ________ it at school.

# FAKE NEWS

## GET THE REAL FACTS!

**We need to know what's happening around us in the world, and there are many ways to get news. We can read print media, such as newspapers and magazines, or we can use digital media, like TV and the internet. However, we have to think carefully about the information those sources provide and watch out for a problem called 'fake news'.**

**THE PRESIDENT IS AN ALIEN**

### 01 ________?

When people talk about fake news, they mean false stories that we sometimes find in the media. For example, a website might post an article with false information about a famous celebrity. Then the story might be shared on social media and go viral before people realise that it's false.

### 02 ________?

The phrase 'fake news' isn't new. In fact, it's more than 100 years old. And of course, rumours and false stories have existed since people started using language! However, fake news is becoming more common today because modern technology makes communication faster and easier than before.

### 03 ________?

In some cases, people invent fake stories to have fun and make jokes, but fake news can also be used to get attention. For example, websites might use fake headlines to attract more readers so they can earn more money. In some cases, fake news gets more attention than real news, and that's not funny!

### 04 ________?

Another negative effect of fake news is that people can stop trusting the media because they don't know who is really telling the truth. Fake news stories can also damage the image of a person or company. For instance, a fake story about a restaurant could suggest that its food is unhealthy or dangerous. Similarly, fake news about other cultures makes people feel negatively about them and changes public opinion.

### 05 ________?

To protect yourself against fake news stories, ask yourself four questions: who, what, where and why.

**Who** wrote the story? Are they experts on the issue? Do you trust them to tell the truth?

**What** do other people say? Check the facts with other sources and people that you trust.

**Where** has this story appeared? Did you find it on a website that usually tells the truth?

**Why** has this story appeared? Is it a joke or is it serious? What is the writer trying to do?

Think carefully about these questions before you share any news on social media. But don't be too negative. Some people tell the truth!

## PROJECT

**A campaign about fake news**

**Organise an information campaign about fake news for your school. Use the questions to help you plan your campaign.**

- Can you define fake news in a simple, clear way?
- Have there been any fake news stories in your area?
- Why do some people believe fake news so easily?
- How can young people avoid or identify fake news?
- How can schools help students notice fake news?
- How can websites be useful for stopping fake news?

**Present your work to the class. Then display it in your school.**

# REVIEW 5 UNITS 17–20

## VOCABULARY

**1 Choose the odd one out in each group of words. Explain your answer.**

| | | | |
|---|---|---|---|
| **1** novel | biography | author | e-book |
| **2** actor | audience | painter | writer |
| **3** sticker | painting | poetry | sculpture |
| **4** artist | director | studio | poet |
| **5** article | gallery | notice | brochure |

**2 Complete the jobs with the missing vowels. Then answer the questions.**

b _ bys _ tt _ r
f _ r _ f _ ght _ r
_ rch _ t _ ct
pr _ s _ nt _ r
j _ _ rn _ l _ st
ph _ rm _ c _ st

Who …

**1** has the most dangerous job? ........
**2** works with children? ........
**3** writes about the news? ........
**4** designs buildings? ........
**5** introduces radio or TV shows? ........
**6** sells medicines? ........

**3 Complete the words in the mini-conversations.**

**1 A:** We have to finish this essay by tomorrow but I'm *so* tired. I keep losing my **c**........ and I can't think of anything to write!
**B:** Your problem isn't being tired, you just need to pay more **a**........ in class.

**2 C:** So what do you want for your birthday? Give us a **h**........!
**D:** No way, I want a surprise. You know me well enough, just use your **i**........ .

**3 E:** I have £12 to spend but I can't make up my **m**........ what to buy. I was going to get a poster for my room but now I'm having second **t**........ .
**F:** Hey, I've just had a **t**........ . What about one of these graphic **n**........ ? The plots are supposed to be amazing.

**4 Complete the sentences. Use the noun or adjective form of the words in brackets.**

-al -er -ful -ian -ist -or

**1** Katy doesn't eat meat. She's ........ . (vegetable)
**2** There's a new ........ on this site who is really funny. (blog)
**3** I love the soundtrack to that film, but the acting isn't very ........ . (nature)
**4** My sister is a brilliant ........ . (piano)
**5** How many ........ are there in this year's marathon? (compete)
**6** I've hurt my leg. It's really ........ . (pain)

## GRAMMAR

**1 Read the first sentence. Then complete the second sentence using the verbs in the box.**

~~advised~~ asked persuaded ordered warned

**0** 'You should publish that story.'
His friends *advised* him *to publish* the story.
**1** 'Sit down!'
The teacher ........ the students ........ .
**2** 'Be careful when you do question five.'
The teacher ........ the students ........ with question five.
**3** 'Can you help me?'
Harry ........ Charlotte ........ him.
**4** 'You really should enter the art competition.'
My mum ........ me ........ the art competition.

**2 Complete the sentences. Use the second conditional form of the verbs.**

**0** My cousins don't live near me, so I don't see them.
If my cousins lived near me, …
*I would see them.*
**1** Marcia doesn't invite me to her parties, so I don't invite her to mine.
If Marcia invited me to her parties, …
**2** They talk all the time, so they're always in trouble.
They wouldn't always be in trouble if …
**3** I never do exercise, so I'm not fit.
If I did exercise, …
**4** He doesn't work hard, so he never gets good marks.
He'd get good marks if …
**5** She doesn't like TV, so she plays computer games all the time.
If she liked TV, …

## 3 Complete the second sentence so that it means the same as the first. Use no more than three words.

1. Leonardo da Vinci painted the *Mona Lisa*.
   The *Mona Lisa* was ________ Leonardo da Vinci.
2. In 2017, a collector sold *Salvator Mundi* by da Vinci for US$400 million!
   In 2017, *Salvator Mundi* by da Vinci ________ for US$400 million!
3. 'I can't imagine life without my phone,' said Nina.
   Nina said ________ life without her phone.
4. I don't think you should paint your bedroom black.
   If I were you, I ________ your bedroom black.
5. Joe said he was going to the exhibition later.
   'I ________ the exhibition later,' said Joe.

## 4 Choose the correct words.

1. The teacher *asked / asked to* us to work together.
2. If they *would want / wanted* to watch a film, they'd need to use my spare screen.
3. I wanted to *say / tell* you that I have a new game.
4. This series *was / is* filmed in 2017.

## 5 Correct the mistake in each sentence.

1. The driver stopped the bus and warns Lisa to sit down.
2. If you came with me to the concert, it will be more fun for me.
3. Someone tells us it was too late to get a bus.
4. The medicine was tasted horrible but it made me feel better.

## 6 Choose the correct word for each space. For each question, choose A, B, C or D.

### DEVELOP YOUR talents!

**Many teenagers dream of becoming celebrities – do you?**

If you have a [1] ________ talent for acting, dancing or singing, why not attend our two-week course and develop all three! Students are taught in small groups to allow you to [2] ________ progress quickly. For the first three days, you will concentrate on the three areas – acting, dancing and singing – with a full day for each skill. The rest of the course is all about the challenges of performing live. On the final afternoon, you will take [3] ________ in a show in front of a real [4] ________, which is always exciting. Past students [5] ________ it's the most fun they've ever had.

The course starts on 15th July and there are ten six-hour classes altogether. To book, simply complete your details on the other side of this [6] ________ and send it in!

| | A | B | C | D |
|---|---|---|---|---|
| 1 | central | cultural | natural | traditional |
| 2 | do | get | have | make |
| 3 | away | back | off | part |
| 4 | audience | character | presenter | performer |
| 5 | say | speak | talk | tell |
| 6 | advert | paper | novel | sticker |

# EXTRA ACTIVITIES

## UNIT 1 GRAMMAR, PAGE 12

**8** **Make questions with the present simple or present continuous. Then ask and answer them.**

1 What subjects / you / study / this year?
2 What / you / do / after school / today?
3 you / own / more than one mobile phone?
4 What TV programmes / you / watch / every week?
5 you / prefer / playing sport or watching TV?
6 What / you / like / doing on Sundays?
7 What / music / you / listen to / regularly?
8 you / have / a party for your next birthday?

## UNIT 1 VOCABULARY, PAGE 12

**3** **Discuss these questions.**

1 Do you ever get **impatient** with anyone?
2 Are you ever **unkind** to people? Who?
3 Do you think you're generally **lucky** or **unlucky**?
4 Do you think your parents are sometimes **unfair**?
5 Do you think you're an **independent** person?
6 How often are you **unwell**?

## UNIT 2 VOCABULARY, PAGE 16

5' **4** **In pairs, write as many sentences as possible using the adverb forms of the adjectives in the box. You have a time limit of five minutes!**

| | | | |
|---|---|---|---|
| accurate | amazing | beautiful | brave |
| dangerous | early | easy | excited |
| happy | hard | last | perfect | safe |
| secret | urgent | | |

*We met secretly.*

**Compare your sentences with other pairs. Who has the most sentences?**

## UNIT 3 VOCABULARY, PAGE 20

**5** **Quiz answers**

1 In England, the majority of children start school the September before their fifth birthday. However, education is not obligatory until the age of five.
2 In Belgium and Germany, students cannot leave school until they are 18.
3 In some states in the USA, the youngest age you can get a driving licence is 14. However, there are often a lot of rules for drivers of this age. For example, in South Dakota young drivers cannot drive between 10 pm and 6 am.
4 In England, 33% of young people go to university after leaving school. Around 6% of these students leave university before they get a degree. The most common reason for leaving is that students don't have enough money.
5 In almost all European countries, women leave home before men. In Italy, over 50% of men leave home in their thirties.
6 In the UK, you can get a job at the age of 13. You can work a maximum of 12 hours a week and 25 hours a week in the holidays.
7 In Spain, the average age at which women and men marry is 33. In India it is 22. In Japan it is 28.
8 In Brazil, the minimum voting age is 16. Between the ages of 18 and 70 in Brazil, it is obligatory to vote.

## UNIT 3 VOCABULARY, PAGE 22

**3** **Complete the sentences with your own ideas. Then compare your answers with a partner.**

1 I never have enough ........ .
2 I don't ........ because I'm too ........ .
3 My parents sometimes aren't ........ enough.
4 I'm ........ enough to ........ .
5 Our school isn't ........ enough and it's too ........ .

## UNIT 4 VOCABULARY, PAGE 26

**3** Student A

**Read the instructions and play the game.**

**a** You are going to explain some words in English without saying the word itself. Student B has to guess each word. Student B can ask questions.
**b** Read the example.
**c** You have a time limit of five minutes! How many can you explain?

| | |
|---|---|
| ~~**0** trainer~~ | **4** rugby |
| **1** coach | **5** athletics |
| **2** exercise | **6** match (noun) |
| **3** fit (adjective) | **7** squash |

Example:
**A:** *This is a noun for a person. They help sports players.*
**B:** *Is it a manager?*
**A:** *No. They help the players to get better at their sport.*
**B:** *A coach?*
**A:** *No, but it's very similar to a coach!*
**B:** *A trainer?*
**A:** *Yes!*

**Listen to Student B and guess the words. You can ask questions. You have a time limit of five minutes! How many words can Student B explain?**

## UNIT 5 VOCABULARY, PAGE 34

**4** Ask and answer the questions with a partner.

1 Do you and your friends buy each other birthday presents?
2 Do you usually enjoy yourself at parties?
3 How do you and your friends greet each other in the mornings?
4 Are you good at introducing yourself to new people?
5 Have you ever taught yourself a new skill?
6 Do you and your teachers email each other?

## UNIT 6 VOCABULARY, PAGE 38

**3** Ask and answer the questions with a partner.

1 Where's the nearest post box to your home?
2 What's the speed limit near your school? Is it too high?
3 How often do cars stop at pedestrian crossings?
4 What do you do while you are waiting at bus stops?
5 How many recycling bins are there in your school?
6 How many different types of road sign can you think of?

## UNIT 7 VOCABULARY, PAGE 44

**4** Student A

**In pairs, put your sentences and Student B's sentences in the correct order to form a story. Don't look at each other's sentences. Read the story together and check.**

**a** **on** very well – in fact, they fell in love. They knew that their relationship would be difficult, because Juliet was a Capulet and Romeo was a Montague, and their families would never **make**
**b** *Once upon a time*, in a town called Verona in Italy, there were two families, the Montagues and the Capulets. The families **had**
**c** **out** many years ago. One day, a young man from the Montague family called Romeo was **hanging**
**d** **round** to their house for a party, so Romeo and his friends decided to go in masks. Then Romeo could **get**
**e** **up** because their love was perfect. They wanted to be together and **look**

**Read the story together and discuss how you think the story ends.**

## UNIT 8 VOCABULARY, PAGE 48

**4** In pairs, write as many sentences as possible using the phrasal verbs in the box. You have a time limit of three minutes!

| | | | |
|---|---|---|---|
| check in | get back | get in | go away |
| look around | pick up | set off | take off |

*My mum picks up my dad if he works late.*

**Compare your sentences with other pairs. Who has the most correct sentences?**

# EXTRA ACTIVITIES

## UNIT 9 VOCABULARY, PAGE 54

**4** Key for quiz

Mostly **a**) answers: You think very carefully about what you spend your money on and you probably find all the best offers. But are you too careful? Money isn't the most important thing in life!

Mostly **b**) answers: The way you think about money is probably just right. You don't waste it, but you don't let it control your life.

Mostly **c**) answers: You need to start thinking about money or you're going to be short of cash your whole life! You don't *have to* spend everything you have. What about saving a bit?

## UNIT 9 GRAMMAR, PAGE 56

**4** **Complete the questions with the correct past participles. Then complete the table for you with ✓ (Yes) or ✗ (No).**

| Have you ever … | You | Your partner |
|---|---|---|
| 1 *sold* (sell) anything online? | | |
| 2 ........ (lend) anyone any money? | | |
| 3 ........ (take) anything back to a shop? | | |
| 4 ........ (lose) your phone? | | |
| 5 ........ (receive) too much change in a shop? | | |
| 6 ........ (regret) buying anything? | | |
| 7 ........ (buy) anything you can't afford? | | |
| 8 ........ (save) up to buy anything? | | |

**Ask and answer the questions in Exercise 4. Complete the table for your partner.**

**A:** *Have you ever sold anything online?*
**B:** *Yes, I have. Lots of times.*

## UNIT 9 VOCABULARY, PAGE 56

**3** **Ask and answer the questions with a partner.**

1. Do you think museums should charge for admission or be free? Why?
2. What's the most you've paid for a small bottle of water?
3. How much does it cost to go to the cinema in your town or city?
4. Will pay be important to you in your future choice of job?
5. Do you know the cost of a typical flat or house in your area?
6. Have you ever eaten at a restaurant free of charge?

## UNIT 10 VOCABULARY, PAGE 60

**3** **Work in pairs. Check you understand the meaning of the items.**

**Student A**
Choose an item to describe using *look, taste* or *smell.* Use the adjectives or your own ideas.

**Student B**
Can you guess what your partner is describing?

**Items**

a chilli   a flower   an ice lolly
fireworks   honey   mustard
strawberries

**Adjectives**

amazing   delicious   disgusting
freezing   fresh   juicy   soft
spicy   sweet

## UNIT 11 VOCABULARY, PAGE 66

**4** Student A

- Say the sentence and act the injury. Student B has to guess what's wrong. (Student B can only ask questions that have *Yes/No* answers.)

**Say:** "Ow, my head!"
**Act:** Put one hand over your right eye and moan with pain.
**Answer:** You walked into a door and cut your forehead.

**B:** *Have you got a fever?*
**A:** *No, I haven't.*

- Guess what's wrong with Student B. You can only ask questions that have *Yes/No* answers.
- Take turns to invent and act out more illnesses and injuries.

## UNIT 12 VOCABULARY, PAGE 70

**2** Photo A is the eye of a goat. Photo B is a horse's foot.

## UNIT 12 VOCABULARY, PAGE 70

**3** Student A

- Write ten sentences about yourself, your family, friends or where you live. Five sentences should be true and five sentences should be false.

*My family originally comes from ….*
*My brother can speak ….*

- Read your sentences one at a time. Student B has to guess which are true and which are false using adverbs of probability.

**A:** *My family originally comes from Ireland.*
**B:** *That's **definitely not** true! You have a Spanish surname, so you must come from a Spanish-speaking country. **Perhaps** your family originally comes from Spain.*
**A:** *You're right! / No, my family originally comes from Colombia.*

- Listen to Student B's sentences. Guess which are true and which are false using adverbs of probability: *definitely* (*not*), *perhaps*, *probably*.

## UNIT 13 VOCABULARY, PAGE 78

**3** Complete the sentences with the *-ed* or *-ing* adjective form of the words. Then write two more questions using *-ed* or *-ing* adjectives. In pairs, ask and answer the questions.

1 Which day of your week is the most ________ (tire)?
2 What's the most ________ (disgust) thing you've ever eaten?
3 Which school subject do you find the most ________ (confuse)?
4 What's the most ________ (amaze) fact you know?
5 Who was the last person you got ________ (annoy) with?
6 When was the last time you felt completely ________ (relax)?
7 How often do you feel ________ (embarrass) by your parents?
8 What's the most ________ (worry) thing happening in the world at the moment?

## UNIT 14 VOCABULARY, PAGE 82

**4** In pairs, write a few sentences about the words in the box, without actually using the words.

| ~~clip~~ | character | plot | review |
|---|---|---|---|
| series | soundtrack | trailer | |

*Example: clip*
*This is a short video that comes from a longer show or film.*
*You can watch it on your phone or on your computer.*
*Usually they show the best parts of a show or film.*

Take turns to read your sentences to other pairs of students. How quickly can they guess the word?

**A:** *This is a short video that comes from a longer show or film.*
**B:** *Is it a trailer?*
**A:** *No. You can watch it on your phone or …*
**B:** *Is it a clip?*
**A:** *Yes!*

# EXTRA ACTIVITIES

## UNIT 12 SPEAKING, PAGE 71

Take turns to describe the photo. Use phrases from the *Prepare to speak* box.

## UNIT 15 GRAMMAR, PAGE 88

**3**
1. The most common type of program that people download is anti-virus software. This is software to check for computer viruses.
2. The most common passwords are often quite simple. Many people just use the word 'password' or the numbers '123456'.
3. This will change every year, but in 2017, the top ten included the Hollywood actors Meghan Markle and Gal Gadot.
4. This figure is increasing every year, but in 2017, we spent more than $200 billion on apps.
5. Most smartphones are made in China, South Korea and India.

## UNIT 15 VOCABULARY, PAGE 88

**3** Take turns to mime an activity using the verbs in Box A and the words in Box B. Can your partner guess what you are doing?

**A**
look up, plug in, shut down, switch/turn off, switch/turn on, turn down, turn up, take out

**B**
your fitness tracker, your games console, a hairdryer, your laptop, a light, the TV, your phone, a printer, a memory card from a phone, the weather on your phone

## UNIT 16 VOCABULARY, PAGE 92

**3** In pairs, write sentences using the phrasal verbs in the box.

| add up | blow up | carry out |
|---|---|---|
| cut up | take away | work out |

**Act them out. Can the class guess your sentences?**

## UNIT 17 VOCABULARY, PAGE 100

**3** **Student A**

**Complete the questions using adjectives formed from the nouns in the box. Then ask Student B the questions.**

| digit | hope | music | person |
|---|---|---|---|
| profession | use | | |

1 What ________ device could you not live without?
2 Can you play any ________ instruments?
3 Do you tell your friends about your problems, or keep ________ issues to yourself?
4 Would you like to be a ________ artist or musician? Why? / Why not?
5 What's the most ________ advice you've ever received?
6 What things do you feel most ________ about in the future?

**Answer Student B's questions.**

## UNIT 18 VOCABULARY, PAGE 104

**3** **Work in pairs. Check you understand the meaning of the words in the box.**

| an actor | an artist | an author |
|---|---|---|
| a banker | a composer | a baker |
| a dentist | a driver | an electrician |
| a film director | a headteacher | a musician |
| a pianist | a politician | |

**Take turns to mime a person in the box. Can you / your partner guess all the words in two minutes?**

## UNIT 19 VOCABULARY, PAGE 110

**3** **Student A**

**Complete the questions using *say, speak, talk* and *tell*. Then ask Student B the questions.**

1 How many languages can you ________?
2 Can you ________ me what your favourite film is?
3 Can you ________ the alphabet backwards in English?
4 Which celebrity would you most like to ________ to? Why?
5 Who do you ________ to when you're in trouble?
6 Can you ________ the English equivalent of your name, or any of your friends' names?

**Answer Student B's questions.**

## UNIT 20 VOCABULARY, PAGE 114

**3** **Write two sentences for each of 1–3 below. Use the ideas in the box or your own.**

1 You're looking at …
2 You've just seen …
3 You're watching …

> a famous actor in the street.
> someone steal a car.
> a fly in your meal at a restaurant.
> a poster about a concert.
> the pictures in a recipe book.
> a soap opera.
> an incredibly exciting football match.
> an eagle in the sky.
> a clip from your favorite TV show.
> a school notice about exam results.

**Work in pairs. Take turns to mime one of your sentences. Can your partner guess your sentence exactly?**

# EXTRA ACTIVITIES

## UNIT 4 VOCABULARY, PAGE 26

**3** Student B

**Read the instructions and play the game.**

**a** You are going to listen to Student A explain some words in English without saying the word itself. You have to guess each word. You can ask questions.
**b** Read the example.
**c** You have a time limit of five minutes! How many can Student A explain?

Example:
**A:** *This is a noun for a person. They help sports players.*
**B:** *Is it a manager?*
**A:** *No. They help the players to get better at their sport.*
**B:** *A coach?*
**A:** *No, but it's very similar to a coach!*
**B:** *A trainer?*
**A:** *Yes!*

**Explain these words without saying the word itself. Student A has to guess each word. You have a time limit of five minutes! How many can you explain?**

~~**0** trainer~~
**1** BMX
**2** champion
**3** jogging
**4** point (noun)
**5** train (verb)
**6** windsurfing
**7** work out (noun)

## UNIT 7 VOCABULARY, PAGE 44

**4** Student B

**In pairs, put your sentences and Student A's sentences in the correct order to form a story. Don't look at each other's sentences. Read the story together and check.**

**f** **after** each other forever. So, the day after the party, they got married in secret.
**g** **arguments** and fought all the time. No one can remember exactly why, but the two families **fell**
**h** **out** with his friends in Verona when they heard about a party at the Capulets' house. Romeo loved a Capulet girl called Rosaline, so he wanted to go to the party to see her. But the Capulets would never let a Montague **come**
**i** **together** with Rosaline and the Capulets would never know. At the party, Romeo didn't speak to Rosaline. Instead, he met a girl called Juliet. Romeo and Juliet **got**
**j** **up** and accept their relationship. After the party, Romeo went into the garden and talked to Juliet through her bedroom window. 'But, soft!' he said. 'What light through yonder window breaks? It is the east, and Juliet is the sun.' They knew they'd never **split**

**Read the story together and discuss how you think the story ends.**

## UNIT 11 VOCABULARY, PAGE 66

**4** Student B

- **Guess what's wrong with Student A. You can only ask questions that have *Yes/No* answers.**
- **Say the sentence and act the illness. Student A has to guess what's wrong. (Student A can only ask questions that have *Yes/No* answers.)**

**Say:** 'Oh, I feel terrible!'
**Act:** Fold your arms, lean forward with your eyes closed and moan.
**Answer:** You feel very sick.

**B:** *Have you injured your arm?*
**A:** *No, I haven't.*

- **Take turns to invent and act out more illnesses and injuries.**

## UNIT 12 VOCABULARY, PAGE 70

**3 Student B**

**Write ten sentences about yourself, your family, friends or where you live. Five sentences should be true and five sentences should be false.**

*My family originally comes from ... .*
*My brother can speak ... .*

**Listen to Student A's sentences. Guess which are true and which are false using adverbs of probability: *definitely* (*not*), *perhaps*, *probably*.**

**A:** *My family originally comes from Ireland.*
**B:** *That's* ***definitely not*** *true! You have a Spanish surname, so you must come from a Spanish-speaking country.* ***Perhaps*** *your family originally comes from Spain.*
**A:** *You're right! / No, my family originally comes from Mexico.*

**Read your sentences one at a time. Student A has to guess which are true and which are false using adverbs of probability.**

## UNIT 17 VOCABULARY, PAGE 100

**3 Student B**

**Complete the questions using adjectives formed from the nouns in the box. Then ask Student A the questions.**

| culture | environment | help | music |
|---|---|---|---|
| stress | tradition | | |

1 Can you cook any ________ dishes from your country or region?
2 Can you play any instruments, or aren't you very ________?
3 Are you worried about ________ issues like global warming?
4 Do you like ________ TV shows about art and literature?
5 What's the most ________ advice you've ever received?
6 Have you been in any ________ situations recently? What happened?

**Answer Student A's questions.**

## UNIT 19 VOCABULARY, PAGE 110

**3 Student B**

**Complete the questions using the correct form of *say, speak, talk* and *tell*.**

1 What would you do if someone was ________ during a film at the cinema?
2 Have you ever ________ your best friend your most secret of secrets?
3 What would you ________ if you saw someone stealing in a shop?
4 Can you ________ any other languages apart from English?
5 What do you ________ about when there's a gap in a conversation?
6 Can you ________ the names of any American states / British cities? How many?

**Answer Student A's questions.**

**Now ask Student A your questions in Exercise 1.**

## UNIT 20 SPEAKING, PAGE 115

**5 Answers to quiz**

1 A and C. In 1889, the Eiffel tower was finished and the company Nintendo was started. At that time, Nintendo made card games.
Contact lenses were invented by Leonardo Da Vinci in around 1508. But they weren't actually produced until 1888 in Germany.

2 A is true in Queensland. In this area of Australia, rabbits cause a lot of damage in the wild. There is also a 2,000-mile fence around this area to stop animals like rabbits getting into Queensland.
B is true in parts of the USA.
C was true until 2017 in Switzerland.

3 A and C. The police first thought the painting was stolen by Guillaume Apollinaire, a French poet and a friend of the Spanish painter, Picasso. They also believed that Picasso was involved.

4 C In theory, if you could fold a piece of paper 42 times, it would be thick enough to reach the moon. However, it is almost impossible to fold a piece of paper more than seven times.

5 A and B. They were both born in 1926. Pele was born in 1940.

# EP VOCABULARY LIST

*adj* = adjective *adv* = adverb
*n* = noun *v* = verb *pv* = phrasal verb
*prn* = pronoun *phr* = phrase

## UNIT 1

### DESCRIBING PEOPLE

**attractive** /ə'træktɪv/ *adj* beautiful or pleasant to look at
**bald** /bɔːld/ *adj* with little or no hair
**blonde** /blɒnd/ *adj* Blonde hair is pale yellow.
**careful** /'keəfəl/ *adj* giving a lot of attention to what you are doing so that you do not have an accident, make a mistake, or damage something
**careless** /'keələs/ *adj* not taking or showing enough care and attention
**cheerful** /'tʃɪəfəl/ *adj* happy
**confident** /'kɒnfɪdənt/ *adj* certain about your ability to do things well
**curly** /'kɜːli/ *adj* shaped like a curl, or with many curls
**dark** /dɑːk/ *adj* nearer to black than white in colour
**elderly** /'eldəli/ *adj* a more polite word for 'old', used to describe people
**fair** /feə/ *adj* having pale skin or a light colour of hair
**funny** /'fʌni/ *adj* making you smile or laugh
**friendly** /'frendli/ *adj* behaving in a pleasant, kind way towards someone
**good-looking** /ˌgʊd'lʊkɪŋ/ *adj* If someone is good-looking, they have an attractive face.
**handsome** /'hænsəm/ *adj* A handsome man is attractive.
**in his/**her early thirties /ɪn hɪz/hər 'ɜːli 'θɜːtiz/ *phr* aged between 30 and 34
**middle-aged** /ˌmɪdl'eɪdʒd/ *adj* in the middle of your life before you are old
**miserable** /'mɪzrəbl/ *adj* very sad
**polite** /pə'laɪt/ *adj* behaving in a way that is not rude and shows that you do not only think about yourself
**pretty** /'prɪti/ *adj* If a woman or girl is pretty, she is attractive.
**rude** /ruːd/ *adj* behaving in a way that is not polite and upsets people
**serious** /'sɪəriəs/ *adj* A serious person is quiet and does not laugh often.
**shy** /ʃaɪ/ *adj* not confident, especially about meeting or talking to new people
**straight** /streɪt/ *adj* not curly
**teenage** /'tiːneɪdʒ/ *adj* aged between 13 and 19 or suitable for people of that age
**unfriendly** /ʌn'frendli/ *adj* not friendly

### PREFIXES: *UN-, IN-, IM-*

**impatient** /ɪm'peɪʃənt/ *adj* easily annoyed by someone's mistakes or because you have to wait
**impolite** /ˌɪmpəl'aɪt/ *adj* not polite
**impossible** /ɪm'pɒsəbl/ *adj* If an action or event is impossible, it cannot happen or be done.
**incorrect** /ˌɪnkər'ekt/ *adj* not correct
**independent** /ˌɪndɪ'pendənt/ *adj* not wanting or needing anyone else to help you or do things for you
**inexpensive** /ˌɪnɪk'spensɪv/ *adj* cheap but of good quality
**invisible** /ɪn'vɪzəbl/ *adj* Someone or something that is invisible cannot be seen.
**unfair** /ʌn'feə/ *adj* not treating people in an equal way
**unfriendly** /ʌn'frendli/ *adj* not friendly
**unhealthy** /ʌn'helθi/ *adj* likely to damage your health
**unkind** /ʌn'kaɪnd/ *adj* slightly cruel
**unknown** /ʌn'nəʊn/ *adj* not known
**unlucky** /ʌn'lʌki/ *adj* having or causing bad luck
**untidy** /ʌn'taɪdi/ *adj* not tidy
**unwell** /ʌn'wel/ *adj* sick

## UNIT 2

### CLOTHES: ADJECTIVES

**badly-dressed** /ˌbædli'drest/ *adj* wearing clothes that are not attractive or are of poor quality
**brand new** /brænd njuː/ *adj* completely new
**casual** /'kæʒjuəl/ *adj* Casual clothing is comfortable and not suitable for formal occasions.
**comfortable** /'kʌmftəbl/ *adj* Comfortable furniture, clothes, rooms, etc. make you feel relaxed and do not cause any pain.
**loose-fitting** /ˌluːs'fɪt.ɪŋ/ *adj* Loose-fitting clothing is quite large and does not fit tightly.
**second-hand** /ˌsekənd'hænd/ *adj* If something is second-hand, someone else owned or used it before you.
**skinny** /'skɪni/ *adj* narrow and fitting closely to the body
**smart** /smɑːt/ *adj* If you look smart or your clothes are smart, you look clean and tidy.
**trendy** /'trendi/ *adj* fashionable at the moment
**uncomfortable** /ʌn'kʌmftəbl/ *adj* not feeling comfortable and pleasant, or not making you feel comfortable and pleasant
**unfashionable** /ʌn'fæʃənəbl/ *adj* not fashionable or popular at a particular time
**well-dressed** /ˌwel'drest/ *adj* wearing attractive, good quality clothes

## ADVERBS

**amazingly** /ə'meɪzɪŋli/ *adv* in an amazing way
**badly** /'bædli/ *adv* in a bad way
**carefully** /'keəfəli/ *adv* in a careful way
**early** /'ɜːli/ *adv* near the beginning of a period of time, or before the usual, expected, or planned time
**fast** /fɑːst/ *adv* in a quick way
**healthily** /'helθəli/ *adv* in a healthy way
**heavily** /'hevəli/ *adv* to a great degree
**honestly** /'ɒnɪstli/ *adv* in an honest way
**lazily** /'leɪzəli/ *adv* in a lazy way
**luckily** /lʌkəli/ *adv* in a lucky way; fortunately
**politely** /pə'laɪtli/ *adv* in a polite way
**quickly** /'kwɪkli/ *adv* fast or in a short time
**rudely** /ruːdli/ *adv* in a rude way
**seriously** /'sɪəriəsli/ *adv* in a serious way
**well** /wel/ *adv* in a good way

# UNIT 3

## LIFE EVENTS

**be born** /biː bɔːn/ *v* When a person or animal is born, they come out of their mother's body and start to exist.
**get a degree** /get ə dɪ'griː/ *phr* get a qualification given for completing a university course
**get a driving licence** /get ə 'draɪvɪŋ ˌlaɪsəns/ *phr* get a document which gives official permission to drive a car, received after passing a driving test
**get a job** /get ə dʒɒb/ *phr* to find regular work in order to earn money
**get married** /get 'mærid/ *v* to begin a legal relationship with someone as their husband or wife
**go to university** /gəʊ tə ˌjuːnɪ'vɜːsəti/ *phr* to go regularly to a place where students study at a high level to get a degree
**have children** /hæv 'tʃɪldrən/ *phr* to become a parent
**leave home** /liːv həʊm/ *phr* to stop living with your parents
**leave school** /liːv skuːl/ *phr* to stop going to school forever
**move home** /muːv həʊm/ *phr* to leave your home in order to live in a new one
**retire** /rɪ'taɪə/ *v* to leave your job and stop working, usually because you are old
**start school** /stɑːt skuːl/ *phr* to begin going to school
**vote** /vəʊt/ *v* to show your choice or opinion in an election by writing a cross on an official piece of paper

## *TOO, ENOUGH, NOT ENOUGH*

**enough** /ɪ'nʌf/ *adv* as much as is necessary
**not enough** /nɒt ɪ'nʌf/ *adv* less than is necessary
**too** /tuː/ *adv* used before adjectives and adverbs to mean 'more than is allowed, necessary, possible, etc.'

# UNIT 4

## SPORTS

**athletics** /æθ'letɪks/ *n* the sports that include running, jumping, and throwing
**boxing** /'bɒksɪŋ/ *n* a sport in which two people hit each other while wearing big, leather gloves (= pieces of clothing for your hands)
**climbing** /'klaɪmɪŋ/ *n* the sport of climbing mountains, hills, or rocks
**cycling** /'saɪklɪŋ/ *n* the sport or activity of riding a bicycle
**gymnastics** /dʒɪm'næstɪks/ *n* a sport in which you do physical exercises on the floor and on different pieces of equipment, often in competitions
**ice hockey** /'aɪs hɒki/ *n* a sport played on ice in which two teams try to hit a small hard object into a goal using long curved sticks
**ice skating** /'aɪs skeɪtɪŋ/ *n* the activity or sport of moving across ice using ice skates
**jogging** /dʒɒgɪŋ/ *n* to run slowly for exercise
**rugby** /'rʌgbi/ *n* a sport played by two teams with an oval ball and H-shaped goals
**squash** /skwɒʃ/ *n* a sport in which two people hit a small rubber ball against the four walls of a room
**surfing** /'sɜːfɪŋ/ *n* the sport of riding on a wave on a special board
**swimming** /'swɪmɪŋ/ *n* the activity of moving through water by moving your body
**table tennis** /'teɪbl tenɪs/ *n* a sport in which two or four people hit a small ball over a low net on a large table
**tennis** /'tenɪs/ *n* a sport in which two or four people hit a small ball to each other over a net
**volleyball** /'vɒlibɔːl/ *n* a sport in which two teams use their hands to hit a ball over a net without allowing it to touch the ground
**windsurfing** /'wɪndsɜːfɪŋ/ *n* a sport in which you sail across water by standing on a board and holding onto a large sail

# VOCABULARY LIST

### WORDS WITH DIFFERENT MEANINGS

**coach** /kəʊtʃ/ *n* a comfortable bus used to take groups of people on journeys

**coach** /kəʊtʃ/ *n* someone whose job is to teach people to improve at a sport, skill, or school subject

**exercise** /ˈeksəsaɪz/ *n* physical activity that you do to make your body strong and healthy

**exercise** /ˈeksəsaɪz/ *n* a piece of written work that helps you learn something

**fit** /fɪt/ *adj* healthy and strong, especially as a result of exercise

**fit** /fɪt/ *v* to be the right size or shape for someone or something

**match** /mætʃ/ *n* a sports competition in which two people or teams compete against each other

**match** /mætʃ/ *v* If two things match, they are the same colour or type

**point** /pɔɪnt/ *n* a unit used for showing who is winning in a game or competition

**point** /pɔɪnt/ *v* to show where someone or something is by holding your finger or a thin object towards it

**train** /treɪn/ *n* a long, thin vehicle that travels along metal tracks and carries people or goods

**train** /treɪn/ *v* to practise a sport or exercise, often in order to prepare for a sporting event, or to help someone to do this

**trainer** /ˈtreɪnə/ *n* a type of light comfortable shoe that is suitable for playing sport

**trainer** /ˈtreɪnə/ *n* a person who teaches skills to people or animals and prepares them for a job, activity or sport

**work out** /wɜːk ˈaʊt/ *pv* to find the answer to a problem

**work out** /wɜːk ˈaʊt/ *pv* to do exercises to make your body stronger

## UNIT 5

### CRIMES AND CRIMINALS

**burglar** /ˈbɜːglə/ *n* someone who gets into buildings illegally and steals things

**burglary** /ˈbɜːgləri/ *n* the crime of getting into a building illegally and stealing things

**hacker** /ˈhækə/ *n* someone who illegally gets into someone else's computer system

**hacking** /ˈhækɪŋ/ *n* the activity of using a computer illegally to get into another computer system to read the information kept there, or to spread a computer virus

**pickpocket** /ˈpɪkˌpɒkɪt/ *n* someone who steals things from people's pockets or bags

**pickpocketing** /ˈpɪkˌpɒkɪtɪŋ/ *n* the crime of stealing things out of people's pockets or bags, especially in a crowd

**rob** /rɒb/ *v* to take money or things from someone or somewhere without their permission

**shoplifter** /ˈʃɒplɪftə/ *n* someone who steals things from a shop

**shoplifting** /ˈʃɒplɪftɪŋ/ *n* the crime of stealing things from a shop

**steal** /stiːl/ *v* to take something that belongs to someone else without their permission

**theft** /θeft/ *n* the action or crime of stealing something

**thief** /θiːf/ *n* someone who steals things

**vandal** /ˈvændəl/ *n* someone who intentionally damages things in public places

**vandalism** /ˈvændəlɪzəm/ *n* the crime of intentionally damaging things in public places

### *OURSELVES, YOURSELVES, THEMSELVES* AND *EACH OTHER*

**each other** /ˌiːtʃ ˈʌðər/ *prn* used to show that each person in a group of two or more people does something to the others

**herself** /həˈself/ *prn* the reflexive form of the pronoun 'she'

**himself** /hɪmˈself/ *prn* the reflexive form of the pronoun 'he'

**itself** /ɪtˈself/ *prn* the reflexive form of the pronoun 'it'

**myself** /maɪˈself/ *prn* the reflexive form of the pronoun 'I'

**ourselves** /ˌaʊəˈselvz/ *prn* the reflexive form of the pronoun 'we'

**themselves** /ðəmˈselvz/ *prn* the reflexive form of the pronoun 'they'

**yourself** /jɔːˈself/ *prn* the reflexive form of the pronoun 'you' (used for one person)

**yourselves** /jɔːˈselvz/ *prn* the reflexive form of the pronoun 'you' (used for two or more people)

## UNIT 6

### CITY PROBLEMS

**crowds** /kraʊdz/ *n* large groups of people who are together in one place

**graffiti** /grəˈfiːti/ *n* writing or pictures painted on walls and public places, usually illegally

**green spaces** /ˌgriːn ˈspeɪsɪz/ *n* areas of grass, trees or other plants in a town or city

**pollution** /pəˈluːʃən/ *n* damage caused to water, air, etc. by harmful substances or waste

**power cut** /paʊə kʌt/ *n* If there is a power cut, the supply of electricity suddenly stops.

**public transport** /ˈpʌblɪk ˈtrænspɔːt/ *n* a system of vehicles such as buses and trains which operate at regular times and that the public use

**rubbish** /ˈrʌbɪʃ/ *n* things that you throw away because you do not want them

**rush hour** /ˈrʌʃ aʊə/ *n* the time when a lot of people are travelling to or from work and so roads and trains are very busy

**traffic jam** /ˈtræfɪk dʒæm/ *n* a line of cars, trucks, etc. that are moving slowly or not moving at all

### COMPOUNDS: NOUN + NOUN

**apartment building** /əˈpɑːtmənt bɪldɪŋ/ *n* a building that is divided into apartments

**bus stop** /ˈbʌs stɒp/ *n* a place where buses stop to let passengers get on or off

**pedestrian crossing** /pəˌdestriən ˈkrɒsɪŋ/ *n* a special place on a road where traffic must stop if people want to cross

**post box** /ˈpəʊst bɒks/ *n* a large, metal container in a public place where you can post letters

**recycling bin** /ˌriːˈsaɪklɪŋ bɪn/ *n* a container for waste that will be recycled, for example, paper or glass

**road sign** /ˈrəʊd saɪn/ *n* a notice at the side of a road which gives information, directions, a warning, etc.

**speed limit** /ˈspiːd ˌlɪmɪt/ *n* the fastest speed that a vehicle is allowed to travel on a particular road

**taxi rank** /ˈtæksi ræŋk/ *n* a place where you can go to get a taxi

## UNIT 7

### *BE, DO, HAVE* AND *MAKE*

**be (someone's) fault** /biː fɔːlt/ *phr* If something bad that has happened is someone's fault, they are responsible for it.

**be annoyed (with somebody)** /biː əˈnɔɪd/ *phr* to be slightly angry

**be on your own** /biː ɒn jər əʊn/ *phr* to be alone

**be wrong** /biː rɒŋ/ *phr* to think or say something that is not correct

**do (someone) a favour** /duː ə ˈfeɪvə/ *phr* to do something to help someone

**do something** /duː ˈsʌmθɪŋ/ *phr* to do an activity with someone

**have (something) in common** /hæv ɪn ˈkɒmən/ *phr* to share interests, experiences, or other characteristics with someone or something

**have an argument** /hæv ən ˈɑːgjəmənt/ *phr* to have an angry discussion with someone in which you both disagree

**have fun** /hæv fʌn/ *phr* to do something that gives you enjoyment or pleasure

**have problems with somebody** /hæv ˈprɒbləmz wɪð ˈsʌmbədi/ *phr* to find someone annoying or offensive

**make angry** /meɪk ˈæŋgri/ *phr* to cause someone to become angry; to annoy someone

**make friends** /meɪk frends/ *phr* to begin to know and like someone

### PHRASAL VERBS: RELATIONSHIPS

**come round** /kʌm ˈraʊnd/ *pv* to visit someone at their house

**fall out (with)** /fɔːl ˈaʊt/ *pv* to argue with someone and stop being friendly with them

**get on** /get ˈɒn/ *pv* If two or more people get along, they like each other and are friendly to each other.

**get together** /get təˈgeðə/ *pv* to meet in order to do something or spend time together

**hang out** /hæŋ ˈaʊt/ *pv* to spend a lot of time in a particular place or with a particular group of people

**look after** /lʊk ˈɑːftə/ *pv* to take care of someone or something by keeping them healthy or in a good condition

**make up** /meɪk ˈʌp/ *pv* to become friendly with someone again after you have argued with them

**split up** /splɪt ˈʌp/ *pv* If two people split up, they end their relationship.

## UNIT 8

### INTERNATIONAL TRAVEL

**baggage** /ˈbægɪdʒ/ *n* all the cases and bags that you take with you when you travel

**baggage hall** /ˈbægɪdʒ hɔːl/ *n* the place at an airport where passengers collect their luggage after their flight

**boarding pass** /ˈbɔːdɪŋ pɑːs/ *n* a piece of paper you must show to get on an aircraft

**check-in desk** /ˈtʃekɪn desk/ *n* one of the places at an airport where you show your ticket so that you can be told where you will be sitting

**customs** /ˈkʌstəmz/ *n* the place where your bags are examined when you are going into a country, to make sure you are not carrying anything illegal

**departure gate** /dɪˈpɑːtʃə geɪt/ *n* the part of an airport where passengers wait and then get on a particular aircraft

**passport** /ˈpɑːspɔːt/ *n* an official document, often a small book, that you need to enter or leave a country

**passport control** /ˈpɑːspɔːt kənˌtrəʊl/ *n* the place where your passport is officially checked when you enter or leave a country

**queue** /kjuː/ *n* a row of people waiting for something, one behind the other

**security check** /sɪˈkjʊərəti tʃek/ *n* an examination before passengers get on a plane to make sure they are not carrying anything that is dangerous

**sign** /saɪn/ *n* a symbol or message in a public place that gives information or instructions

# EP VOCABULARY LIST

### PHRASAL VERBS: TRAVEL

**check in** /tʃek ˈɪn/ *pv* to go to the desk at an airport in order to say that you have arrived and to get the number of your seat

**get back** /get ˈbæk/ *pv* to return to a place after you have been somewhere else

**get in** /get ˈɪn/ *pv* to succeed in entering a place, especially a building

**go away** /gəʊ əˈweɪ/ *pv* to leave your home in order to spend time in a different place, usually for a holiday

**look around** /lʊk əˈraʊnd/ *pv* to visit a place and look at the things in it

**pick up** /pɪk ˈʌp/ *pv* to collect someone who is waiting for you, or to collect something that you have left somewhere

**set off** /set ˈɒf/ *pv* to start a journey

**take off** /teɪk ˈɒf/ *pv* If an aircraft takes off, it begins to fly.

## UNIT 9

### MONEY AND SHOPPING

**bank account** /bæŋk əˈkaʊnt/ *n* an arrangement with a bank to keep your money there and take it out when you need to

**change** /tʃeɪndʒ/ *n* the money that you get back when you pay more for something than it costs

**checkout** /ˈtʃekaʊt/ *n* the place in a large shop, especially a food shop, where you pay for your goods

**give away** /gɪv əˈweɪ/ *pv* to give something to someone without asking for any money

**price** /praɪs/ *n* the amount of money that you pay to buy something

**receipt** /rɪˈsiːt/ n a piece of paper which proves that you have paid for something

**save up** /seɪv ˈʌp/ *pv* to keep money so that you can buy something with it in the future

**special offer** /ˈspeʃəl ˈɒfə/ *n* a price that is lower than usual

**take back** /teɪk ˈbæk/ *pv* to return something to the place you borrowed or bought it from

### EASILY CONFUSED WORDS: *PAY, CHARGE, COST*

**charge** /tʃɑːdʒ/ *n* the amount of money that you have to pay for something, especially for an activity or a service

**charge** /tʃɑːdʒ/ *v* to ask someone to pay an amount of money for something, especially for an activity or a service

**cost** /kɒst/ *n* the amount of money that you need to buy or do something

**cost** /kɒst/ *v* If something costs a particular amount of money, you have to pay that in order to buy or do it.

**pay** /peɪ/ *n* the money you receive from your employer for doing your job

**pay** /peɪ/ *v* to give money to someone because you are buying something from them, or because you owe them money

## UNIT 10

### FOOD AND DRINK ADJECTIVES

**bitter** /ˈbɪtə/ *adj* having a strong, sharp, usually unpleasant taste

**delicious** /dɪˈlɪʃəs/ *adj* If food or drink is delicious, it smells or tastes extremely good.

**disgusting** /dɪsˈgʌstɪŋ/ *adj* extremely unpleasant

**fresh** /freʃ/ *adj* Fresh food has been produced or collected recently and has not been frozen, dried, etc.

**frozen** /ˈfrəʊzən/ *adj* Frozen food has been made so that it will last a long time by freezing.

**horrible** /ˈhɒrəbl/ *adj* very unpleasant or bad

**juicy** /ˈdʒuːsi/ *adj* full of juice

**raw** /rɔː/ *adj* not cooked

**sour** /saʊə/ *adj* having a sharp, sometimes unpleasant, taste or smell, like a lemon, and not sweet

**spicy** /ˈspaɪsi/ *adj* containing strong flavours from spice

**sweet** /swiːt/ *adj* with a taste like sugar

**tasty** /ˈteɪsti/ *adj* Food that is tasty has a good flavour and is nice to eat.

### *LOOK, TASTE, SMELL*

**look** /lʊk/ *v* used to describe the appearance of a person or thing

**smell** /smel/ *v* to have a particular quality that people notice by using their nose

**taste** /teɪst/ *v* If food tastes a particular way, it has that flavour.

# UNIT 11

## BODY AND HEALTH

**aches** /eɪks/ *n* feelings of pain over an area of your body which continue for a long time
**ankle** /ˈæŋkl/ *n* the part of your leg that is just above your foot
**back** /bæk/ *n* the part of your body from your shoulders to your bottom
**broken** /ˈbrəʊkən/ *adj* This describes an arm/leg, etc. with a damaged bone.
**cheek** /tʃiːk/ *n* the soft part of your face below your eye
**chest** /tʃest/ *n* the front of your body between your neck and your waist
**chin** /tʃɪn/ *n* the bottom part of your face, below your mouth
**cold** /kəʊld/ *n* a common illness that makes you sneeze and makes your nose produce liquid
**cough** /kɒf/ *n* an illness that makes you cough a lot
**cut** /kʌt/ *n* an injury made when the skin is cut with something sharp
**earache** /ˈɪəreɪk/ *n* pain in your ear
**elbow** /ˈelbəʊ/ *n* the part in the middle of your arm where it bends
**fever** /ˈfiːvə/ *n* a high body temperature because you are sick
**finger** /ˈfɪŋgə/ *n* one of the five, long, separate parts at the end of your hand, including your thumb
**flu** /fluː/ *n* an illness like a very bad cold, that makes you feel hot and weak
**forehead** /ˈfɔːhed/ *n* the part of your face between your eyes and your hair
**knee** /niː/ *n* the middle part of your leg where it bends
**neck** /nek/ *n* the part of the body between your head and your shoulders
**shoulder** /ˈʃəʊldə/ *n* where your arm joins your body next to your neck
**sore** /sɔː/ *adj* painful, especially when touched
**stomach ache** /ˈstʌmək eɪk/ *n* pain in your stomach
**throat** /θrəʊt/ *n* the back part of your mouth and the passages inside your neck
**thumb** /θʌm/ *n* the short, thick finger on the side of your hand that can touch the top of all your other fingers
**toe** /təʊ/ *n* one of the five separate parts at the end of your foot
**toothache** /ˈtuːθeɪk/ *n* a pain in one or more of your teeth

## ILLNESSES AND INJURIES: VERBS

**be sick/ill** /biː sɪk/ɪl/ *phr* not feel well, or be suffering from a disease
**break** /breɪk/ *v* to damage a bone in your arm/leg, etc.
**catch** /kætʃ/ *v* to get an illness or disease
**cut** /kʌt/ *v* to injure yourself on a sharp object that makes you bleed
**feel better** /fiːl ˈbetə/ *phr* to feel healthy, or less sick than before
**feel ill** /fiːl ɪl/ *phr* to not feel well
**feel sore** /fiːl sɔː/ *phr* If a part of your body feels sore, it is painful, especially when you touch it or move it.
**get** /get/ *v* If you get an illness or a disease, you start to develop it or suffer from it.
**get better** /get ˈbetə/ *phr* to be well again after being ill
**have** /hæv/ *v* If you have an illness or disease, you are suffering from it.
**hurt** /hɜːt/ *v* If a part of your body hurts, it is painful.
**injure** /ˈɪndʒə/ *v* to hurt a person, animal, or part of your body

# UNIT 12

## ANIMALS

**ant** /ænt/ *n* a small, black or red insect that lives in groups under the ground
**bat** /bæt/ *n* a small animal like a mouse with wings that flies at night
**bee** /biː/ *n* a flying insect that has a yellow and black body and makes honey
**butterfly** /ˈbʌtəflaɪ/ *n* an insect with large, patterned wings
**deer** /dɪə/ *n* a large, wild animal that that has antlers (= long horns) if it is male
**donkey** /ˈdɒŋki/ *n* an animal that looks like a small horse with long ears
**eagle** /ˈiːgl/ *n* a large, wild bird with a big, curved beak, that hunts smaller animals
**fly** /flaɪ/ *n* a small flying insect with two wings
**fox** /fɒks/ *n* a wild animal like a dog with red-brown fur, a pointed nose, and a long, thick tail
**frog** /frɒg/ *n* a small, green animal with long back legs for jumping that lives in or near water
**mosquito** /mɒˈskiːtəʊ/ *n* a small flying insect that drinks your blood
**shark** /ʃɑːk/ *n* a large fish with very sharp teeth
**wolf** /wʊlf/ *n* a wild animal like a large dog
**worm** /wɜːm/ *n* a small creature with a long, thin, soft body and no legs that lives in the ground

# VOCABULARY LIST

### ADVERBS OF PROBABILITY

**definitely** /'defɪnətli/ *adv* used to emphasise that there is no doubt that something is true, or will happen
**definitely not** /'defɪnətli nɒt/ *adv* used to emphasise that there is no doubt that something is not true, or will not happen
**perhaps** /pə'hæps/ *adv* possibly
**probably** /'prɒbəbli/ *adv* used to mean that something is very likely

## UNIT 13

### ADJECTIVES: MOODS AND FEELINGS

**amazed** /ə'meɪzd/ *adj* very surprised
**brave** /breɪv/ *adj* showing no fear of dangerous or difficult situations
**confused** /kən'fjuːzd/ *adj* unable to think clearly or to understand something
**disappointed** /ˌdɪsə'pɔɪntɪd/ *adj* unhappy because someone or something was not as good as you hoped or expected, or because something did not happen
**embarrassed** /ɪm'bærəst/ *adj* feeling ashamed or shy
**exhausted** /ɪg'zɔːstɪd/ *adj* very tired
**grateful** /'greɪtfəl/ *adj* feeling or showing thanks
**hopeful** /'həʊpfəl/ *adj* feeling positive about a future event or situation
**proud** /praʊd/ *adj* feeling very pleased about something you have done, something you own, or someone you know
**relaxed** /rɪ'lækst/ *adj* feeling happy and comfortable because nothing is worrying you
**scared** /skeəd/ *adj* frightened or worried
**stressed** /strest/ *adj* worried and not able to relax

### ADJECTIVES: *-ED* OR *-ING*

**annoyed** /ə'nɔɪd/ *adj* slightly angry
**annoying** /ə'nɔɪɪŋ/ *adj* making you feel annoyed
**bored** /bɔːd/ *adj* feeling tired and unhappy because something is not interesting or because you have nothing to do
**boring** /'bɔːrɪŋ/ *adj* not interesting or exciting
**confused** /kən'fjuːzd/ *adj* not able to think clearly or understand something
**confusing** /kən'fjuːzɪŋ/ *adj* difficult to understand
**disappointed** /ˌdɪsə'pɔɪntɪd/ *adj* unhappy because something was not as good as you expected, or because something did not happen
**disappointing** /ˌdɪsə'pɔɪntɪŋ/ *adj* making you feel disappointed
**embarrassed** /ɪm'bærəst/ *adj* feeling ashamed or shy
**embarrassing** /ɪm'bærəsɪŋ/ *adj* making you feel embarrassed
**relaxed** /rɪ'lækst/ *adj* feeling happy and comfortable because nothing is worrying you
**relaxing** /rɪ'læksɪŋ/ *adj* making you feel relaxed
**tired** /taɪəd/ *adj* feeling that you want to rest or sleep
**tiring** /'taɪərɪŋ/ *adj* making you feel tired

## UNIT 14

### TV AND FILM

**action thriller** /'ækʃən 'θrɪlə/ *n* a film that has a lot of exciting action
**animation** /ˌænɪ'meɪʃən/ *n* a film or television programme containing moving drawings or models
**chat show** /'tʃæt ʃəʊ/ *n* a television or radio programme where people are asked questions about themselves
**comedy** /'kɒmədi/ *n* entertainment such as a film, play, etc. that is funny
**crime drama** /kraɪm 'drɑːmə/ *n* a film or television programme about solving a crime
**documentary** /ˌdɒkjə'mentəri/ *n* a film or television programme that gives facts about a real situation or real people
**horror film** /'hɒrə fɪlm/ *n* a film that entertains people by shocking or frightening them
**period drama** /'pɪəriəd 'drɑːmə/ *n* a film or television programme that happens in a particular historical period
**reality show** /ri'æləti ʃəʊ/ *n* a television programme about ordinary people who are filmed in real situations
**science fiction** /saɪəns 'fɪkʃən/ *n* a film, television programme or story about life in the future or in other parts of the universe
**soap opera** /səʊp 'ɒpərə/ *n* a series of television programmes that continues over a long period and is about the lives of a group of characters
**the news** /ðə njuːz/ *n* information about important events on television, radio, and in newspapers

### TALKING ABOUT FILMS AND SHOWS

**character** /'kærəktə/ *n* a person in a book, film, television programme, etc.
**clip** /klɪp/ *n* a short part of a film or television programme
**plot** /plɒt/ *n* the things that happen in a story
**review** /rɪ'vjuː/ *n* a report in a newspaper, magazine or programme that gives an opinion about a new book, film, etc.
**series** /'sɪəriːz/ *n* a group of television or radio programmes that have the same main characters or deal with the same subject
**soundtrack** /'saʊndtræk/ *n* the music used in a film or television programme
**trailer** /'treɪlə/ *n* short parts of a film or television programme which are shown in order to advertise it

# UNIT 15

## COMPUTER PHRASES

**delete a file** /dɪ'liːt ə faɪl/ *phr* to remove a file from your phone's, tablet's or computer's memory
**do a search** /duː ə sɜːtʃ/ *phr* to use a computer to find information, especially on the internet
**have a virus** /hæv ə 'vaɪərəs/ *phr* have a program on your computer that destroys or steals the information that is stored on it
**install an app** /ɪn'stɔːl ən æp/ *phr* put an application on a mobile phone, tablet, computer, etc.
**share links** /ʃeə 'lɪŋks/ *phr* to put links (= connections to other websites) on social media so that other people can see them
**upload photos/videos** /ʌp'ləʊd fəʊtəʊz/vɪdiəʊz/ *phr* to copy photos/videos from a mobile phone, tablet or computer to the internet
**download a podcast** /ˌdaʊn'ləʊd ə 'pɒdkɑːst/ *phr* to copy a podcast (= a radio programme) from the internet to a phone, tablet or computer

## PHRASAL VERBS: TECHNOLOGY

**look up** /lʊk 'ʌp/ *pv* to look at a book or computer in order to find information
**plug in** /plʌg 'ɪn/ *pv* to connect a piece of electrical equipment to an electricity supply
**shut down** /ʃʌt 'daʊn/ *pv* to turn off a large device, such as a computer
**switch off** /swɪtʃ 'ɒf/ *pv* to turn off a light, television, etc. by using a switch
**switch on** /swɪtʃ 'ɒn/ *pv* to turn on a light, television, etc. by using a switch
**take out** /teɪk 'aʊt/ *pv* to remove something from somewhere
**turn down** /tɜːn 'daʊn/ *pv* to reduce the level of sound or heat that a machine produces
**turn off** /tɜːn 'ɒf/ *pv* to move the switch on a machine, light, etc. so that it stops working, or to stop the supply of water, electricity, etc.
**turn on** /tɜːn 'ɒn/ *pv* to move the switch on a machine, light, etc. so that it starts working, or to start the supply of water, electricity, etc.
**turn up** /tɜːn 'ʌp/ *pv* to increase the level of sound or heat that a machine produces

# UNIT 16

## DOING EXPERIMENTS

**blow** /bləʊ/ *v* to force air out through your mouth
**boil** /bɔɪl/ *v* to cook food in water that is boiling (= 100° C or higher)
**cover** /'kʌvə/ *v* to put something over something else, in order to protect or hide it
**fill** /fɪl/ *v* to make a container or space full, or to become full
**pour** /pɔː/ *v* to make a liquid flow from or into a container
**rub** /rʌb/ *v* to press your hand or a cloth on a surface and move it backwards and forwards
**shake** /ʃeɪk/ *v* to make quick, short movements from side to side or up and down, or to make something or someone do this
**stir** /stɜː/ *v* to mix food or liquid by moving a spoon, or similar object, round and round in it
**tie** /taɪ/ *v* to fasten something with string, rope, etc.
**wrap** /ræp/ *v* to cover something or someone with paper, cloth, etc.

## PHRASAL VERBS: SCIENCE

**add up** /æd 'ʌp/ *pv* to put numbers together in order to reach a total
**blow up** /bləʊ 'ʌp/ *pv* to make something explode
**carry out** /kæri 'aʊt/ *pv* to do or complete something, especially something that you have said you would do or that you have been told to do
**cut up** /kʌt 'ʌp/ *pv* to cut something into pieces
**take away** /teɪk ə'weɪ/ *pv* to remove a number from another number
**work out** /wɜːk 'aʊt/ *pv* to understand something or decide something after thinking very carefully

# EP VOCABULARY LIST

## UNIT 17

### ARTS AND ENTERTAINMENT

**audience** /ˈɔːdiəns/ *n* the people who sit and watch a performance at a theatre, cinema, etc.
**biography** /baɪˈɒgrəfi/ *n* the story of a person's life written by another person
**director** /dɪˈrektə/ *n* someone who tells the actors in a film or play what to do
**gallery** /ˈgæləri/ *n* a room or building that is used for showing paintings and other art to the public
**novel** /ˈnɒvəl/ *n* a book that tells a story about imaginary people and events
**painter** /ˈpeɪntə/ *n* someone who paints pictures
**painting** /ˈpeɪntɪŋ/ *n* a picture that someone has painted
**poet** /ˈpəʊɪt/ *n* someone who writes poems
**poetry** /ˈpəʊɪtri/ *n* poems in general, or the writing of poetry
**sculpture** /ˈskʌlptʃə/ *n* a piece of art that is made from stone, wood, clay, etc.
**studio** /ˈstjuːdiəʊ/ *n* a room where an artist or photographer works
**writer** /ˈraɪtə/ *n* someone whose job is writing books, stories, articles, etc.

### ADJECTIVES: *-AL* AND *-FUL*

**central** /ˈsentrəl/ *adj* in the main part of a town or city
**cheerful** /ˈtʃɪəfəl/ *adj* happy
**colourful** /ˈkʌləfəl/ *adj* having bright colours
**historical** /hɪˈstɒrɪkəl/ *adj* relating to events or people in the past, or the study of history
**natural** /ˈnætʃərəl/ *adj* If you have a natural characteristic, it is something you have been born with.
**original** /əˈrɪdʒənəl/ *adj* special and interesting because of not being the same as others
**painful** /ˈpeɪnfəl/ *adj* causing physical pain
**peaceful** /ˈpiːsfəl/ *adj* quiet and calm
**political** /pəˈlɪtɪkəl/ *adj* relating to or involved in politics
**stressful** /ˈstresfʊl/ *adj* making you stressed
**successful** /səkˈsesfəl/ *adj* having achieved a lot or made a lot of money through your work

## UNIT 18

### JOBS

**architect** /ˈɑːkɪtekt/ *n* someone who designs buildings
**babysitter** /ˈbeɪbisɪtə/ *n* someone who takes care of your child while you are out
**builder** /ˈbɪldə/ *n* someone who makes or repairs buildings as a job
**coach** /kəʊtʃ/ *n* someone whose job is to teach people to improve at a sport, skill, or school subject
**firefighter** /ˈfaɪəfaɪtə/ *n* someone whose job is to stop fires burning
**hairdresser** /ˈheəˌdresə/ *n* someone whose job is to wash, cut, colour, etc. people's hair
**journalist** /ˈdʒɜːnəlɪst/ *n* someone whose job is writing for newspapers, magazines, television or radio
**lawyer** /ˈlɔɪə/ *n* someone whose job is to understand the law and deal with legal situations
**pharmacist** /ˈfɑːməsɪst/ *n* someone who is trained to prepare or sell medicines
**politician** /ˌpɒlɪˈtɪʃən/ *n* someone who works in politics, especially a member of the government
**presenter** /prɪˈzentə/ *n* someone who introduces a radio or television programme
**vet** /vet/ *n* someone whose job is to give medical care to animals that are sick or hurt

### SUFFIXES: *-ER*, *-OR*, *-IST*, *-IAN*

**actor** /ˈæktə/ *n* someone whose job is to perform in plays and films
**artist** /ˈɑːtɪst/ *n* someone who creates art, especially paintings and drawings
**blogger** /ˈblɒgə/ *n* a person who writes a blog
**cleaner** /ˈkliːnə/ *n* someone whose job is to clean houses, offices, public places, etc.
**comedian** /kəˈmiːdiən/ *n* someone who entertains people by telling jokes
**competitor** /kəmˈpetɪtə/ *n* a person, team, or company that is competing with others
**film director** /ˈfɪlm daɪrektə/ *n* a person who is in charge of making a film and tells the actors how to play their parts
**goalkeeper** /ˈgəʊlˌkiːpə/ *n* the player in a sport such as football who tries to stop the ball going into the goal
**guitarist** /gɪˈtɑːrɪst/ *n* someone who plays the guitar, especially as their job
**journalist** /ˈdʒɜːnəlɪst/ *n* someone whose job is writing for newspapers, magazines, television or radio
**musician** /mjuːˈzɪʃən/ *n* someone who plays a musical instrument, often as a job
**novelist** /ˈnɒvəlɪst/ *n* someone who writes novels
**politician** /ˌpɒlɪˈtɪʃən/ *n* someone who works in politics

**receptionist** /rɪ'sepʃənɪst/ *n* someone who works in a hotel or office building, answering the telephone and dealing with guests
**runner** /'rʌnə/ *n* someone who runs, usually in competitions
**scientist** /'saɪəntɪst/ *n* someone who studies science or works in science
**supporter** /sə'pɔːtə/ *n* someone who supports a particular idea, group or person
**teacher** /'tiːtʃə/ *n* someone whose job is to teach in a school, college, etc.
**vegetarian** /ˌvedʒɪ'teəriən/ *n* someone who does not eat meat or fish
**visitor** /'vɪzɪtə/ *n* someone who visits a person or place

# UNIT 19

## THINGS THAT YOU READ

**advert** /'ædvɜːt/ *n* an advertisement (= a picture, short film, etc. that is designed to persuade people to buy or do something)
**article** /'ɑːtɪkl/ *n* a piece of writing in a magazine, newspaper, etc.
**brochure** /'brəʊʃə/ *n* a thin book with pictures and information, usually advertising something
**e-book** /'iːbʊk/ *n* a book that is published in electronic form, for example on the internet or on a disk, and not printed on paper
**graphic novel** /'græfɪk 'nɒvəl/ *n* a book containing a long story told mostly in pictures but with some writing
**note** /nəʊt/ *n* a short piece of writing
**notice** /'nəʊtɪs/ *n* a sign giving information about something
**paper** /'peɪpə/ *n* thin, flat material used for writing on, covering things in, etc.
**poster** /'pəʊstə/ *n* a large, printed picture or notice that you put on a wall, in order to decorate a place or to advertise something
**sticker** /'stɪkə/ *n* a piece of paper or plastic with writing or a picture on it that you stick onto a surface

## *SAY*, *SPEAK*, *TALK* AND *TELL*

**say** /seɪ/ *v* to speak words
**speak a language** /spiːk ə 'læŋgwɪdʒ/ *phr* to be able to say things in a language
**talk** /tɔːk/ *v* to say things to someone
**tell** /tel/ *v* to say something to someone, usually giving them information

# UNIT 20

## COLLOCATIONS: THINKING

**cross your mind** /krɒs jə maɪnd/ *phr* If an idea crosses your mind, you think about it for a short time.
**give someone a hint** /gɪv 'sʌmwʌn ə hɪnt/ *phr* to give someone a piece of advice that helps them do something
**have a thought** /hæv ə θɔːt/ *phr* to have an idea suddenly
**have second thoughts** /hæv 'sekənd θɔːts/ *phr* to change your opinion about something or start to doubt it
**lose your concentration** /luːz jə ˌkɒnsən'treɪʃən/ *phr* to stop being able to think only about the thing you are doing
**make up your mind** /meɪk ʌp jə maɪnd/ *phr* to make a decision
**use your imagination** /juːz jər ɪˌmædʒɪ'neɪʃən/ *phr* to create ideas or pictures in your mind

## *LOOK (AT)*, *SEE*, *WATCH*

**look (at)** /'lʊk (ət)/ *v* to turn your eyes in the direction of something or someone so that you can see them
**see** /siː/ *v* to notice people and things with your eyes
**watch** /wɒtʃ/ *v* to look at something for a period of time

# GRAMMAR REFERENCE AND PRACTICE

## UNIT 1 PRESENT SIMPLE AND CONTINUOUS

### Present simple

- The present simple has two forms.

| I, You, We, They | get, study, watch, go | |
|---|---|---|
| He, She, It | + -s | gets |
| | or + -es | watches, goes |
| | or -~~y~~ + -ies | studies |

- We use *do/does not* + infinitive to make negatives.

| I, You, We, They | don't get, study, watch, go |
|---|---|
| He, She, It | doesn't get, study, watch, go |

- We use *do/does* + infinitive to make questions.

| Do | I, you, we, they | get, study, watch, go? |
|---|---|---|
| Does | he, she, it | get, study, watch, go? |

We use the present simple for:

- things that happen regularly.
  *I **walk** to school with a friend every day.*
  *My sister **doesn't go** to the sports club very often.*
  *What **do** you **do** on Sundays?*
- facts.
  *We **live** near my grandparents.*
  *The weather **doesn't get** very cold here.*
- verbs called **state verbs** (we don't normally use these verbs in a continuous form) which describe what we think or feel.
  ***believe, hate, know, like, love, mean, need, own, prefer, understand, want***
  *Mike **knows** the answer to your question.*
  *Alice **doesn't understand** what you want.*
  *I **don't remember** your address.*
  *What **does** this word **mean**?*
  ***Does** your teacher **own** a sports car?*

### Practice

**1 Complete the sentences. Use the present simple form of the verbs.**

1 ________ (you / prefer) volleyball or basketball?
2 Angelo never ________ (choose) sandwiches for lunch because he ________ (not like) bread.
3 We ________ (not see) our cousins very often because they ________ (live) in America.
4 Where ________ (he / go) after school?
5 We ________ (not want) to go home.
6 Sara ________ (not play) football but she ________ (watch) it on TV.
7 ________ (he / know) the time?
8 Emma ________ (study) French.

### Present continuous

- We use *am, are, is* + *-ing* to make the present continuous.

| I | am ('m) | playing. |
|---|---|---|
| You, We, They | are ('re) | working. |
| He, She, It | is ('s) | helping. |

- We use *'m not, aren't, isn't* to make negatives.

| I | 'm not | working. |
|---|---|---|
| They | aren't | helping. |
| She | isn't | playing. |

- We use *am, are, is* to make questions.

| Am | I | helping? |
|---|---|---|
| Are | you | working? |
| Is | he | playing? |

We use the present continuous for:

- something that is happening now or around now.
  *We**'re doing** our homework.* (= We're in the middle of it now.)
- temporary situations.
  *I**'m helping** my dad in his office this week.* (= I don't help him every week.)
- future plans.
  *They**'re playing** table tennis after school.* (= They plan to play table tennis.)

### Practice

**2 Complete the sentences. Use the present continuous form of the verbs.**

1 I ________ (cycle) to the beach with some friends next weekend.
2 My brother ________ (not watch) sport on TV this week because of his exams.
3 **A:** What ________ (you do) at the moment?
**B:** We ________ (watch) a nature film because we ________ (study) insects at school now.

**3 Choose the correct form of the verbs.**

[1] *I sit / I'm sitting* on the bus with my friends. [2] *We go / We're going* to the match in London. Our team [3] *plays / is playing* in the final this afternoon, so we're very excited. Our team [4] *doesn't play / isn't playing* in the final very often, but this season [5] *they play / they're playing* really well. [6] *I believe / I'm believing* they can win. After the match [7] *we have / we're having* dinner in London. [8] *I want / I'm wanting* to go to a restaurant near the stadium but [9] *they get / they're getting* very busy on match days, so [10] *we eat / we're eating* at a place in another part of the city.

# UNIT 2 PAST SIMPLE

## Regular verbs

- The past simple of regular verbs is verb + **-ed**.
- Verbs ending consonant + *-y* change *-y* to **-ied**.
- It is the same for *I*, *you*, *he*, *she*, *it*, *we* and *they*.
  *I **looked***  *He **watched***  *We **studied***  *They **played***

## Irregular verbs

- The past simple of irregular verbs has different forms.
- They are the same for *I, you, he, she, it, we* and *they*.

| | | | | | |
|---|---|---|---|---|---|
| buy | → | bought | make | → | made |
| do | → | did | meet | → | met |
| feel | → | felt | put | → | put |
| get | → | got | run | → | ran |
| give | → | gave | say | → | said |
| go | → | went | take | → | took |
| have | → | had | think | → | thought |
| know | → | knew | wear | → | wore |

***See page 158 for a list of irregular verbs.***

## Regular and irregular verbs: negatives and questions

- We use ***didn't** (**did not**)* + verb to make negatives with all verbs in the past simple.

| | | |
|---|---|---|
| I, You, He, She, It, We, They | didn't | **buy** it. |
| | | **get** it. |
| | | **look**. |

- We use ***did*** + verb to make questions with all verbs in the past simple.

| | | |
|---|---|---|
| **Did** | I, you, he, she, it, we, they | **buy** it? |
| | | **get** it? |
| | | **look**? |

## *be*

- The verb ***be*** has two forms in the past simple.

| | | |
|---|---|---|
| I, He, She, It | **was/wasn't** | **Was she?** |
| You, We, They | **were/weren't** | **Were you?** |

- We use the past simple to talk about finished past actions, feelings and states.
  *I **had** coffee with some friends.*
  *I **didn't eat** anything.*
  ***Did** your sister **enjoy** the concert?*
- We often mention the time when things happened.
  *I **met** my mum **after school**.*
  *The teacher **didn't give** us any homework **yesterday**.*
  ***Did** you **go** out **last night**?*

## Practice

**1 Complete the conversation. Use the past simple form of the verbs.**

**Lara:** I [1] ______ One Direction at a concert last Saturday. (see)
**Kay:** No! Really? Where [2] ______ it? (be)
**Lara:** In Glasgow.
**Kay:** [3] ______ by train or on the bus? (you / go)
**Lara:** Neither. I [4] ______ by car. (go) The chauffeur [5] ______ us right to the door. (drive)
**Kay:** A chauffeur? That's amazing. So, what [6] ______? (you / wear)
**Lara:** Jeans and a top and my new necklace.
**Kay:** Cool! How many people [7] ______ at the concert? (be)
**Lara:** About ten thousand.
**Kay:** Where [8] ______? (you / sit)
**Lara:** In the front row.
**Kay:** What? How much [9] ______? (your ticket / cost)
**Lara:** I [10] ______ for it. (not pay) I [11] ______ it in a competition. (win)
**Kay:** Wow! You [12] ______ (be) lucky!

**2 Make sentences in the past simple.**

1. she / be / late again?
   ______
2. I / not like / Andrea's new dress
   ______
3. we / sleep / really well last night
   ______
4. you / find / my bag?
   ______
5. he / wear / his new trainers
   ______
6. they / not know / about Bill Haley and the Comets
   ______

**3 Complete the text. Use the verbs in the box in the past simple.**

| | | | |
|---|---|---|---|
| be | not be | catch | come |
| decide | not eat | have | know |
| start | want | walk | |

My friend Callum and I [1] ______ into town yesterday evening. We [2] ______ to buy some trainers but there [3] ______ any good ones. Callum [4] ______ a good café so we [5] ______ to try that. We [6] ______ some drinks there but the food [7] ______ very expensive so we [8] ______ anything. We [9] ______ a bus home because it [10] ______ to rain when we [11] ______ out of the café.

# GRAMMAR REFERENCE AND PRACTICE

## UNIT 3 COMPARATIVES AND SUPERLATIVES

To make comparative and superlative adjectives:

- with one-syllable adjectives, add *-er* and *-est*.
- with adjectives ending in *-e*, add *-r* and *-st*.
  *new newer (the) newest*
  *nice nicer (the) nicest*
- with one-syllable adjectives ending in vowel + consonant, we usually double the consonant.
  *big bigger (the) biggest*
- with two-syllable adjectives ending in *-y*, change *-y* to *-i* and add *-er* and *-est*.
  *funny funnier (the) funniest*
- with other adjectives of two or more syllables, we usually use ***more*** and ***the most***.
  *interesting more interesting (the) most interesting*
  *beautiful more beautiful (the) most beautiful*
- Some adjectives are irregular.
  *good better (the) best*
  *bad worse (the) worst*

### Comparative structures

- To compare two people or things in a positive way, we can use a comparative adjective + ***than***.
  *Your laptop is **faster than** mine.*
  *The girls were **more friendly than** the boys.*
- To say two people or things are not the same, we can use ***not as*** (adjective) ***as***.
  *My laptop **isn't as fast as** yours.*
  *The boys **weren't as friendly as** the girls.*

### Superlative structures

- We often use ***the*** before superlative adjectives.
  *This laptop is **the fastest** in the shop.*
  *The Brazilians were **the most friendly**.*

### Practice

**1 Complete the sentences with the comparative form of the adjectives. Add *than* if it is necessary.**

1 I usually do my homework in the school library because my home internet is ________ (slow) my school's and my house is ________ (noisy).
2 Exams these days are ________ (hard) they were in the past, but the preparation classes are ________ (good).
3 Most teenagers prefer to wear casual clothes, partly because they're ________ (fashionable) these days and also because they're ________ (cheap) formal clothes.
4 I usually take the bus to school. It's ________ (fast) walking and it's also ________ (warm).
5 Stop worrying! Katy isn't ________ (attractive) you and she isn't ________ (funny) you either.
6 The weather forecast is for today to be ________ (wet) and ________ (windy) yesterday.
7 Now I'm even ________ (confused). Your brother's explanation was ________ (complicated) the original question.
8 We're looking for something a bit ________ (bright) and ________ (colourful), sorry.

**2 Complete the second sentences using *not as … as*.**

1 Football is more tiring than yoga.
Yoga ________
2 Electric cars are cleaner than petrol cars.
Petrol cars ________
3 Most ballet dancers are fitter than many athletes.
Many athletes ________
4 Salads are healthier than burgers.
Burgers ________
5 I had more work last week than this week.
I don't have ________

**3 Complete the sentences. Use *the* + the superlative form of the adjectives.**

1 This website has ________ (cool) music and it's also ________ (cheap).
2 My brother's ________ (good) student in his class but he is ________ (bad) at sport.
3 The beach road is ________ (safe) for cycling and it has ________ (interesting) views.
4 When we go on holiday, my bag is always ________ (light) and my sister's is always ________ (big) and ________ (heavy).
5 This is a competition to find ________ (brilliant) and ________ (creative) people in the music industry.
6 It's freezing! Let's go to your house. It's ________ (close) and it's always ________ (cosy) in winter.
7 Simon really is ________ (untidy) person I've ever met. But he's also ________ (charming).
8 'You're ________ (sociable) person I know. What good cafés can we go to?'
'Let's go to CoCo's. It's ________ (lively) place I know.'

# UNIT 4 PAST CONTINUOUS

- The past continuous is similar to the present continuous, but uses the past of the verb *be*.
- We use *was* or *were* + the *-ing* form of the verb.

| I, He, She, It | was | running. |
|---|---|---|
| You, We, They | were | talking. |

- We use *wasn't (was not)* and *weren't (were not)* to make negatives.

| I, He, She, It | wasn't | running. |
|---|---|---|
| You, We, They | weren't | talking. |

- We make questions with *was* or *were*.

| Was | he | running? |
|---|---|---|
| Were | you | talking? |

- We use the past continuous to talk about actions and events in progress at a particular time in the past.
  *I **was chatting** to my friends online.*
  *We **were texting** my mum.*
  *It **wasn't raining** at that time.*
  *They **weren't listening** to me.*
  ***Was** it **snowing**?*
  ***Were** the boys **watching** us?*

## Practice

**1 Complete the sentences. Use the past continuous form of the verbs.**

1 I ________ (dream) about my holiday last night.
2 How many hours ________ (you / play) tennis?
3 You ________ (not watch) television in the kitchen.
4 ________ (you / talk) to your brother at lunchtime?
5 Belinda ________ (not do) her homework in front of the television.
6 The cat ________ (sit) on the car.
7 ________ (we / use) the wrong kind of paint on that wall?
8 The students ________ (chat) quietly in the computer room.
9 Charlie ________ (not look) at the cars, he ________ (shout) at his friends on the beach.
10 I ________ (not ask) your opinion, I ________ (explain) my plan.

**2 Complete the text. Use the past continuous form of the verbs in the box.**

| argue | lie | listen | not listen | look |
|---|---|---|---|---|
| make | not sell | tell | wait | |

It was a peaceful summer afternoon in the park. The students [1] ________ on the grass. Derek and Armando [2] ________ about football, as usual. Henri [3] ________ a story about his holiday in Florida. Penelope and Doris [4] ________ to him and Doris [5] ________ a necklace of wooden beads. Margherita [6] ________ to anyone. She [7] ________ at the ice cream van which was near the gate. Twenty people [8] ________ to buy an ice cream. There was a burger van as well, but the owner [9] ________ many burgers.

**3 Look at Exercise 2 and write questions for the answers, using the past continuous.**

0 Where *were the students lying?*
On the grass.
1 What ________________?
Football, as usual.
2 What ________________?
His holiday in Florida.
3 What ________________?
Listening to Henri's story.
4 What ________________?
A necklace.
5 Who ________________?
No one.
6 How many people ________________?
Twenty.

**4 Read this paragraph and compare it with Exercise 2. Some of the facts are wrong. Correct them by writing sentences with negative verbs.**

The students were sitting on the grass. Derek and Armando were arguing about music. Henri was describing the scenery in Florida. Penelope and Doris were waving at Henri and Doris was making a necklace. Margherita was taking a photo of the other students.

0 The students *weren't sitting on the grass, they were lying on it.*
1 Derek and Armando ________________
2 ________________
3 ________________
4 ________________

# GRAMMAR REFERENCE AND PRACTICE

## UNIT 5 PAST SIMPLE AND CONTINUOUS

FOR THE PAST CONTINUOUS FORM, SEE GRAMMAR REFERENCE AND PRACTICE, UNIT 4, PAGE 141

- We use the past continuous to talk about actions and events in progress at a particular time in the past.
  *At lunchtime, I **was texting** a friend.*
  *It **was raining**.*
  *The students **weren't playing** computer games.*
  ***Was** the teacher **riding** her motorbike?*

SEE UNIT 2, PAGE 139 FOR THE PAST SIMPLE FORM

- We use the past simple to talk about:
  - completed actions in the past, often with the time when they happened.
    *I **met** my friends at the shopping centre yesterday.*
    *We **didn't buy** anything, but we **looked** at some new phones.*
  - two or more actions which happened after one another.
    *Amy **showed** me her new bag and then I **went** home.*
    *When Jules **lost** his key, we all **helped** to look for it.*
    *I **finished** my drink and **washed** the glass.*
- We use the past simple and past continuous together when a shorter action in the past interrupted an action or event that was in progress. We use the past simple for the action that interrupts and the past continuous for the action that was in progress.
  *I **was chatting** with some friends when I **saw** you on the bus.*
  *The singer **threw** his guitar at some fans because they **were annoying** him.*
  *She **didn't eat** anything for lunch because she **was feeling** nervous.*

### Practice

**1** **Complete the sentences with the verbs in the box.**

| | | |
|---|---|---|
| emailed | talked | were talking |
| watched | was watching | waited |
| were emailing | were waiting | |

1 I ________ the TV when the phone rang.
2 I got to the airport and ________ for my friend to arrive.
3 I ________ a film, and then I went to sleep.
4 We chatted while we ________ for the bus.
5 I ________ to Ben two days ago.
6 They ________ to each other when I saw them.
7 She ________ me ten times yesterday!
8 When we ________ each other, we sent lots of jokes and photos.

**2** **Choose the correct form of the verbs.**

1 I *didn't hear / wasn't hearing* Elinor come into my room because I *wore / was wearing* headphones.
2 We *all celebrated / were all celebrating* when we *got / were getting* our exam results.
3 My grandad *found / was finding* some gold coins when he *worked / was working* in his garden.
4 I *broke / was breaking* my arm when I *learned / was learning* to ski.
5 My mum *drove / was driving* home from work when she *got / was getting* my text, so she couldn't answer it.
6 When Sonja *opened / was opening* the garage door she *discovered / was discovering* her new bike.
7 I *chatted / was chatting* to a friend on the phone when the train *went / was going* into a tunnel and I never *heard / was hearing* the end of her story.
8 Tomas *emailed / was emailing* me twice while I *mended / was mending* my bike but I *didn't check / wasn't checking* my laptop until later.

**3** **Complete the story. Use the past simple or past continuous form of the verbs.**

Marcus Jones was very lucky last weekend. He [0] *was cycling* (cycle) home from the city centre. It [1] ________ (snow) and the road was icy. Suddenly his bike [2] ________ (slip) and he [3] ________ (fall off) onto the pavement. He [4] ________ (pick up) his bike off the road when he [5] ________ (see) something in the sky. It [6] ________ (move) towards him very fast. He [7] ________ (jump) back onto the pavement and the object [8] ________ (hit) the road. It was a piece of a meteorite. 'I was glad I [9] ________ (not stand) there!' he [10] ________ (tell) journalists later.

**4** **Make sentences. Use the past continuous or past simple form of the verbs.**

1 I / visit / my friends. Afterwards, I / take / the bus home.
________
2 Luke / walk / into the door because he / not look / ahead.
________
3 It / snow / at lunchtime, so I / not go / for a walk.
________
4 I / not be / hungry, so I / not have / anything to eat.
________
5 My sister / crash / into a traffic light when she / ride / her scooter.
________
6 I / think / about the holidays. Then suddenly, I / realise / the time.
________

# UNIT 6 SOME/ANY, MUCH/MANY, A LOT OF, A FEW / A LITTLE

## *some*/ *any*

- We use ***some*** and ***any*** with plural countable nouns and uncountable nouns.
- We use ***some*** in positive sentences.
  *We bought **some petrol** and **some sweets** at the garage.*
- We use ***any*** in questions and negative sentences.
  *I haven't got **any homework** tonight.*
  *Are there **any** good **clubs** near here?*
  *Is there **any fruit** in the fridge?*
  *They **don't** want **any salad**.*

## *much*/ *many* and *a lot of*

- We use these words to talk about large amounts.
- We use ***a lot of*** with plural countable nouns and with uncountable nouns, in positive and negative sentences and questions.
  *I took **a lot of photos** last night.*
  *There's **a lot of milk** in the fridge.*
  *We **haven't** got **a lot of** money for clothes.*
- We often use ***many*** with plural countable nouns in questions and negatives.
  *We **haven't** got **many photos** of our holiday.*
  *Are **many people** coming to your party?*
- We often use ***much*** with uncountable nouns in negative sentences and questions.
  *I **haven't** got **much time** to help you.*
  *Is there **much traffic** on this road at night?*

## *a few* / *a little*

- We use these words to talk about small amounts.
- We use ***a few*** and ***a little*** in positive sentences and questions. We don't use these words in negative sentences.
- We use ***a few*** with plural countable nouns.
  *I invited **a few friends** to a barbecue on my birthday.*
  *Do you want **a few grapes** with the cheese?*
- We use ***a little*** with uncountable nouns.
  *I'd like **a little sugar** in my coffee, please.*
  *Have you got **a little time** to spare?*

## Practice

**1 Match the sentence halves.**

1 Do you need
2 Tom hasn't got
3 I need
4 Is there
5 I had
6 I didn't have

a any time to phone me today.
b any news about the date of the exam?
c any time to work yesterday.
d any help?
e some good news yesterday.
f some more time.

**2 Complete the sentences with *some* or *any*.**

1 Don't make ________ noise near the exam room.
2 My brother had ________ problems with his phone, so he couldn't text me.
3 Did you have ________ help when you made that cake?
4 There isn't ________ rubbish in the bin.
5 There's ________ fruit in the cupboard if you want it.
6 Were there ________ children at the party?

**3 Choose the correct words.**

1 I didn't play *many* / *much* matches last season.
2 I haven't got *a little* / *much* paper, so I need to buy some soon.
3 My earphones aren't working, so I can't listen to *some* / *any* music on the bus.
4 We had *a little* / *a few* problems with the password but in the end we remembered it.
5 I've got *a lot of* / *much* cousins in Germany.
6 How *much* / *many* students are there at your school?
7 I found *some* / *much* information for my project online.
8 We haven't got *any* / *some* time for shopping today.
9 Did you spend *many* / *a lot of* time at the park?
10 There's *a little* / *a few* space left for your name at the bottom of the page.

**4 Complete the sentences with *much*, *many*, *a few* or *a little*.**

1 There isn't ________ traffic at this time in the morning, so it only takes ________ minutes to get to the centre.
2 I only have ________ money with me, so I can't buy ________ food.
3 Did you have ________ trouble finding the address you needed?
4 We've got ________ exercises to do for homework but they won't take ________ time.
5 I made ________ phone calls about the screen problems with your tablet but I didn't get ________ helpful answers.
6 Were there ________ cars on the road this morning?
7 We only had ________ time at the party but we still made ________ new friends.
8 'Have you got ________ sandwiches left?' 'Yes, there are ________.'
9 There are too ________ people in this room. There isn't ________ space here.
10 We haven't got ________ time left, so we need to leave in ________ minutes.

# GRAMMAR REFERENCE AND PRACTICE

## UNIT 7 *HAVE TO* AND *MUST*; *SHOULD*

### *have to* and *must*

- ***Have to*** changes form.
  *I **have to go** to school.*
  *We **don't have to go** in the car.*
  *You **had to go** to school.*
  *She **has to be** home by 10 pm.*
  *He **doesn't have to do** any homework today.*
  *They **didn't have to clean** the car.*
  We don't use contractions in the positive:
  ~~*You've to go. He's to stay.*~~
- ***Must*** has only one form. There is no past tense of ***must***. We use the past form ***had to***.

| I, You, He, She, We, They | **must catch** the early bus. |
|---|---|
| | **mustn't be** late. |

- We use ***must*** and ***have to*** to talk about rules and things that are necessary.
  *You **must be** 18 to see that film.*
  *He **has to practise** the guitar every day.*
- In the past tense we use ***had to***. There is no past form of ***must***.
  *You **had to be** 18 to see that film.*
  *He **had to practise** the guitar every day.*
- We use ***mustn't*** when something isn't allowed.
  *I **mustn't sleep** in class.*
  *You **mustn't read** that letter.*
- ***Don't/Didn't have to*** means that it is/was not necessary to do something.
  *She **doesn't have to answer** that email.*
  *I **didn't have to do** a test.*

### *should* and *shouldn't*

- ***Should*** has only one form.

| I, You, He, She, We, They | **should tidy** the living room. |
|---|---|
| | **shouldn't** make a mess. |

- We use ***should*** when we think it is a good idea to do something.
  *I **should buy** a present for my mum.*
  *They **should build** a new sports centre.*
- We use ***shouldn't*** when we think it isn't a good idea to do something.
  *You **shouldn't do** your homework in front of the TV.*
  *We **shouldn't eat** too many chips.*
- We use ***should*** in questions when we ask for advice.
  *What **should** I **say** in my interview?*
  *Which shoes **should** I **wear** with this dress?*

### Practice

**1** Choose the correct verbs.

OUTDOOR ADVENTURE CAMP

**Welcome!**

**PLEASE READ THIS NOTICE CAREFULLY.**

There are eight different activities to choose from. You 1 *should / don't have to* look at the list of activities for the week and decide which ones you want to do. You can choose to do something different every day. You 2 *must / should* talk to your friends before you sign up if you want to do the same things.

You 3 *shouldn't / must* try at least three different activities in the week but you 4 *don't have to / must* try everything. You 5 *mustn't / should* sign up for activities before breakfast every day.

You 6 *don't have to / mustn't* miss the safety lesson before each new activity. You 7 *should / have to* ask a teacher if you aren't sure what to do.

**2** **Rewrite the sentences, using the correct form of *must, have to* and *should.* For one sentence two of these verbs are correct. Which sentence is it?**

1. We're not allowed to text our friends in lessons.
   We ..............................
2. It's a good idea to read through your work before you show it to anyone.
   You ..............................
3. My brother can wear any clothes he likes to school.
   He .............. school uniform.
4. Can you advise me which phone to buy?
   Which phone ..............................?
5. It wasn't necessary to book seats for the concert.
   We ..............................
6. It isn't very sensible to wear your best shirt when you mend your bike.
   You ..............................
7. Seat belts are compulsory for both drivers and passengers.
   Both drivers and passengers ..............................

## UNIT 8 FUTURE: *BE GOING TO* AND PRESENT CONTINUOUS

### Present continuous for plans and arrangements

» FOR THE PRESENT CONTINUOUS FORM SEE GRAMMAR REFERENCE AND PRACTICE, UNIT 1, PAGE 138

- We use the present continuous, usually with the time mentioned, for definite plans we already know about.
  *I'm **flying** to Spain **at the weekend**.*
  *He's **not working next week**.*
  ***What time are** you **leaving**?*

### *be going to* for intentions

- We use ***am/is/are (not)*** + ***going to*** + verb to make the ***be going to*** future.
  *I'm going to run.*
  *We're going to finish.*
  *You're not going to win.*
  *They're not going to arrive.*
  ***Is** she **going to leave**?*
  ***Are** you **going to play**?*
- We use ***be going to***:
  - for things we intend to do in the future.
    *I'm **going to visit** Italy one day.*
    *We're **going to work** really hard.*
    *I'm **not going to eat** any more chocolate.*
  - for things we know are likely to happen.
    *You drive well now. I'm sure you're **going to pass** your driving test.*
    *Look at that blue sky! It's **not going to rain** today.*

### Practice

**1** **Choose the correct form of the verbs.**

1 The traffic is awful this evening. I'm sure *it's going to take* / *it's taking* hours to get home.
2 I can't come to the cinema with you on Saturday; it's my parents' wedding anniversary and *we're going to organise* / *we're organising* a big family party.
3 Look at the mess in this kitchen! *I'm going to get* / *I'm getting* really angry if you don't clean it up right now.
4 Mum really enjoyed that cake we had at my cousin's party. *I'm going to ask* / *I'm asking* my aunt how to make it.
5 *I'm going to take* / *I'm taking* my driving test on Monday morning, so *I'm going to do* / *I'm doing* lots of practice this weekend.
6 I can't wait to go on holiday! *We're catching* / *We're going to catch* the train from St Pancras at 9 am tomorrow. *We're going to play* / *We're playing* card games all the way to Paris.
7 Can you hear thunder? *It's going to rain* / *It's raining* soon.
8 *We're meeting* / *We're going to meet* in the library, after lunch.

**2** **Complete the conversation. Use the correct form of *be going to*.**

**A:** [1] ________ (you, go) to my cousin Felix's party?
**B:** Yes, I think so.
**A:** What [2] ________ (wear)?
**B:** I'm not sure. My blue dress, probably.
**A:** And which shoes?
**B:** Well, the weather forecast says it [3] ________ (be) hot so I [4] ________ (buy) some sandals.
**A:** [5] ________ (you, take) him a present?
**B:** I guess I should give him something.
**A:** I [6] ________ (give) him this belt.
**B:** Oh, that's cool. I know he [7] ________ (be) so pleased with it. But the problem is, I [8] ________ (not find) anything as good as that.
**A:** We can give it as a shared present, if you like.
**B:** Oh, that's great, thanks very much. But I [9] ________ (tell) him you found it for him.

**3** **Read the descriptions of the situations and complete the sentence about what is going to happen. Use *be going to* and the verb in brackets.**

1 A man is climbing out of a window with a bag in his hand. A police officer is watching him. She's waiting for him.
She ________ (arrest)
2 A boy is walking along the pavement. He's looking at a beautiful motorbike on the road. He doesn't know there's a rubbish bin two metres in front of him.
He ________ (fall over)
3 There are some sausages cooking in a frying pan but there's no one in the kitchen.
They ________ (burn)
4 A man is in bed. The people in the flat downstairs are talking loudly.
He ________ (not sleep) well.
5 A girl is singing on a TV talent show. All the judges are smiling and clapping.
She ________ (win)
6 A man and a woman are playing the guitar and drums on a TV talent show. One of the judges has his hands over his ears.
They ________ (not win)

# GRAMMAR REFERENCE AND PRACTICE

## UNIT 9 PRESENT PERFECT

- We form the present perfect of regular and irregular verbs with ***has/have*** + the past participle.
  *I, you, we, they **'ve / have (haven't) bought***
  ***Have** I, you, we, they **bought** ...?*
  *He, She, It **'s / has (hasn't) lived***
  ***Has** he, she, it **lived** ...?*
- In regular verbs the past participle looks the same as the past simple (verb + *-(e)d*).

| Verb | Past simple | Past participle |
|---|---|---|
| turn | turned | turned |
| like | liked | liked |

- In irregular verbs the past participle sometimes looks the same as the past simple and is sometimes different.

| Verb | Past simple | Past participle |
|---|---|---|
| | The same | |
| make | made | made |
| find | found | found |
| | Different | |
| be | was/were | been |
| do | did | done |
| break | broke | broken |
| know | knew | known |

SEE PAGE 158 FOR A LIST OF IRREGULAR VERBS

- We use the present perfect to talk about experiences in the past which have some link to the present.
  *We**'ve spent** all our money.* (= We haven't got any now.)
  *We **haven't eaten** lunch.* (= We're hungry.)
  ***Have** you **visited** Paris?* (= Do you know Paris?)

### *been* and *gone*

- The verb ***go*** has two forms in the present perfect: ***have gone*** and ***have been***. They have different meanings.
- ***Have / Has gone*** means that someone is in another place.
  *Tessa **has gone** to the club.* (= Tessa isn't here, she's at the club.)
  *Jack**'s gone** to the city centre.* (= He isn't here, he's in the city centre.)
- ***Have / Has been*** means that someone went to that place in the past but is not there now.
  *Tessa **has been** to the club.* (= Tessa visited the club some time in the past, but she isn't there now.)
  *Jack**'s been** to the city centre.* (= He's not there now. He was there some time before now.)

### *ever, never* and short answers

- We use ***ever*** and ***never*** with the present perfect to mean 'in your whole life' or 'not in your whole life'.
- We can use ***Yes, I have*** and ***No, I haven't*** to answer these questions.
  *Have you **ever** been to Lapland?*
  *Yes, I **have**.* (= some time before now)
  *No, I **haven't**.* (= he/she has **never** been to Lapland in his/her life)

### Practice

**1 Complete the sentences. Use the present perfect form of the verbs in the box and the words in brackets.**

| | | | | |
|---|---|---|---|---|
| beat | eat | fall | fly | forget |
| give | go | hurt | know | tear |
| text | write | | | |

1 Zoe ________ (not) anything all day. I'm going to make her a sandwich.
2 Yolanda ________ (never) a thank you letter to anyone.
3 Vincent and I ________ Tom all our lives.
4 Urs ________ (never) me at chess.
5 I ________ to Paris twice, but usually I go by train.
6 Olga ________ (not) me her number, so I ________ (not) her.
7 Nigel ________ off his bike. He ________ (not) himself but he ________ his best jeans.
8 Mark ________ to the sports club but he ________ his membership card. I hope they let him in without it.

**2 Complete the conversations. Use the present perfect form of the verbs.**

**A:** [1] ________ (you / finish) your history homework?
**B:** Not quite. I [2] ________ (find) three websites with the right sort of information but I [3] ________ (not read) it all.
**A:** Well, I [4] ________ (go) to the library and I [5] ________ (borrow) this old book for you.
**B:** Thanks, that's great.

**C:** [6] ________ (you / tidy) your room?
**D:** No, I [7] ________. I'm going to do it now.
**C:** But I [8] ________ (make) a pizza for our lunch. It's going to be cold before you can eat it.
**D:** That's OK. I [9] ________ (have) some chips, so I'm not really hungry.

**E:** Where [10] ________ (you / be)? The match starts in five minutes!
**F:** I [11] ________ (be) in that café. Look, I [12] ________ (buy) you some chocolate.
**E:** But I don't like chocolate. [13] ________ (you / ever / see) me eating chocolate?
**F:** Oh, sorry. No, I [14] ________.

## UNIT 10 PRESENT PERFECT AND PAST SIMPLE; *HOW LONG?* AND *FOR/SINCE*

### Present perfect

» FOR THE PRESENT PERFECT FORM SEE GRAMMAR REFERENCE AND PRACTICE, UNIT 9, PAGE 146

- We use the present perfect to talk about experiences in our life up to the present.
- We don't use past time phrases with the present perfect.
  *She's **seen** that film.*
  *They've **heard** that song.*
  *We **haven't visited** this museum.*
  ***Have** you **tried** Thai food?*

### Past simple

» SEE UNIT 2, PAGE 139 FOR THE PAST SIMPLE FORM

- We can use the past simple to say exactly when something happened.
  *She **saw** the film last week.*
  *They **heard** that song at a concert.*
  *We **visited** this museum last time we came to London.*
  ***Did** you **try** Thai food when you were in Bangkok?*

### *How long?* and *for/ since*

- We use *How long* with the present perfect to ask a question about a period of time up to now.
  ***How long have you lived** here?*
  ***How long have you known** your best friend?*
- We use *for* to introduce the length of time something lasted.
  ***for** ten years, **for** a long time, **for** six weeks*
- We use *since* to introduce when something began.
  ***since** six o'clock, **since** my birthday party, **since** last year*
- When there is a verb after *since*, it is in the past simple.
  *I have known him **since** I **was** eleven, **since** I **started** school, **since** I **arrived** in Madrid.*

### Practice

**1 Match the sentence halves.**

1 I went to Paris
2 I've been to France
  a two years ago.
  b twice in my life.

3 I've read two books
4 I read an interesting book
  a last week.
  b since the beginning of the month.

5 I've had a lot to eat
6 I ate a lot
  a yesterday.
  b so I won't eat any more.

**2 Choose the correct form of the verbs.**

1 I hope you're all hungry. *I've made / I made* a big paella and a salad.
2 Emerald *has gone / went* to the cinema with her friends. I'm not sure when she'll be home.
3 Gary *has cooked / cooked* a fantastic meal last night. I *haven't met / didn't meet* anyone who can cook as well as he can.
4 I don't know why Toby *hasn't come / didn't come* to see me. *I've asked / I asked* him yesterday to come as soon as possible.
5 My friends *haven't enjoyed / didn't enjoy* the trip to the beach at the weekend because the wind *has been / was* so cold.

**3 Complete the sentences with *for* or *since*.**

1 I've supported Liverpool ________ I was at primary school. They've always been a great team, although they haven't won the cup ________ quite a long time.
2 We haven't eaten meat ________ five years. It was a bit difficult at first but we've all been very healthy ________ we became vegetarians.
3 They've only owned that car ________ about three months but they've had two accidents ________ they bought it.
4 I'm so tired! I've cycled ten kilometres ________ breakfast and I've had all this shopping in my backpack ________ most of the time.
5 My dad hasn't seen his parents ________ the beginning of the year. They've been in Australia ________ six months, visiting my aunt and her family.

**4 Complete the text. Use the present perfect or the past simple form of the verbs.**

I [1] ________ (be) a member of the swimming team for two months. I [2] ________ (enjoy) swimming since I [3] ________ (be) small. Last year I [4] ________ (start) using the swimming pool at our local sports club and one day I [5] ________ (see) a notice about the team. The next week they were practising in the pool when I [6] ________ (arrive) and I [7] ________ (think) it looked like fun.
We train twice a week. I [8] ________ (not miss) any training sessions, although sometimes it's hard to find the time. When I [9] ________ (have) exams last summer I almost [10] ________ (give) up. But I'm so pleased I [11] ________ (not leave) because since then we [12] ________ (enter) three competitions and we [13] ________ (have) a lot of fun together.
Unfortunately, we [14] ________ (not win) any prizes for quite a long time.

# GRAMMAR REFERENCE AND PRACTICE

## UNIT 11 *WILL* AND *BE GOING TO*

### *will*

- We form the future with ***will/won't*** + verb.
  *We'**ll (will) write***
  *She **won't go***
  ***Will** they **want** … ?*
- We use ***will***:
  - for general predictions about the future.
    *People **will be** healthier.*
    *Medicines **won't cure** everything.*
    ***Will** everyone **live** longer?*
  - when we decide to do something while we are speaking.
    *I'**ll have** a cake with my coffee.*
    *I **won't wait** any longer.*

### *be going to*

» FOR THE FORM OF *BE GOING TO* SEE GRAMMAR REFERENCE AND PRACTICE, UNIT 8, PAGE 145

- We use ***be going to***:
  - to talk about something we have already decided to do.
    *Our teacher **is going to give** us the test results soon.*
    *I'**m not going to spend** a lot of money today.*
    *What **are we going to eat** tonight?*
  - to predict the future based on something we can see or know.
    *Business is good – we'**re going to be** rich!*
    *Look at the crowd round the table – the food'**s going to run out**.*

### Practice

**1 Choose the correct form of the verbs.**

1. Scientists are working on new crops that *will help / are going to help* to feed us all.
2. I can't meet you tomorrow. *I'll help / I'm going to help* my brother paint his bedroom.
3. This new bike *will save / is going to save* me lots of money on bus fares.
4. I've got a headache now but I think *I'll feel / I'm going to feel* OK when I get outdoors.
5. Please hurry up, the bus *will leave / is going to leave* any minute.
6. I must get another pen. This one *will run / is going to run* out of ink in a minute.
7. Some people say that air fares *will be / are going to be* much more expensive in the future.
8. We don't have much food at home. I think *I'll go / I'm going to go* to the shops this afternoon.

**2 Complete the conversation. Use the *will* or *be going to* form of the verbs.**

**Jane:** Hi, Angie. What are you doing?
**Angie:** I'm trying to pack, but I'm not getting on very well. I've got so much stuff, my case [1] ________ (be) too heavy.
**Jane:** Don't worry, I [2] ________ (help) you. I'm good at packing. What [3] ________ (do) on your holiday?
**Angie:** Oh, I [4] ________ (have) a good rest after my exams. I [5] ________ (lie) on the beach under an umbrella and listen to the waves.
**Jane:** OK. So you need a swimming costume. What else?
**Angie:** Well my dad wants to visit some ancient city, so probably I [6] ________ (walk) around there with him one day.
**Jane:** Right, shorts and a T-shirt and a pair of trainers. But what are all these heavy bottles?
**Angie:** Shampoo, shower gel, face cream …
**Jane:** I don't think you [7] ________ (use) that much in one week! I've got some small travel bottles. I [8] ________ (lend) them to you. They [9] ________ (not weigh) as much. Now, what about sun cream?
**Angie:** I've got that in my hand luggage, see?
**Jane:** But that tube's 120 ml. It's too big – the security people at the airport [10] ________ (take) it away from you. I [11] ________ (put) it in your suitcase.
**Angie:** Thanks. I hope we can have a holiday in this country next year. Then I [12] ________ (not care) about the weight of my bag!

**3 Write sentences using *will* or *be going to*.**

1. Lucy and Linda are running a race. Lucy is running very fast, Linda is tired.
   ________________ (win)
2. Jonah is on a boat. The sea is very rough. Jonah feels ill.
   ________________ (be sick)
3. Joe has got a difficult science project. His sister is good at science.
   ________________ (help)
4. Alicia and Paula are in a beauty salon preparing for a birthday party.
   ________________ (look / great)
5. Inez is cooking some burgers on a barbecue and talking to her friends at the same time.
   ________________ (burn)
6. Tomasz likes studying.
   ________________ (go / university)

# UNIT 12 MODALS OF PROBABILITY

- Modal verbs do not change form. Modal verbs of probability are always followed by another verb.

| | |
|---|---|
| I, You, He, She, It, We, They | **must** be tired. |
| | **might** die. |
| | **could** bite. |
| | **can't** exist. |

- To talk about something we think is certain, we use **must** + verb.
  *The explorers found two new species. They **must be** very excited.* (= I'm certain they're very excited.)
  *They've walked through the jungle for four days. They **must feel** tired.* (= I'm certain they feel tired.)
- To talk about something we think is possible, we use **might** or **could** + verb.
  *I've never seen an animal like this before. It **could be** / **might be** a new species.* (= Perhaps it's a new species.)
  *Other new species **could exist** in these mountains.* (= Perhaps other new species exist in these mountains.)
  *Don't touch it, it **might bite** you.* (= Perhaps it will bite you if you touch it.)
- To talk about something we think is impossible, we use **can't** + verb (**NOT** *mustn't* + verb).
  *I've seen a picture of this animal in an old book, so it **can't be** a new species.* (= I'm sure it isn't a new species.)
  *He's an intelligent person; he **can't believe** those silly stories!* (= I'm sure he doesn't believe those stories.)

## Practice

**1 Rewrite the underlined words in the sentences using *must*.**

1 Jon's gone out without a coat. I'm sure he's cold.
..........

2 I put the potatoes in the oven an hour ago. I'm certain they're ready to eat by now.
..........

3 I know this parcel is my new phone because I ordered it last week.
..........

4 My computer is very slow. I'm sure it's broken.
..........

**2 Rewrite the underlined words in the sentences using *might*.**

1 That cat wants something. Perhaps he's hungry.
..........

2 I don't know where my phone is. Perhaps it's in the car.
..........

3 It's possible that my teacher speaks three languages. I'm not sure.
..........

**3 Look at your answers to Exercise 2. Can you replace *might* with a different modal verb?**

**4 Rewrite the underlined words in the sentences using *can't*.**

1 This fish smells terrible. I'm certain it isn't fresh.
..........

2 I don't believe that coat belongs to you. It's much too small.
..........

3 It's not possible that you feel tired. You've been asleep for twelve hours!
..........

**5 Choose the correct verbs.**

*Liz has come to visit Becca on her birthday.*

**Becca:** Hi, Liz, come in. I'm having a great day. I've got lots of cards and some great presents. But what's this parcel? I didn't notice it before. Oh dear, there's no card with it.
**Liz:** Is it from your sister?
**Becca:** It [1] *can't be / must be* from her – I've already opened her present.
**Liz:** Is it from your parents?
**Becca:** No, it [2] *can't be / could be* from them either because they're giving me a new bike. We're going to get it later.
**Liz:** Is it from your grandparents?
**Becca:** It [3] *could be / must be* from them, I guess. They usually send me something, but I don't know how it got here.
**Liz:** Well, the card [4] *might be / can't be* inside.
**Becca:** Yes, but it's a strange shape. I wonder what it is. The wrapping paper is really beautiful. It [5] *must be / can't be* something special.
**Liz:** It's not very big. It [6] *could be / must be* a new phone. Did you ask for one?
**Becca:** No. Anyway, it's hard at one end and softer at the other, so it [7] *can't be / might be* a phone. OK, I'm going to open it. Oh, wow, it's some of those brushes I saw in the art shop last week! And here's the card. It says 'Love from Liz'! I didn't see you bring the parcel in.
**Liz:** Well, I knew you wanted some and so I thought they [8] *could be / must be* a good present.
**Becca:** They're perfect, thank you so much!

# GRAMMAR REFERENCE AND PRACTICE

## UNIT 13 JUST, ALREADY AND YET

We use *just*, *already* and *yet* with the present perfect.

### just

- means 'only a short time ago'.
- goes before the main verb in positive sentences.
  *I've **just passed** my driving test.*
  *The match **has just started**.*
  *We**'ve just moved** house.*

### already

- means 'some time before now'.
- emphasises that the action is now complete – we are not so interested in how long ago.
- sometimes means 'sooner than expected'.
- goes before the main verb in positive sentences.
  *I'**ve already driven** five hundred kilometres, I don't want to drive any more.*
  *My brother **has already left** school. He's at university now.*
  *My dad had flu last week but he'**s already gone** back to work.*
  *Our little sister'**s already learned** how to open cupboards, although she's only one!*

### yet

- means 'up to now'.
- often emphasises that we expected something to happen before now.
- goes at the end of a negative sentence.
  *I **haven't finished** my sandwich **yet**.* (= I'm eating it now, I need more time.)
  *We **haven't decided** which film to watch **yet**.* (= We're still thinking about it.)
- sometimes suggests that something might happen in the future.
  *You **haven't seen** my new bike **yet**.* (= You might see it sometime soon.)
- goes at the end of a question.
  ***Have** you **phoned** Jade **yet**?* (= I think you planned to phone Jade around now.)
  ***Has** Francis **bought** Mum a birthday card **yet**?*
  (= I think he should do it soon.)

### Practice

**1 Choose the correct words.**

1 Wow! I've *just* / *yet* seen our street on TV.
2 I've worked at the café for the last two weekends but I haven't been paid *already* / *yet*.
3 We've *just* / *yet* heard our exam results.
4 Oh no! I've *already* / *just* dropped a litre of olive oil on the kitchen floor!
5 Have you got an invitation to Janie's party *just* / *yet*?

**2 Put the words in brackets in the correct position in each sentence.**

1 The lesson has begun. (already)
2 Have you been to the new shopping centre? (yet)
3 This parcel has arrived for you. (just)
4 I haven't saved much money for my holiday. (yet)
5 It's only eleven o'clock but everyone's gone home. (already)
6 My parents have bought a new car. (just)
7 Have you done this exercise? (yet)
8 We've finished the last sentence. (just)

**3 Mark the sentences *S* if they mean the same thing or *D* if they mean different things.**

1 I saw the doctor a few minutes ago.
I've just seen the doctor. ........
2 We've already had one holiday this year.
We haven't had a holiday yet. ........
3 My brother has a job although he only left school last week.
My brother left school last week and he's already found a job. ........
4 I've already been to Australia twice but I haven't visited New Zealand yet.
I've just left Australia and I'm going to New Zealand. ........
5 I've just finished cleaning the kitchen and I'm going to have a shower.
I've already cleaned the kitchen but I haven't had a shower yet. ........

**4 Nick has an exam tomorrow. He's made a list of things to do. Write sentences about what he's already done and what he hasn't done yet.**

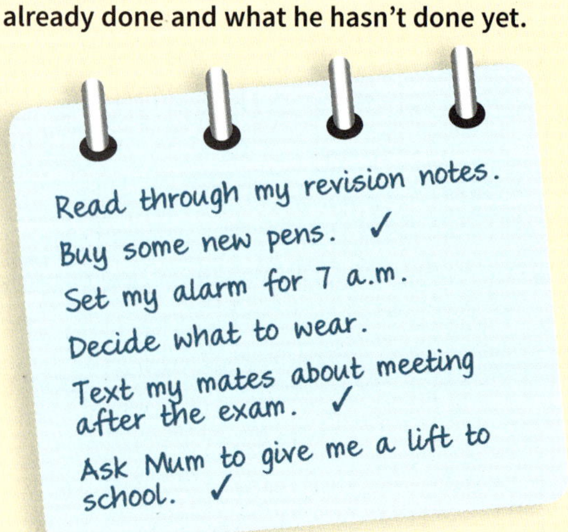


0 *He hasn't read through his revision notes yet.*
1 ........
2 ........
3 ........
4 ........
5 ........

# UNIT 14 RELATIVE CLAUSES

- We use relative clauses to explain who, what or where we are talking about.
  *The film **that we saw last night** was really funny.*
  (We need the words ***that we saw last night*** to know which film the speaker is talking about.)
  *The actor **that played Mrs Wood** was brilliant.* (We need the words ***that played Mrs Wood*** to know which actor the speaker is talking about.)
- We use the pronouns ***who*** or ***that*** to talk about people.
  *There's the woman **who** I met at the singing competition.*
  *I preferred the singer **that** got the second prize.*
- We use the pronouns ***which*** or ***that*** to talk about things.
  *I enjoy singing songs **which** make people laugh.*
  *My friend sang a song **that** she wrote about her home town.*
- Relative clauses can have ***who, which*** or ***that*** as their subject or as their object.
  *I preferred the singer **that** got the second prize.* (***that*** is the subject of the relative clause)
  *I enjoy singing songs **which** make people laugh.* (***which*** is the subject of the relative clause)
  *There's the woman **who** I met at the singing competition.* (***who*** is the object of the relative clause, ***I*** is the subject)
  *My friend sang a song **that** she wrote about her home town.* (***that*** is the object of the relative clause, ***she*** is the subject)
- We use the pronoun ***where*** to talk about places.
  *We went to the house **where** the film director lives.*
  (= which the film director lives in)
  *I know a website **where** you can find all kinds of films.*
  (= You can find all kinds of films there.)

## Practice

**1** **Complete the sentences with *who or which*.**

1. I've just met someone ________ has a part in a soap opera.
2. The chat show ________ I usually watch has lots of interesting people on it.
3. I like programmes ________ make me laugh.
4. This is the animated film ________ my teacher recommended to me.
5. I really admire the actor ________ plays the main character in this thriller.
6. I'm not a big fan of murder mysteries ________ have complicated stories.
7. I know a girl ________ is a TV actor.
8. This documentary is by a woman ________ my mum was at school with.

**2** **Malcolm is telling Kirsty about a film. Complete the conversation. Use the relative clauses from the box.**

| |
|---|
| who was always unkind to him<br>who hasn't seen it<br>who was called Millie Moop<br>who lived in an old bus<br>which you need to see to understand<br>which was really funny<br>where Millie put shampoo into a toothpaste tube<br>where Mr Scratch lived |

**Malcolm:** I saw this film last weekend [1] ________. There was a family called the Moops [2] ________. They had a teenage daughter [3] ________ and she was very intelligent. Her dad had a job which he hated, and he worked for a man called Mr Scratch [4] ________. So one day, Millie went to the house [5] ________ and got a job as a cleaner. Then she played all kinds of tricks on Mr Scratch and his family. The best scene was one [6] ________. I laughed all the time.
**Kirsty:** Really?
**Malcolm:** Oh, well, perhaps it's one of those films [7] ________. It maybe doesn't sound so funny to someone [8] ________.

**3** **Make each pair of sentences into one sentence, using a relative clause. Make other changes if necessary.**

1. This is a photo of my friend. She wants to be a TV presenter.
   ________________
2. We have a goldfish. He is called Bubbles.
   ________________
3. That man wrote a song. Everyone knows it.
   ________________
4. I visited a house. John Lennon lived there as a boy.
   ________________
5. Do you remember the woman? She had 20 cats.
   ________________
6. Our teacher gave us some exercises for homework. No one could understand them.
   ________________
7. I have a neighbour. He is a famous designer.
   ________________
8. Kington is a small town. I grew up near there.
   ________________

# GRAMMAR REFERENCE AND PRACTICE

## UNIT 15 PRESENT SIMPLE PASSIVE

- We form the present simple passive with the present tense of *be* + the **past participle** of a verb.

| | |
|---|---|
| I | **am given** |
| You, We, They | **are helped** |
| He, She, It | **is recommended** |

*I'm* ***given*** *a maths test every week.*
*I'm* ***not given*** *a maths test every week.*
***Are*** *you* ***given*** *a maths test every week?*
*Robbie* ***is helped*** *with his homework.*
*Robbie* ***isn't helped*** *with his homework.*
***Is*** *Robbie* ***helped*** *with his homework?*
*These apps* ***are recommended*** *on lots of websites.*
*These apps* ***aren't recommended*** *on many websites.*
***Are*** *these apps* ***recommended*** *on many websites?*

- When we include who or what does the action, we use ***by***.
  ***My teacher gives*** *me a maths test every week.* (active)
  *I'm* ***given*** *a maths test* ***by my teacher*** *every week.* (passive)
  *Robbie's parents* ***don't help*** *him with his homework.* (active)
  *Robbie* ***isn't helped*** *with his homework* ***by his parents***. (passive)
  ***Do a lot of people admire*** *the girls for their courage?* (active)
  ***Are*** *the girls* ***admired by a lot of people*** *for their courage?* (passive)
- We use the passive:
  - when it isn't important to say who or what does the action.
    *This app* ***is used*** *for sharing photos.*
    *Our exam results* ***are published*** *online.*
    *Teenagers* ***are allowed*** *to drive in my country.*
  - when we do not know who or what does the action.
    *These new phones* ***are made*** *in China.*
    *The streets* ***are cleaned*** *at night.*
    *My dad* ***is sent*** *lots of brochures.*
- We include ***by*** when we want to emphasise who or what does the action.
  *This app* ***is used by millions of people*** *for sharing photos.*
  *My dad* ***is sent*** *lots of brochures* ***by car companies.***

## Practice

**1 Decide if the sentences are active (A) or passive (P).**

1. Thousands of new apps are downloaded every day.
2. We need more computers in my school.
3. Computer viruses are often sent by email.
4. A lot of money is spent on developing new smartphones.
5. A virus deleted all the information on my laptop.

**2 Complete the sentences. Use the active form.**

1. I'm always given money for my birthday by my granny.
   My granny ________ for my birthday.
2. All our vegetables are grown by my parents.
   My parents ________ vegetables.
3. Cambridge is visited by lots of tourists.
   Lots of tourists ________ Cambridge.
4. Computers are used by most schoolchildren nowadays.
   Most schoolchildren ________ computers nowadays.
5. This computer is used by everyone in my class.
   Everyone in my class ________ this computer.

**3 Complete the sentences. Use the passive form of the verb. Only include *by* if it is important.**

1. You need a password to enter this website.
   A password ________ this website.
2. My brother cleans Dad's car once a month.
   Dad's car ________ once a month.
3. We don't send children to prison in this country.
   Children ________ in this country.
4. Thieves steal ten bicycles every day in this town.
   Ten bicycles ________ in this town.
5. People play football all the year round.
   Football ________ all the year round.
6. My parents don't allow me to have a TV in my bedroom.
   I ________ a TV in my bedroom.
7. Someone designs a clever new app every day.
   A clever new app ________ every day.
8. A local company pays for our school trips.
   Our school trips ________.
9. Criminals hide viruses in software.
   Viruses ________ in software.
10. A film star owns that house.
    That house ________.

## UNIT 16 ZERO AND FIRST CONDITIONAL

- Conditional sentences tell us about a possible situation and a result. They use two clauses: the conditional clause and a result clause.
- The conditional clause begins with ***if*** or ***unless***.
- The conditional clause or the result clause can come first without changing the meaning.

### Zero conditional

- The zero conditional uses the present simple in the conditional clause and in the result clause.
- ***If*** + present tense, + present tense
  ***If*** *plants* ***have*** *enough light, they* ***grow*** *well.*
  ***If*** *plants* ***don't have*** *enough light, they* ***don't grow*** *well.*
  We use a comma when the *if* clause comes first.
- We can also put the ***if*** clause at the end of a sentence.
  *Plants* ***grow*** *well* ***if*** *they* ***have*** *enough light.*
- We use the zero conditional to talk about things that are true or always happen.
  ***If*** *you* ***give*** *plants enough food and water, they* ***grow*** *well.*
  ***If*** *you* ***don't give*** *plants enough food and water, they* ***don't grow*** *well.*
- ***If*** usually means the same as ***when*** in zero conditional sentences.
  *Plants* ***grow*** *well* ***when*** *you* ***give*** *them enough food and water.*

### Practice

**1 Complete the zero conditional sentences with the correct form of the verbs.**

1 Everyone ________ sleepy if the weather ________ too hot. (feel, be)
2 If my brother ________ any money, he always ________ it on clothes. (earn, spend)
3 Students ________ stressed if their teacher ________ them too many tests. (get, give)
4 If I ________ a film, I ________ it to the end. (not like, not watch)
5 If I ________ well in my school exams, my parents usually ________ me extra pocket money. (do, give)
6 It ________ difficult to remember facts if you ________ studying that subject. (be, not enjoy)

### First conditional

- The first conditional uses the present simple in the conditional clause and the ***will*** future in the result clause.
- ***If*** + present tense, + ***will/won't***
  ***If*** *we* ***share*** *a taxi, we'****ll*** *save money.*
  ***If*** *we* ***take*** *a taxi, we* ***won't*** *get wet.*
  ***If*** *we* ***don't take*** *a taxi, we'****ll*** *get wet.*
  We use a comma when the *if* clause comes first.
- We can also put the ***if*** clause at the end of a sentence.
  *We'****ll*** *save money* ***if*** *we* ***share*** *a taxi.*
- We use the first conditional to talk about possible or probable future events.
  ***If*** *this café* ***closes****, we'****ll*** *lose our jobs.*
  *We'****ll*** *lose our jobs* ***if*** *this café* ***closes****.*
  *We* ***won't*** *lose our jobs* ***if*** *this café* ***doesn't close****.*
- ***If*** does not mean the same as ***when*** in first conditional sentences.
  ***If*** *this café closes, we'll lose our jobs.* (= The speaker believes it is possible that the café will close, but is not sure.)
  ***When*** *this café closes, we'll lose our jobs.* (= The speaker knows that the café is going to close.)

### Practice

**2 Choose the correct form of the verbs.**

1 If *I don't go* / *I won't go* to bed right now, *I'm not able* / *I won't be able* to get up in the morning.
2 *I'll buy* / *I buy* some ice cream later if the café *is* / *will be* still open.
3 *You pass* / *You'll pass* your driving test if *you won't forget* / *you don't forget* to wear your lucky ring.
4 *We'll phone* / *We phone* my dad after the party if *we'll need* / *we need* a lift home.
5 If anyone *finds out* / *will find out* where my brother is today, *he'll be* / *he's* in big trouble when he comes home.
6 *You won't feel* / *You don't feel* cold if *you put* / *you'll put* this sweater on.

### *unless*

- ***Unless*** means ***if not***.
  *Plants don't grow* ***unless*** *they* ***have*** *light.* (= ***if*** *they* ***don't have*** *light*)
  *I'll stay at home* ***unless*** *it* ***stops*** *raining.* (= ***if*** *it* ***doesn't stop*** *raining*)
  ***Unless*** *I'****m*** *invited, I won't go to the party.* (= ***if*** *I'****m not*** *invited*)

### Practice

**3 Rewrite the sentences using *unless*.**

1 I can't get up in the morning if I don't have enough sleep.
________
2 We'll all have dinner together if my mum doesn't get home too late.
________
3 My parents will go mad if we don't clear up this mess.
________
4 If we don't find a taxi soon, we'll miss the train.
________

# GRAMMAR REFERENCE AND PRACTICE

## UNIT 17 REPORTED COMMANDS

- When we want someone to do something or not to do something, we say things like:
  *Open the door! / Don't open the door!* **(command)**
  *Please open the door. / Please don't open the door.* **(request)**
  *You must open the door! / You mustn't open the door!* **(command)**
  *You should open the door. / You shouldn't open the door.* **(advice/suggestion)**
- When we report commands, requests, suggestions, etc., we use:
  - a reporting verb + object pronoun + ***to*** + infinitive for positive commands and requests.
    *Dad said to me, 'Open the door!'* → *Dad **told me to open** the door.*
    *Dad said to me, 'Please open the door!'* → *Dad **asked me to open** the door.*
    *I said to the boys, 'You must close the door!'* → *I **told them to close** the door.*
    *I said to the boys, 'You should close the door.'* → *I **advised them to close** the door.*
  - a reporting verb + object pronoun + ***not to*** + infinitive for negative commands and requests.
    *Dad said to me, 'Don't open the door!'* → *Dad **told me not to open** the door.*
    *Dad said to me, 'Please don't open the door!'* → *Dad **asked me not to open** the door.*
    *I said to the boys, 'You mustn't close the door!'* → *I **told them not to close** the door.*
    *I said to the boys, 'You shouldn't close the door.'* → *I **advised them not to close** the door.*

### Reporting verbs

- In sentences like the ones above, we can use different verbs to tell people what we want them to do, e.g.
  *She **convinced** me to stay, but my friend **warned** me not to listen to her.*
  Examples of reporting verbs are: ***advise, ask, convince, encourage, order, persuade, remind, tell, warn***
  **NOTE** We cannot use ***say*** in this way. (**NOT** ~~He said me to open the door~~.)

### Practice

**1 Write what the speakers said. Include the words in brackets.**

**0** Our teacher reminded us not to leave our bags on the bus.
He said, '*Don't leave your bags on the bus.*' (don't)
**1** My brother persuaded me to try a new hairstyle.
He said, '………………………' (should)
**2** The inspector asked us to show him our tickets.
He said, '………………………' (please)
**3** My cousin convinced me not to put my address on the website.
She said, '………………………' (shouldn't)
**4** I told my friends not to text me in the morning.
I said, '………………………' (mustn't)
**5** The police officer ordered the driver to get out of his car.
She said, '………………………' (please)
**6** I asked my sister to help me with the washing-up.
I said, '………………………' (please)
**7** My friend encouraged me to join the sports club.
He said, '………………………' (should)
**8** My mum advised me to phone the school.
She said, '………………………' (should)
**9** The fire officer warned us not to go into the house.
He said, '………………………' (mustn't)

**2 Report what each speaker said. Use the reporting verb and a suitable pronoun.**

**1** The detective shouted to the thief, 'Put the gun on the floor!' (order)
The detective ………………………
**2** The electrician said to us, 'You mustn't open the box.' (warn)
The electrician ………………………
**3** The hairdresser said to me, 'You shouldn't use this shampoo.' (advise)
The hairdresser ………………………
**4** I texted my friends, 'Remember to come to my party.' (remind)
I ………………………
**5** The teacher said to the students, 'Please tell me your names.' (ask)
The teacher ………………………
**6** I whispered to my brother, 'Please don't tell anyone!' (ask)
I ………………………
**7** My friend said to me, 'You should tell your mum about your problem.' (encourage)
My friend ………………………
**8** My dad said to my brother, 'You really should apply for another job.' (persuade)
My dad ………………………
**9** My mum said to my dad, 'Don't invite the neighbours on Saturday.' (tell)
My mum ………………………

## UNIT 18 SECOND CONDITIONAL

- Conditional sentences tell us about a possible situation and a result. They use two clauses: the conditional clause and a result clause.
- The conditional clause begins with ***if*** or ***unless***.
- The conditional clause or the result clause can come first without changing the meaning.
- The second conditional uses the past simple in the conditional clause and ***would*** (***'d***) / ***wouldn't*** + verb in the result clause.
  ***If*** + past tense, + ***would*** + verb: ***If I was*** *a journalist,* ***I'd (would) meet*** *lots of famous people.*
  We use a comma when the *if* clause comes first.
- We can also put the ***if*** clause at the end of a sentence.
  ***I'd (would) meet*** *lots of famous people* ***if I was*** *a journalist.*
- We sometimes use ***I were*** instead of ***I was*** in the conditional clause.
  ***If I were*** *a journalist,* ***I'd (would) meet*** *lots of famous people.*
- We never use ***when*** instead of ***if*** in second conditional sentences.
- We use the second conditional to talk about an unlikely or impossible situation in the present or future, and its results.
  ***If I were*** *a millionaire,* ***I'd buy*** *a desert island.* (= I'm not a millionaire, so I won't buy a desert island.)
  *We* ***wouldn't send*** *many texts* ***if*** *they* ***cost*** *a lot of money.* (= It's cheap to send texts, so we send lots.)
  ***If*** *my brother* ***got up*** *earlier, he* ***wouldn't have*** *to run for the train every morning.* (= My brother doesn't get up early enough, so he has to run for the train every morning.)
  ***If I could*** *get a job,* ***I'd (would) have*** *enough money to go out.* (= I can't get a job, so I don't have enough money to go out.)
  *The students* ***wouldn't play*** *football* ***unless*** *they* ***enjoyed*** *it.* (= They enjoy playing football, that's why they do it.)
- We often use the second conditional to ask questions.
  ***If*** *you* ***had*** *the chance,* ***would*** *you* ***visit*** *California?*
  ***Wouldn't*** *you* ***be*** *angry* ***if*** *you* ***were*** *me?*
  *What* ***would*** *you* ***do if*** *someone* ***told*** *you a secret?*
  ***If*** *you* ***could do*** *any job at all, what* ***would*** *you* ***choose?***
- We answer the questions with the conditional tense.
  *I* ***wouldn't visit*** *California,* ***I'd go*** *to Florida.*
  ***Yes, I would.*** / ***No, I wouldn't.***
  *I* ***wouldn't tell*** *anyone else.*
  ***I'd be*** *a racing driver.*

## Practice

**1 Match the questions and answers.**

1 If you could leave school tomorrow, what would you do? ......
2 If you saw someone stealing, who would you tell? ......
3 What would you say if I told you I'd bought a motorbike? ......
4 How would you get to school if you missed the bus? ......
5 What colour would you choose if you repainted your room? ......

a I'd go for light blue, I think.
b I'd probably talk to my dad about it.
c I'd travel round Europe with a friend.
d I'd say you were mad!
e I'd have to walk, I suppose.

**2 What would be your answers to the questions in Exercise 1?**

**3 Make second conditional questions.**

1 What / you / do / if / you / win / lots of money?
..............................
I'd buy presents for all my friends.

2 Who / you / ask / if / you / not / understand / some grammar?
..............................
I'd ask my teacher.

3 What / you / do / if / you / see / a burger for $50?
..............................
I'd find somewhere cheaper to eat.

4 What / you / do / if / someone / ask / you / about advanced physics?
..............................
I'd try to find some information online.

5 Who / help / you / if / you / miss / the school bus?
..............................
My dad would give me a lift.

**4 Complete the sentences. Use *would* and the past simple form of the verbs.**

1 You .......... (have) more friends if you .......... (not tell) stories about people.
2 If I .......... (be) you, I .......... (take) a warm coat today, but I guess it's up to you.
3 If Kirsty .......... (stay) in France, she .......... (learn) French quickly.
4 My parents .......... (not get) angry with us unless we .......... (do) something very bad.
5 If we all .......... (eat) as much as you, there .......... (not be) any food in the fridge!
6 If you .......... (save) a little money every week, you .......... (have) enough to buy new boots quite soon.

# GRAMMAR REFERENCE AND PRACTICE

## UNIT 19 REPORTED SPEECH

When we report what people said in the past:

- the tense of the verbs changes.
- the pronouns change if necessary.
- we can use ***that*** after ***said*** but it isn't always necessary.

| Direct speech | | Reported speech |
|---|---|---|
| **Present simple** | → | **Past simple** |
| 'I often **go** sailing,' said Ed. | → | Ed said (that) **he** often **went** sailing. |
| **Present continuous** | → | **Past continuous** |
| 'Doug **is cycling** fast,' said Megan. | → | Megan said (that) Doug **was cycling** fast. |
| ***will*** | → | ***would*** |
| 'Olga **will win** the race,' said the coach. | → | The coach said (that) Olga **would win** the race. |
| ***can*** | | ***could*** |
| They said to us, **'You can** sit with **us.'** | → | They said (that) **we could** sit with **them**. |

- When we use ***told***, we need to use an object.
  *Mark **told me** that he went to Italy on holiday.*
- We don't use an object with ***said***.
  *Mark **said** that he went to Italy on holiday.* (NOT ~~*Mark said me that he went to Italy*~~.)

### Practice

**1 Change the sentences from reported to direct speech.**

1 Andy said he was texting his parents.
Andy said, 'I ________ my parents.'
2 My brothers said they couldn't find any pictures of their favourite singers.
My brothers said, 'We ________ any pictures of our favourite singers.'
3 Andrea said she always laughed at the letters page in her magazine.
Andrea said, 'I always ________ the letters page in my magazine.'
4 My sister said I could borrow her new shoes.
My sister said, 'You ________ new shoes.'
5 Phil said he often bought a newspaper for his dad.
Phil said, 'I often ________ for my dad.'
6 Alexi said he was looking for an article about his local team.
Alexi said, 'I ________ an article about my local team.'
7 We said we'd design the front cover.
We said, 'We ________ the front cover.'

**2 Complete the sentences with *said* or *told*.**

1 Harry ________ that he wanted to leave.
2 I ________ my mother that I would help her today.
3 We ________ the teacher that we couldn't do the homework.
4 My teacher ________ that we had to finish the homework before Monday.
5 My dad ________ me that he had a new job.

**3 Complete the reported sentences.**

1 'I'm starting a blog about my sailing club,' said Saskia.
Saskia told me ________ a blog about her sailing club.
2 'Readers can get free gifts with fashion magazines,' said Lewis.
Lewis said that readers ________ free gifts with fashion magazines.
3 'The writers don't know much about teenagers, in my opinion,' said my mum.
My mum told me that in her opinion, the writers ________ much about teenagers.
4 'I'll take some photos for you,' said Derek.
Derek said ________ some photos for me.
5 'We are making a lot of progress with our stories,' said the twins.
The twins said ________ a lot of progress with their stories.
6 'The celebrities are sitting in my garden,' said the photographer.
The photographer said that the celebrities ________ in his garden.

# UNIT 20 PAST SIMPLE PASSIVE

- We form the past simple passive with *was*/*were* (*not*) + the **past participle**

| I, He, She, It | **was(n't) allowed** to go. |
|---|---|
| You, We, They | **were(n't) told** about the party. |

*I **was told** to phone home.*
*She **wasn't told** the correct time.*
***Were** you **told** what to do?*
*The story **was told** to a journalist.*
*The journalist **wasn't told** the truth.*
***Was** the story **told** to make trouble for someone?*
*The pictures **were found** in a second-hand shop.*
*They **weren't found** in good condition.*
***Were** the pictures **found** by chance?*

- When we want to say the person or thing that did the action, we use *by*.
*__Two school students found__ the pictures in a second-hand shop.* (active)
*The pictures __were found__ in a second-hand shop __by two school students__.* (passive)
***The shop owner didn't tell** the journalist the truth.* (active)
*The journalist __wasn't told__ the truth __by the shop owner__.* (passive)
*Did __the students__ find the pictures?* (active)
***Were** the pictures __found by the students__?* (passive)
- We use the passive:
  - when it isn't important to say who or what did the action.
  *That picture **was sold** for a thousand pounds.*
  *My brother's drawings **were shown** in a gallery.*
  *I **wasn't allowed** to watch horror movies when I was younger.*
  - when we do not know who or what did the action.
  *My friend **was interviewed** about his invention.*
  *The story **wasn't published** until yesterday.*
  *The students **were offered** a reward.*
- We include *by* when we want to emphasise who or what did the action.
*That picture was sold __by the artist's mother__ for a thousand pounds.*
*The story wasn't published __by the national newspapers__ until yesterday.*
*The students were offered a reward __by the owner of the painting__.*

## Practice

**1 Underline the past passive forms in this text.**

I have lived in my apartment for five years, but it is much older than that. The building that my apartment is in was built over 100 years ago. It was designed by a famous architect who also designed many other buildings in the city. It was created for a local businessman who wanted his own building. It was used by his family for about 50 years. Then, it was sold and it was made into lots of smaller apartments.

**2 Rewrite the sentences in the active form.**

1 The celebrity artist was interviewed by lots of journalists.
Lots of journalists ________ the celebrity artist.
2 The best drawing wasn't done by Picasso.
Picasso ________ the best drawing.
3 Were the pictures copied by the students?
Did ________ the pictures?
4 These sculptures weren't made by Henry Moore.
Henry Moore ________ these sculptures.
5 These pictures weren't described in the coursebook.
The coursebook ________ these pictures.

**3 Rewrite the sentences. Use the passive form of the verbs.**

1 Our teacher **reminded** us about the school trip.
We ________ teacher.
2 Someone **copied** my card details and **stole** all my money.
My card details ________ and all my money ________.
3 My classmates **gave** me a good luck card before my interview.
I ________ my classmates before my interview.
4 Did you **prepare** these salads this morning?
Were ________ this morning?
5 No one **told** me where to sit.
I ________ to sit.

**4 Choose the correct form of the verbs.**

Last month a class of secondary school students [1] *was given / gave* a half-day holiday by their school after their exams. Two of the students went for a walk but it [2] *was started / started* to rain, so they went into a second-hand shop to keep dry. All kinds of old furniture [3]*left / were left* around the shop. There were bowls and plates everywhere and old photographs and paintings [4] *were pushed / pushed* under tables. The students [5] *were decided / decided* to look at the pictures to pass the time. Most of them [6] *were covered / covered* in dust. Then one of the students [7] *was noticed / noticed* a small picture which [8] *was almost hidden / almost hid* behind a cupboard.
It [9] *was shown / showed* a vase of flowers which [10] *were painted / painted* in great detail. The picture [11] *wasn't signed / didn't sign* but the shop owner thought it [12] *was probably painted / probably painted* about fifty years ago. The students [13] *were paid / paid* £5 for it and [14] *were taken / took* it away. Later they [15] *were discovered / discovered* it was five hundred years old. It [16] *was sold / sold* by a gallery in London last week for one million pounds!

# LIST OF IRREGULAR VERBS

| Infinitive | Past simple | Past participle |
|---|---|---|
| be | was, were | been |
| become | became | become |
| begin | began | begun |
| break | broke | broken |
| bring | brought | brought |
| build | built | built |
| burn | burnt/burned | burnt/burned |
| buy | bought | bought |
| catch | caught | caught |
| choose | chose | chosen |
| come | came | come |
| cost | cost | cost |
| cut | cut | cut |
| do | did | done |
| draw | drew | drawn |
| dream | dreamed/dreamt | dreamed/dreamt |
| drink | drank | drunk |
| drive | drove | driven |
| eat | ate | eaten |
| fall | fell | fallen |
| feel | felt | felt |
| find | found | found |
| fly | flew | flown |
| forget | forgot | forgotten |
| get | got | got |
| give | gave | given |
| go | went | gone/been |
| grow | grew | grown |
| have | had | had |
| hear | heard | heard |
| hit | hit | hit |
| hold | held | held |
| hurt | hurt | hurt |
| keep | kept | kept |
| know | knew | known |
| learn | learned/learnt | learned/learnt |
| leave | left | left |

| Infinitive | Past simple | Past participle |
|---|---|---|
| lend | lent | lent |
| lie | lay | lain |
| lose | lost | lost |
| make | made | made |
| mean | meant | meant |
| meet | met | met |
| pay | paid | paid |
| put | put | put |
| read | read /red/ | read /red/ |
| ride | rode | ridden |
| ring | rang | rung |
| run | ran | run |
| say | said | said |
| see | saw | seen |
| sell | sold | sold |
| send | sent | sent |
| show | showed | shown |
| shut | shut | shut |
| sing | sang | sung |
| sit | sat | sat |
| sleep | slept | slept |
| speak | spoke | spoken |
| spell | spelled/spelt | spelled/spelt |
| spend | spent | spent |
| stand | stood | stood |
| steal | stole | stolen |
| swim | swam | swum |
| take | took | taken |
| teach | taught | taught |
| tell | told | told |
| think | thought | thought |
| throw | threw | thrown |
| understand | understood | understood |
| wake | woke | woken |
| wear | wore | worn |
| win | won | won |
| write | wrote | written |

# Acknowledgements

The authors would like to thank everyone who worked on the first edition of *Prepare*, and also Jacqueline French and Alyson Maskell for their hard work on the second edition. James Styring dedicates this book to Jude Robert Alver Styring. Nicholas Tims thanks Clare, Ismay and Elodie for their endless support.

The authors and publishers are grateful to the following for reviewing the material during the writing process:

Argentina: Diana Ogando; Italy: Sarah Brocklebank; Spain: Isabel Sobrino

**The authors and publishers acknowledge the following sources of copyright material and are grateful for the permissions granted. While every effort has been made, it has not always been possible to identify the sources of all the material used, or to trace all copyright holders. If any omissions are brought to our notice, we will be happy to include the appropriate acknowledgements on reprinting and in the next update to the digital edition, as applicable.**

Key: U = Unit, LS = Life Skills, C = Culture, R = Review, EA = Extra Activities.

Text

**U6**: Ann Makosinski for the text about Ann Makosinski. Copyright © Ann Makosinski. Reproduced with permission; **U14:** Kameron R. Badgers for the text about Kameron R. Badgers. Copyright © Kameron R. Badgers. Reproduced with permission of Deb McAlister-Holland; **C5**: Royal Ballet School for the text about Royal Ballet School. Copyright © Royal Ballet School. Reproduced with permission; Idyllwild Arts Academy for the text about Idyllwild Arts Academy. Copyright © Idyllwild Arts Academy. Reproduced with kind permission; National Circus School of Montreal for the text about National Circus School of Montreal. Copyright © National Circus School of Montreal. Reproduced with kind permission.

Photography

The following images are sourced from Getty Images.

**U1**: Hero Images/DigitalVision; Westend61; mixetto/E+; Fuse/Corbis; Tetra Images; golubovy/iStock/Getty Images Plus; **U2**: Nicholas Hun/Getty Images Entertainment; Raymond Hall/GC Images; Kevin Winter/WireImage; Dimitrios Kambouris/Getty Images Entertainment; Michael Ochs Archives; H. Armstrong Roberts/ClassicStock/Archive Photos; PYMCA/Universal Images Group; Matthias Clamer/Stone; PeopleImages/iStock/Getty Images Plus; Jan Olofsson/Redferns; BURGER/Canopy; Juanmonino/iStock/Getty Images Plus; **C1**: Mike Powell/The Image Bank; Mark Hawkins/Barcroft Images/Barcroft Media; kobbydagan/iStock Editorial/Getty Images Plus; Neil Mcallister/Photolibrary; Pawel Libera/LightRocket; VisitBritain/Britain on View; **U3**: Just One Film/Photonica; Caiaimage/Sam Edwards; YinYang/E+; Dave G Kelly/Moment; Sami Sarkis/Photographer's Choice RF; bizoo_n/iStock/Getty Images Plus; Joe Sohm/Visions of America/Universal Images Group; Jamie Grill; Robert Daly/OJO Images; **U4**: Peter Muller/Cultura; gbh007/iStock/Getty Images Plus; M_a_y_a/E+; Tony Anderson/Taxi; SolStock/E+; Westend61; Mikael Vaisanen/Corbis; FatCamera/E+; Carlos Herrera/Icon Sportswire; Carlos Herrera/Icon Sportswire; Carlos Herrera/Icon Sportswire; Mike Hewitt; Thomas Barwick/Stone; **LS1:** Westend61; **R1:** Helene Wiesenhaan/Getty Images Sport; **U5:** fstop123/iStock/Getty Images Plus; AndreyPopov/iStock/Getty Images Plus; noonland/Westend61; amesy/iStock/Getty Images Plus; Marc Volk; Tony Bee/Photolibrary; NatalieShuttleworth/Moment Open; Yuki Cheung/EyeEm; Ken Chernus/The Image Bank; 4x6/iStock/Getty Images Plus; Klaus Vedfelt/DigitalVision; BFG Images; Peter Dazeley/Photographer's Choice; **U6**: Chris Stowers/Dorling Kindersley; DebraLee Wiseberg/E+; Richard Newstead/Moment; Luca Calogero Mazzarella/EyeEm; CribbVisuals/ iStock Unreleased; Levi Bianco/Moment; Boston Globe; Photography taken by Mario Gutiérrez./Moment; ConstantineV/iStock/Getty Images Plus; Ante Badzim/EyeEm; Tom and Steve/Moment; Influx Productions/DigitalVision; visual2020vision/Westend61; Anshu/Moment Open; Thomas M. Scheer/EyeEm; bluecinema/iStock/Getty Images Plus; Sino Images; Geography Photos/Universal Images Group; Matteo Colombo/DigitalVision; Scott Jordan Levy/The LIFE Images Collection; Az Jackson/Moment; Alexander Spatari/Moment; mizoula/iStock Editorial/Getty Images Plus; **C2**: Matthias Haker Photography/Moment; German Conejo/EyeEm; Jos Badillo/EyeEm; **U7**: Mallika Wiriyathitipirn/EyeEm; Teti Nurhayati.r/EyeEm; kate_sept2004/E+; ljubaphoto/E+; monkeybusinessimages/iStock/Getty Images Plus; **U8:** baona/iStock/Getty Images Plus; Robert Alexander/Archive Photos; Lawrence Manning/Corbis; Bounce/Cultura; Joe Raedle/Getty Images News; Santiago Urquijo/Moment; Paul J. Richards/AFP; pjohnson1/E+; Clare Lawrence/EyeEm; aluxum/iStock Unreleased; David Clapp/Photolibrary; Sino Images; Toru Yamanaka/AFP; Kazuhiro Nogi/AFP; Greg Elms/Lonely Planet Images; Westend61/Brand X Pictures; fazon1/iStock Editorial/Getty Images Plus; **LS2:** Universal Images Group; Alys Tomlinson/Cultura; **R2:** DaydreamsGirl/iStock/Getty Images Plus; **U9:** eclipse_images/iStock/Getty Images Plus; moodboard/Cultura; Tetra Image; Hill Street Studios/Blend Images; JGI/Jamie Grill/Blend Images; Roy Hsu/UpperCut Images; Le Club Symphonie/Cultura; Westend61; Mark Chaves/EyeEm; Trina Dopp Photography/Moment; Terry Vine/Blend Images; **U10:** Andrew Pini/Photolibrary; Patrick Foto/Moment; rez-art/iStock/Getty Images Plus; HandmadePictures/iStock/Getty Images Plus; Chatiyanon/iStock/Getty Images Plus; Pinghung Chen/EyeEm; Fuse/Corbis; Debby Lewis-Harrison/Cultura; Lepro/iStock/Getty Images Plus; reisegraf/iStock/Getty Images Plus; simonlong/Moment; Minjoon Lee/EyeEm; Brian Macdonald/DigitalVision; Kirill Rudenko/Moment Open; Dorling Kindersley; Nastasic/iStock/Getty Images Plus; **C3:** VisitBritain/Britain on View; Foodcollection RF; Szakaly/iStock/Getty Images Plus; agmit/E+; StockSolutions/iStock/Getty Images Plus; David Bishop Inc./Photolibrary; manyakotic/iStock/Getty Images Plus; travellinglight/iStock/Getty Images Plus; Mark Thomas/StockFood Creative; bloodstone/iStock/Getty Images Plus; Lesyy/iStock/Getty Images Plus; **U11:** moodboard/Cultura; Fabricio Bomjardim/Brazil Photo Press/LatinContent; OGphoto/E+; Jakob Helbig/The Image Bank; **U12**: RolfAasa/iStock/Getty Images Plus; proxyminder/iStock/Getty Images Plus; alarifoto/iStock/Getty Images Plus; hkuchera/iStock/Getty Images Plus; Jose Triguero/EyeEm michaklootwijk/iStock/Getty Images Plus; CraigRJD/E+; Viorika/E+; Samantha Nicol Art; Photography/Moment; JB Parrett Photography/Moment; Reinhard Dirscherl/Corbis Documentary; M_MUC1968/iStock/Getty Images Plus; Michelle Valberg/All Canada Photos; Jasmin Brough/iStock/Getty Images Plus; Visuals Unlimited, Inc./Ken Catania; John Cancalosi/Oxford Scientific; Cigdem Uzun/Moment; Dietmar Heinz/Picture Press; Visuals Unlimited, Inc./Thomas Marent; Douglas Vigon/EyeEm; Jack Taylor/EyeEm; ritfuse/Shutterstock; Eric Isselee; CHAIWATPHOTOS/iStock/Getty Images Plus; Photoshot Holdings Ltd/Alamy; Tsuneya Kudoh/EyeEm; rollover/E+; ALEXANDER JOE; Valeriy Kirsanov; Don Farrall/Photodisc; Altrendo images; dpa picture alliance/Alamy; **LS3:** Tang/Anadolu Agency; Tuned_In/iStock/Getty Images Plus; P A Thompson/Corbis Documentary; T2 Images/Cultura; **R3:** South_agency/E+; **U13:** oRethwill images/ Moment; Umberto Leporini/EyeEm; Westend61; Jack Smith/EyeEm Premium; SensorSpot/E+; Jackson Kersine/EyeEm; Brainsil/iStock/Getty Images Plus; Nikodash/iStock/Getty Images Plus; **U14:** Peter Beavis/Stone; Loungepark/Stone; JGI/Jamie Gril; UpperCut Images; Richard Wear/Design Pics; ConeyLJay/Stone; Feverstockphoto/E+; Tashi-Delek/E+; Fuse/Corbis; BaloOm Studios/Moment; Michael Klippfeld/Moment; simonkr/E+; MEHAU KULYK/Science Photo Libra; William Attard McCarthy - McCarthy's PhotoWork; Westend61; gremlin/iStock/Getty Images Plus; **C4:** American Stock Archive/Moviepix; RichLegg/E+; **U15:** JGI/Jamie Grill/Blend Image; Bruno Gori/Cultura; **U16:** STAN HONDA/AFP; martinrlee/iStock/Getty Images Plus; Riou, Jean-Christophe; Dale Sutton/Nature Picture Library; Bryce Duffy/Corbis via Contour; Artyom Geodakyan/TASS; Education Images/Universal Images Group; **LS4:** Manchan/Photographer's Choice RF; biglike/iStock/Getty Images Plus; eclipse_images/

iStock/Getty Images Plus; Daisy-Daisy/iStock/Getty Images Plus; Ryhor Bruyeu/iStock/Getty Images Plus; Stephen Derr/ The Image Bank; FrancescoCorticchia/iStock/Getty; Ian Walton; Ed Freeman; Images Plus; **U17:** Tom Merton; Siri Stafford/ Stone; Theo Wargo/Getty Images Entertainment; Paul Archuleta/ WireImage for Fashion Media; Antoine Antoniol/Getty Images Entertainment; Mint Images RF; ason Kempin/TAS18/Getty Images Entertainment; **U18:** Hero Images; microgen/iStock/ Getty Images Plus; Jorge Cruz/Canopy; UpperCut Images; GoodLifeStudio/E+; vm/E+; Mihajlo Maricic/EyeEm; Boris Suntsov/Moment; Chris Ryan/OJO Images; Monty Rakusen/ Cultura; alvarez/E+; Steve Debenport/E+; maurusone/iStock/ Getty Images Plus; Image Source/DigitalVision; Hero Images; **C5:** Hans Neleman/The Image Bank; **U19:** KLH49/iStock/Getty Images Plus; Carla Gottgens/Bloomberg; ivanmollov/iStock/ Getty Images Plus; Bill Oxford/E+; Yin Jiang/EyeEm; calvindexter/ DigitalVision Vectors; zmeel/E+; Manakin/iStock Editorial/Getty Images Plus; Hero Images; JDawnInk/DigitalVision Vectors; bubaone/DigitalVision Vectors; Martin Seras Lima/Action Plus; Marco Quintarelli/EyeEm; Westend61; **U20:** Fine Art Images/ Heritage Images/Hulton Archive; bgblue/DigitalVision Vectors; Luca Ghidoni/Getty Images Entertainment; Jon G. Fuller/ VW Pics/Universal Images Group; Feature China/Barcroft Media; RAUL ARBOLEDA/AFP; Dan Kitwood/Getty Images News; Bernadett Csatri/EyeEm; Darren Rogers/Moment; **LS5:** Caiaimage/Tom Merton; Caiaimage/Sam Edwards; Stocktrek Images; botamochi/iStock/Getty Images Plus; MirageC/Moment; **R5:** Hill Street Studios/Blend Images; **EA:** James D. Morgan/ Getty Images News.

The following photographs have been sourced from other library/ sources.

**U4**: Rajah Bose/AP/Press Association Images; Jonathan Larsen/ Diadem Images/Alamy Stock Photo; **U6**: ©Don Chaput; **R2:** Steven Day/AP/Press Association Images; **U10:** Africa Studio/ Shutterstock; ZUMA Press, Inc/Alamy Stock Photo; **U14:** Courtesy of Deb McAlister-Holland; **U16:** Courtesy of Taylor Wilson; **LS4:** PSL Images/Alamy Stock Photo; **R4:** Ruth Amos/ Stair Steady Products Ltd; **U17:** Allyson Scott/Alamy Stock Photo; WENN UK/Alamy Stock Photo; **U18**: Image Source/Alamy Stock Photo; **C5:** ©Royal Ballet School/Schuhlelewis.com; Courtesy of Idyllwild Arts Academy; © Sylvie-Ann Paré/National Circus School; **U19:** CBW/Alamy Stock Photo; ©Neil Matthews; **U20:** Science History Images/Alamy Stock Photo; © Julian Beever.

Front cover photography by Priscilla Gragg/Blend Images/Getty Images.

Illustration
Ludovic Salle (Advocate Art); Chris Challik (The Bright Agency)

**The publishers are grateful to the following contributors:**
cover design and design concept: restless; typesetting: emc design Ltd; audio recordings: produced by Leon Chambers and recorded at The SoundHouse Studios, London; Life Skills and Culture sections: Robert Quinn; Texts and exercises on pp. 11, 106-7: Emma Heyderman; Grammar reference and practice section: Louise Hashemi and Andrew Reid